Westsiders

Westsiders

WILLIAM SHAW

BLOOMSBURY

For Jane

First published in Great Britain in 2000
This paperback edition published 2001

Copyright © 2000 by William Shaw

The moral right of the author has been asserted

Bloomsbury Publishing Plc, 38 Soho Square, London, W1D 3HB

A CIP catalogue record for this book
is available from the British Library

ISBN 0 7475 5250 9

10 9 8 7 6 5

Typeset by Hewer Text Ltd, Edinburgh
Printed in Great Britain by Clays Ltd, St Ives plc

CONTENTS

Part Four

PART ONE

'All I ever wanted was to be a man.'

Chester Himes,
If He Hollers Let Him Go, Los Angeles, 1945

1

The New Dope Game

BABYBOY

The 110 freeway ignores the strict perpendicular below, curving at palm-top level above the streets. From this elevated vantage point, the speeding drivers can see for miles, out towards the Pacific in the west, to Customs Island in the south, northwards to the skyscrapers of Downtown, or towards the hazy San Bernardino Mountains far to the north-east. The territory beneath their wheels is invisible, blanked out by the sound walls on either side. Once a wide flood plain, it is now divided into square lots of streets and houses that you barely notice from up here. Only the occasional billboard, apartment block, minaret or tower reaches high enough to merit attention.

The wide 110 is a futuristic ride, two car-pool lanes each way, four lanes on either side of them, with complex, beautiful interchanges that sweep the cars upwards through elegant curves and then lower them to rejoin other routes, all equally busy. A quarter of a million vehicles hurtle over this fat freeway every day, unslowed by South Central's massive sprawl below.

I drop my speed in preparation for the off-ramp to Martin Luther King. For all its vastness, South Central is avoidable. A trickle of tourists occasionally venture into the post-industrial wasteland of Watts to visit the Watts Towers, those strange, dream-like sculptures built by a lonely Italian immigrant in the fifties, but there is no other advertised reason for the casual visitor to enter it. I have been visiting Los Angeles for 12 years, yet I have strayed into South Central on only a few occasions. They were usually when I lost my way and discovered myself in some neighbourhood on Western where I could make out no other white faces, where I pressed down the door locks on my hire car, embarrassed at my own timorousness.

Though it stretches right into the middle of the huge expanse of Los Angeles, South Central has become somehow detached from it. I had few reasons to go there until now. The times I did find myself there, I remember a sense of disappointment. How ordinary and undramatic these rows of small, neat houses looked, with their clipped grass and their palm trees; and how different from the image of the place I had built up from the hip-hop records, videos, news reports and movies.

South Central's reputation precedes it, in garish news stories about gang murders, or in that single helicopter shot that travelled the world swamping all the other stories from the 1992 riots, of a mob dragging a white truck driver from his cab and beating him until he was almost dead.

It is the culture of hip hop, though, which has done more than anything in recent years to define this geography. Young people all over the world now know about South Central, or at least have some vivid image of what they think it must be like. From the records and movies they would probably imagine it as a crime-ridden hell-hole. Some parts of it are. They might imagine too that nearly all the people who live there are black. Once upon a time they were, but the last 20 years have seen a massive influx of Latinos. Today African-Americans make up only half the population, yet through their music black Americans have somehow repopulated the region.

All music is about geography, in a way. It's either about the place in which it's made, or the place where the maker wants to be;

rarely, though, is music as explicit about its sense of place as hip hop. Hip hop in particular is about where you're from. It's about what where you're from says about you, and what you say about where you're from. Since its beginning, Los Angeles hip hop has revelled in listing specific locations, street intersections, schools, stores, parks, housing projects, gang turfs and 'hoods'. The only other genre which is as needily specific about place names is emigrant music, whose songs nostalgically detail the names of old home towns, hillsides and rivers. To my ears, hip hop can sometimes sound just as woebegone, just as romantic about the geography it's trying to claim as any emigrant music.

In 1987 a young member of a Crip gang from LA's Compton district called Eric 'Eazy-E' Wright and his group Niggaz Wit' Attitude, or NWA, released their first single. It was called 'Boyz In Tha Hood'. Crudely produced though it was by the standards of New York rap, it was also a simple, effective conjunction of masculinity and geography: boys in the 'hood – men and the territory they wished to claim as their own. The phrase was later purloined and made famous by the young film director John Singleton, for his 1991 movie of the same name, starring one of NWA's original rappers, Ice Cube.

Bored as hell and I want to get ill
So I went to a place where my homeboys chill . . .

'Homeboy'. 'Homie'. Even that word, such a staple of hip-hop vocabulary, works to join men to a location. More than that, it contains hidden memories of the great northward migration of the first half of this century, when the rural populations of the old South moved to the booming industrial cities. Ghettos began to fill with migrants who clustered together with others they knew from back home. In those days 'homeboy' meant, more literally, my boy from home – from Arkansas, or Mississippi, or Alabama.

The following year, after 'Boyz In Tha Hood', NWA became more geographically specific with 'Straight Outta Compton':

Straight outta Compton, crazy motherfucker named Ice Cube
From the gang called Niggaz Wit' Attitudes
When I'm called off, I got a sawed off
Squeeze the trigger and bodies are hauled off . . .

Geography and masculinity; manhood and place.

Up until then, hip-hop culture had been largely owned by New Yorkers who had filled their music with references to the communities they had grown up in, the Bronx, Brooklyn, Harlem and Queens. With the album *Straight Outta Compton*, a little-heard-of city in South Central Los Angeles was demanding its share of attention too, for the first time. And when Eazy-E filmed the video for tracks like '100 Miles And Runnin'' he was showing America parts of South Central which had almost certainly never been seen on television before. The choice of location wasn't just accidental: in some ways this was the point of the whole enterprise. There's an African-American verb beloved by hip-hoppers: to represent. Its meaning is broader than it is standard English. To represent is not only to portray something, but also to throw your whole self into doing it. Eazy-E and NWA were representing.

Creating culture is the act of writing yourself into land. That's what hip hop does, more literally than any other pop culture yet. But if hip hop invented itself as a way for young men to find themselves in the ghettos they lived in, it quickly became more than that. It became a way of getting the hell out of those ghettos too. By the late eighties, when Los Angeles began to contribute to the canon, hip hop was also a potentially very viable way of building a life away from the conflict and poverty of the inner city. Hip hop made money. As Ice-T, a former Los Angeles pimp and armed robber turned rapper, once announced: 'Rhyme Pays':

Rhyme pays — buys my food every night and day
Pays my rent, my bills, I guess I'm doin' OK . . .

Stars were already facing a peculiar dilemma: if they were successful, they were automatically distanced from their own subject matter, from the environment which gave their music meaning. Ice-T moved up into a fancy house in the Hollywood Hills, to the derision of some of his former followers.

The wide, east–west thoroughfare of Martin Luther King is slow today. In front of me is a pick-up truck, in the back two Latino children, each tugging at the same blanket. A car cuts in front, between the truck and me. Its bumper sticker reads: 'I MAY BE FAT BUT YOU'RE UGLY – AND I CAN LOSE WEIGHT.'

Once, before I ever came to South Central, I asked Ice Cube, one of the fiercest mythologists of this land, for some stories about growing up here. He told me about the year when he turned 17. It was the year he bought his first car, an old VW Bug. It was also the year he saw his first two people killed.

The first was at a KFC restaurant. He had just got into his VW, and was trying to find a place on the seat to put his drink so that it wouldn't spill, when he saw a man walking past with a gun in his hand. Oh shit! thought Cube. He struggled to get the car into reverse.

The murderer had just robbed a store. He was looking for a car to make a getaway in. Still tugging at his gear-stick, Cube watched him walk up to a car three vehicles ahead. 'Get out,' the gunman ordered.

Probably the driver just hesitated too long. The gunman fired four times. Uh-uh-uh-uh. The driver slumped over. Shit, thought Cube. Shit.

The second time was at a fast-food restaurant too, a Brolly Hut – one of those stands with seats all around on the outside. Cube was on the inside, just about to place his order. The first thing he noticed was the glass breaking all around him, then the popping sound. He dived down, but by the time he had hit the floor, it was all over.

When it was safe, he walked outside and looked at the victim, head bleeding on the kerb, feet still up on the chair, stone dead, his friends all around him crying.

Cube never found out what it was about. This time he was cooler about the whole experience. He walked back to the counter and asked, 'You still talking orders?'

'No,' shouted the frightened man behind the counter. 'Closed!'

'South Central,' Cube told me, '. . . it ain't the most terrible place to live in the world, but it's just so unpredictable.'

For the last couple of weeks, I've been visiting talent shows, record stores and clubs in South Central, and scouring the small ads in the local hip-hop press, trying to find the would-be hip-hoppers, the African-American boys who haven't made it yet, the ones who are still trying to make something of themselves. I'm driving westwards on King because I want to meet those who are still trying to find a voice, who are still dreaming about their houses in the hills, away from this flat landscape, dulled by cheap real estate and corner liquor stores. The rappers I think I'm looking for don't necessarily have to be destined to be great: they just have to be dreaming of greatness.

Two days earlier I had called up one of the people who run one of the local hip-hop showcases on cable TV. He had passed me the pager number of a young man who called himself Babyboy. Carefully checking the street names at the unfamiliar intersections as I cross them, I'm on the way to meet him.

On the phone, Babyboy gave me instructions to meet him on Wilton Place, two blocks north of King.

He is there standing under a small tree, clutching a briefcase. His friends turn and look at me, briefly, then resume their conversation.

'I'll be a minute, OK?' says Babyboy. He is about six foot, with a closely shaved head, and wearing a plaid shirt over his trousers; thin in a muscular way, and good-looking. His brown eyes have the red rims of a heavy grass smoker.

This is a typical South Central neighbourhood: small houses, laid out on even lawns – sometimes with even smaller guest houses built in their backyards – set on an endless criss-cross of streets. In the forties this was a white neighbourhood, back when the African-American ghetto was still restricted to small sections of the city to the east of here.

There are almost always one or two men leaning against the tree, or sitting on doorsteps, at the corner of Wilton and Leighton. A few of the cars that cruise slowly up and down Wilton pause here, uncertainly: this is a well-known spot for buying weed. The drivers peer at me out of their side windows, then rev up and drive on, put off by my presence. White people are conspicuous in this part of town.

I too feel uncomfortable, standing on this concrete sidewalk, dressed in a suit. I don't normally like to wear a suit, but when I imagined what it was going to be like, travelling here to Los Angeles to mingle with the young men of South Central, a suit seemed appropriate. I have met so many white hip-hop fans who like to dress like the boys of the inner cities, even adopt their language, deeming the world around them either 'dope' or 'wack' by turns, and who practise elaborate street-corner handshakes. Perhaps it is just as perverse for me to dress up as it is for them to dress down, but I was born and raised in rural England and have little obvious in common with the people I want to meet here. I would be embarrassed if I was thought to be pretending otherwise. Now, of course, not only am I overdressed for the summer weather, but I feel faintly ridiculous to be so dressed up; but then I always expected to.

I wait about ten minutes before Babyboy leaves with his

companions and wanders over to meet me. With him is his friend and cousin, a big, round-faced boy called Rahiem, whom he introduces as 'O.G. Budman'.

Budman has a dream. He wants to record an album of songs entirely about weed. Marijuana is a substance Budman has developed a profound respect for. It's not like other drugs. The way he sees it, you smoke it and it doesn't make you want to kill someone; it just makes you want to eat something. It's a handy source of income too.

Budman's group is called Ya Highness – highness, as in stoned. Ya Highness have been together for a year: the group consists of him and a friend who calls himself Payback whom Budman knows from their days together at Birmingham High School. They weren't even friends until they smoked their first joint together: this, Budman believes, is proof of the great transformational value of weed. 'Marijuana can't end world violence,' declares Budman. 'But it's a start.'

Since they shared that first joint they've written a bunch of rhymes about weed. Like 'So High', 'Bud 4 Life', 'Another Day With A J.', and one for the ladies that's called 'I Wanna Smoke Wit' Ya'. Their rhymes attempt to dissect every possible stoned experience. Budman writes ambitious couplets in praise of the drug, like:

There's nothing wrong with havin' a bong and fillin' the cap with chronic
You want the best then come to the west and purchase hydroponic.

There's even one called 'Creeper', about those times when you smoke and you don't feel a thing until it creeps up on you later on. The high point of their career so far has been opening a show for Playa Hamm – the LA rapper who was once half of a group called the Penthouse Players, who recorded for Eazy-E's label, Ruthless.

In the meantime the large, bear-like Budman, who always seems to wear a shy grin on his face, gets by selling a little weed and smoking a little of it too. 'A friend with weed is a friend indeed,' he proclaims profoundly.

Becoming a rapper is a dream for Budman. You couldn't exactly call it an ambition, because Budman isn't really the ambitious sort. It's his friend Babyboy who has all the ambition.

Babyboy has pulled a video camera out of his car. 'This is for my cable show,' he explains as he zooms in on Budman. He doesn't have a cable show yet, but he's planning to get one. Babyboy is full of plans. 'Welcome, everybody,' he supplies his own voice-over to the camcorder, 'to the N Entertainment video volume . . .'

Babyboy tells me he has his own entertainment company. It's a loose collection of local rappers and producers that he has marshalled from the area. He's a rapper too: Babyboy Delatorres is one of his rap names. His real name is Kimeyo Daniels. Sometimes he uses another rap name, Keydawg. The name implies drugs: a key is a kilo of cocaine. Drug dealers are, to their credit, forward-looking; they have gone metric well before the rest of pounds-'n'-ounces America. 'Keydawg' is also an unwieldy acronym for 'Kimeyo Extra Yard Dickin' All Women Good', but these days he usually just calls himself Babyboy. The name Keydawg harks back to an earlier time a few years ago when he made a serious effort to become a cocaine dealer himself. These days Babyboy still deals drugs, but in a minor way. 'I'm a hustler, man. I don't hustle cocaine, heroin' – he pronounces it 'hero-wine' – 'speed, sherm. That ain't my forte. That ain't me.'

What he really dreams about doing is creating a music business empire right here in South Central.

'Music,' he tells me, repeatedly, 'is the new dope game.' In the seventies, when cocaine first began to flood the inner cities, it was glamorous to be a drug dealer. It was also, of course, a hazardous occupation, and careers were often brought to an abrupt halt, but it was a way in which poor boys with little education could become rich and earn respect. But the last decade has seen the young men of the inner cities turn to a new money-spinner that appears to offer incredible riches.

'That's what it is. It's the new dope game,' Babyboy says again. He gives me his card: 'Kimeyo Daniels, CEO N Entertainment. No Respekt Mob Records.'

I meet Babyboy a few days later at M+M's Diner – 'Tennessee Homestyle Cooking' – at the junction of King and Crenshaw. He sits, proprietorially, in a Naugahyde booth, laying his briefcase down beside him, and tells me a little about himself and his dreams for N Entertainment.

He's 24 now and lives with his girlfriend Marlene and their newly born daughter Chanel – Babyboy's second child. Their small apartment is in Culver City, a few miles west of here, where many of the film studios are based. Marlene pays the rent. She works as a secretary at Fox.

Babyboy doesn't have a job. After Marlene has gone to work in the mornings, he gets in his old silver Mercury Cougar and rides back out to Wilton Place and King, where I met him. It's where he grew up. He calls it 'the hood' or 'the dub'. It's where his people are. Marlene's family live just around the corner.

Babyboy hangs out. He hatches plans to break into the music business and he smokes grass with Budman and his friends on the dub. 'On the dub,' he says, peering over the menu, 'we barbecue maybe four or five times a week, you know what I'm sayin'?'

As Keydawg, he once wrote a rap called 'Hoodlife', which romanticizes the boyish indolence of life here:

Spendin' all the day walkin' back and forth to the store
To get another blunt and two four-ohs
And I'm the only homie that will drink the O.E.
But I'm down to put ends on a fifth of Hennessy

I'm gonna kick back, relax and chill
On the 'W' where the niggas show love and stay real . . .

A 'blunt' is a cigar, usually used to roll a joint in; a 'four-oh' is shorthand for a 40-ounce bottle of beer, usually a brand like O.E., Old English; 'ends' is slang for money, and 'the W' is Wilton Place, the dub.

Babyboy's love for the hood is powerful. It is his identity, his place. He could happily pass his life here, if it were not for his ambition to make something big of himself. He has been around here all his life, apart from a spell in prison, and another in North Carolina, when he was a Marine.

As a schoolboy, all Babyboy wanted to be was a Marine. He was in ninth grade when the recruiter came to his school and dazzled him with the white cap with the anchor badge on it. There was a school legend that if you actually reached out and touched the cap, you'd end up joining up. Babyboy picked up the hat right away and signed on the moment he was old enough. He wanted to see the world. He dreamed of going to Okinawa. They sent him to North Carolina instead. The entire experience was a sorry disappointment. Instead of having a real taste of Marine Corps action, he ended up in Bravo Company, 7th Engineers, which he will happily deride as a 'bitch-ass company of pencil-whippin' motherfuckers'. So he quit the Marines and went made his way back to the dub. 'I got out of that shit. As long as I been living, I ain't been a motherfucker that played no games,' he says, ordering his pork chop and biscuits. The menu is strictly Southern.

When he arrived back on Wilton and King in 1992, the Los Angeles rap scene had already taken off. People like Hamm and DJ Quik were making a lot of money. He started scheming right back then, fancying himself as one of the new rap moguls of Los Angeles. 'I always wanted to be in the spotlight,' he says. 'I always thought I was somebody special.'

When the chop arrives, he leans over it and whispers a few words of grace.

Eazy-E had enjoyed a great run with his Ruthless Records empire by the time Babyboy returned to LA. Now a new record company had emerged from South Central, run by another man connected with the Compton gangs, a big, violent, heavy-set man called Marion Knight, also known as Suge Knight, short for the Sugar Bear. Suge was known to have connections with the Mob Piru Bloods. Rumours were flying around LA that Suge Knight had strong-armed the former Crip Eazy-E, turning up to a business meeting with a gang of thugs armed with baseball bats. The rumours were largely true. Knight had used threats of violence to force Eazy-E into signing over the contracts to some of his most profitable artists, including NWA member Dr Dre. By this time Dr Dre had become the hottest record producer in Los Angeles, and was working with a new artist, a one-time Long Beach Crip known as Snoop Doggy Dogg. Thuggery aside, the LA rap scene had never been healthier. Millions were being made.

For a couple of years Kimeyo, as he was then, didn't do anything serious about his ambition. It was enough for him to make money by what Babyboy calls the CSC, the California Street Code: selling cocaine. His first attempts at getting into the music business were not auspicious. In '93, he, Payback and Budman formed a group they called No Respekt Mob and took their very first demo to Suge Knight's Death Row record company, at its offices at 10900 Wilshire Boulevard. By this time Death Row had become the number-one rap label in America, with Snoop's Dre-produced album *Doggystyle* and Dre's own *The Chronic*. Babyboy had a chance to let Knight's promotions man, Kevin 'DJ Black' Connell, hear the tape. The Death Row man played a little of it, then shooed Babyboy straight out of the office. The tape was so badly recorded he could hardly hear it on the huge office system.

Babyboy was homeless, staying with whoever would put him

up. Things went from bad to worse. While cheating on his girlfriend, he made another girl pregnant. She gave birth to his first daughter, Kimaree. To top it all, the police caught up on him when he was trying to pull off a scam involving forged cheques and he ended up in prison.

It was his first offence, so he was back on the streets soon. He weighed his options. He'd had some success dealing in cocaine, but the money came and went. On 13 August 1996, the day before his twenty-third birthday, he decided it was time to start taking the music business seriously. 'Man,' he says, 'I got tired of doing the shit I was doing.' That was the day he decided to form N Entertainment – which stood for No Respekt Mob Entertainment.

He turns his back to me. 'See?' he pulls down the collar of his plaid shirt and shows me the five-inch-wide tattoo on the back of his neck. Poking out of the top of his shirt and curving around the dark-olive skin of his neck is the logo he designed for his business, a large black letter 'N' inside a circle.

'Hey!' he hails a waitress. 'Can you give me a couple more napkins, hon?'

'Coming up.' The restaurant is filling. It's lunch-time. Shoppers from the nearby Crenshaw–Baldwin Hills Mall enter clutching bags of shopping.

'The reason I like entertainment,' he considers, 'is 'cause there ain't no career where you can kick it as much as you work . . .'

After we've eaten, he promises to keep in touch. He writes down my number and puts it in his wallet. I notice a picture of a pretty girl inside.

'Is that your girlfriend?' I ask.

He looks horrified. 'Hell no.'

Outside, I take a look around. King and Crenshaw is one of west South Central's best-known corners. To the left of me, on the same block as M+M's, is King of Music Records, opposite the large shopping mall. Recently the Crenshaw–Baldwin Hills Mall has thrived. Magic Johnson has opened up his new movie theatre on the far side of it. It lies between two major gang territories, the Harlem Crips to the east and the P Stone Bloods to the west. The local businessmen have fought hard to establish what they call 'the Crenshaw corridor' here. They hate the bad image this area has earned.

Babyboy walked up here from the dub. I offer him a ride back there. As we drive out of the car park he points at a couple of boys who watch us drive past and says, 'Look at those motherfuckers staring at us. A thug and a white boy.' He laughs. He says they're staring because they can't figure out why I'm in the same car with him. 'That's the trouble with Los Angeles. It's all about stereotypes.'

2

Crenshaw Hustlers

C-DOUBLE-E

Herman Collins, a 24-year-old who raps under the name of C-Double-E, has booked a session at the studio he's been using for a while now. 'Like an underground location,' he explains grandly. Herman has a group called A Nu Creation.

All over South Central there are little home studios charging only ten or so bucks an hour to make you a demo. They're part of a food chain fed by dreams so many people have that they're going to make it. The studios are owned by musicians who are hoping for a break themselves, and who spread their cost by renting their equipment out to other young musicians. Each year there are more studios, each year it gets cheaper to make a quality demo and each year more demos will pass, usually very briefly, across the desks of the A&R men north of here in Hollywood.

Casa Terris studios is actually the spare bedroom in Terence Robinson's apartment. Terence painted the ceiling black and set up his racks of synths, mixers and sequencers there. Now he rents it out for $10 an hour.

'So. What are we doing today?' Terence asks Herman.

'I want to do the vocals to "Nine Times Out Of Ten" over.'

'I thought we had already finished them.'

'Yeah, but I want to do them over.'

Terence exhales. He's not a big rap fan anyway. He prefers r'n'b and jazz. He's a keyboard player himself. There was a time, back in the mid-eighties, when he had a solo deal, writing complex jazzy songs under the name 'Robi', but the whole thing fell through. The independent label that was going to release his CD belly-flopped, leaving him with an album's worth of material and no one who wanted to put it out. So he put his own studio together with an idea of forming his own record label, updating his material and releasing it himself.

Terence recorded the backing track for 'Nine Times Out Of Ten' months ago from a loop that A Nu Creation's DJ had brought him, but privately he doesn't like working from samples. He doesn't find that sort of work very creative at all.

'What was wrong with the vocals?' he asks.

'It was the tone,' explains Herman. 'My first verse sounded like a different tone from the second verse.'

'Well, if you're not happy with them, do them again.' Terence shrugs. 'But I don't have a lot of time,' he says, with a note of tetchiness in his voice. 'Tell you the truth, I was happy with they way you did it before.'

'I don't like the tone,' insists Herman. He is slim, tall, long-limbed and gawky, with a strikingly angular, dark-skinned face. He wears long, dark-blue denim shorts that end below his knees and a matching loose denim jacket that seem to emphasize his boniness. 'If I don't do my vocal right,' he grins, 'you can call me MC Wack.'

Herman is a well-intentioned, amiable boy, but highly strung. He keeps up a nervy chatter.

'Just a minute,' says Terence. He closes the door to shut out the noises of air-conditioners and Latino children playing in the yard outside. Terence feels his way around the room to close the window. Glaucoma contracted when he was growing up in Mississippi before his parents moved to LA left him with extremely limited vision. His left eye bulges out slightly. For his recording work he has made himself a pair of special glasses with magnifying attachments that flip down in front, taped and glued on to the frames. They give him the air of a mad scientist as he works in the studio, pushing buttons and lowering his face to within six inches of the mixing desk to scan the dials.

By day Terence works in the laundry room at a Veterans Administration hospital – he calls it 'textile care'. He's hoping that when he starts his own record label he'll be able to give all that up.

'OK,' says Terence, and presses the record button on his eight-track.

Herman closes his eyes and nods his head to the rhythm, then starts to speak to the microphone:

Nine times out of ten if you done visit my vicinity
You'd be one in a bunch that recognize my identity
Deep down in ya subconscious I know that you remember me
From various locations within the black community
Like Crenshaw and Stocker where I got my hustle on
Selling Krazy Kut T-shirts and body eau de Cologne . . .

White rock music communicates in a vague, opaque way. Listeners are required to bring their own interpretation of what a song might mean. Rarely does its message contain any sense of urgency. Meanings are deliberately open-ended. In general, apart from the odd feisty punk-rock or protest song, it has no crucial message to pass on. Hip hop is the reverse. If it fails to communicate directly, it fails. Herman's verse is as literal a description of his everyday life as you could get.

Most days of the week, including Sundays, Herman pushes his small cart up towards the junction of Crenshaw and Stocker, where he has, like the rhyme says, 'his hustle on'. He sits on the small wall outside the liquor store just a few blocks down from M+M's, where I lunched with Babyboy. There he sells what he calls his 'Krazy Kut T-shirts' – T-shirts that he has carefully shredded with a razor until they turn into cheap, hole-filled dresses. He sells perfumes too, as well as incense sticks he makes in his own apartment. This year he's trying out a new scent: bubblegum. He'll give you one incense stick for free to tempt you back to buy more. There are about 20 guys who work the area: they call themselves the Crenshaw Hustlers. They all keep an eye out for each other.

Herman grew up in the projects to the west of the Compton area, near Avalon. His father was a Vietnam Vet; he moved out before Herman was born.

Now Herman lives north-west of Compton in the Crenshaw district, just south of Martin Luther King Boulevard. As a Crenshaw Hustler, he works long hours. At the beginning of the month when people receive their pay-cheques he earns a decent income. That dwindles as the month goes on and money runs dry. But he likes it: he is his own boss, he says. Of course, it's not what he really wants to do with his life. He wants to rap. He's been working towards it for years.

Herman is gabbling the words of his verse; his timing is jerky. Terence, peering through his glasses, stops the playback halfway through. 'You're all, eeehehehehehe,' Terence squeaks like a mouse. He is wearing a black Million Man March T-shirt bearing the slogan 'Let My People Go'. He didn't manage to join Louis Farrakhan's march himself, but he thinks it was a great thing: black men, all coming together for a change.

On the next run-through, Herman tries harder, but that makes it worse. Now he's swallowing his words, taking breaths in odd places: the line 'Crenshaw and Stocker' comes out mashed: 'Cr'nshaw'nstocker'.

'Just take your time,' instructs Terence calmingly.

Like any young rapper with a few songs, Herman is proud of what he's written. It's the story of his life, after all. Rap is autobiography: a form of testimony. If Herman has a talent, it is writing: he's always coming up with simple but effective little ideas for hooks for rap songs which nail down the minutiae of his life. Like the poppy, straightforward chorus for this track:

Nine times out of ten when you're clocking them ends
Everybody and they momma want to be your friend
But when you're down and out
Money all ranned out
Don't nobody wanna hear what you're talking about . . .

'Clocking them ends' means to make money. It says a lot that the topic of wealth is such a rich source of rap slang. There are dozens of words, all meaning basically the same thing. The origins of some are clear: for instance, 'ends' comes from 'making ends meet'. 'Dead presidents', 'Franklins', 'Benjamins', 'green' and 'paper' all mean paper money. 'Flow' is short for cash flow. Less obviously, 'cream' is an acronym, invented by the Staten Island group the Wu-Tang Clan, for Cash Rules Everything Around Me. Other, harder-to-fathom dairy-product slang for money includes 'cheese', 'mozzarella' and 'cheddar'. 'It's all about the cheddar', declared LA rapper Dub C on a recent hit. Still more obscure is 'scrilla', a piece of slang that seems to have originated in the San Francisco Bay area. More words seem to be invented each week, faster than any Webster's could keep track: 'G', 'grip', 'bank', 'mail', 'feddy', 'scratch', 'snaps', 'stack', 'chips', 'gravy'. It is the fecund vocabulary of desire.

Herman is nodding earnestly at the advice Terence is giving him: he tries again. He has said the words of his verse to himself a thousand times and it's almost as if he's so familiar with them that the sense has gone missing.

Finally, after eight takes he stops. 'You think that's OK?'

'It's OK,' says Terence reassuringly.

There are two rappers in A Nu Creation. The other is a solid, muscular-looking boy called Stephen Kennedy Jr, who goes under the rap name of Diamond DX. In contrast to Herman, DX lays down his verse in just two takes in his deep, big-bodied voice. DX's voice is slick and confident. He was born in Tennessee: his mother moved here when he was just two years old and he still has a hint of a Southern accent that gives his delivery a slight drawl. 'I get people that even say I all be country, that I talk country,' DX says shyly.

The quality of the voice is all-important. Unlike Herman, DX is a natural, but Herman is the one with the drive. It's Herman's dollars, earned vending on street corners, that are going towards paying for this session.

Terence switches off the playback, turns and grabs DX's hand. 'That was the bomb,' he says enthusiastically. 'You sounding like you got that gangsta shit down.'

'Thank you,' says Diamond DX bashfully. And he yawns broadly. He was up late last night.

DX isn't particularly tall, but he is heavy. He works late nights as a nightclub bouncer. The pay is terrible, but it's regular work. 'I tell you what,' he announces. 'By the time I paid for my transport last night, I'm lucky if I had $5 left in my pocket.'

DX always wears black, and a wooden pendant in the shape of a black fist hangs from his neck. His trademark is the black baseball cap he wears with the letters 'DX' embroidered on it in silver.

DX doesn't say much – not to me, at least. He is ill at ease talking about himself. I ask about what he got up to before he started working as a security guard. He answers vaguely, 'We all do some good and we all do some bad.'

I prod: 'What sort of bad?'

DX looks at the ground. 'Well,' he sighs. 'Like selling drugs. You know, killing off the community. Shooting somebody over something material.'

'You did that? You shot people?'

'Well . . .' – he looks at me uncomfortably – 'I was part of it.'

Some rappers love to talk up their wild teenage days, real or imaginary. DX clearly doesn't. 'And then a lot of people did say that I had a voice for rapping. At first I didn't believe it, until I tried. And then I started to come up with songs with a partner. But we really didn't do nothing with it . . . and then, as I was growing up, I got into some more bad stuff and I went to jail . . .'

I interrupt: 'What for?'

'Drugs.'

'You mean possession?'

'Yeah,' he says quietly.

'What jail was that?'

'That was in juvenile [hall – young offenders' prison]. And then I went to jail too again.'

'What was that like?

He exhales. 'My mom had to come and see me in jail and I was embarrassed,' he says unhappily.

Once, he tells me, his crew were chasing some rivals who had offended them in some way, the way that boys in gangs do. 'Somebody had did something to us and we had went back and tried to do something to him. That day I almost shot a kid. Just a kid, you know?' he says. 'I still remember that . . . I stopped when I realized what I was doing.'

He shuffles in his seat and says, 'I used to have nightmares about it.'

'About what? Nearly shooting the boy?'

He nods. These days he says he prays every day.

'That's the only thing that really changed me,' he says, looking up. 'Praying every day.'

Herman, sitting across the room all the while, nods. Herman always avoided gangs himself. He tells me, 'A lot of people say you are forced into gangs, but you know, you have to make your own decisions. I knew everybody that was out there in gangs, but thank God, I never was.' Herman isn't that sort. For all his apparent geekiness, he's a single-minded boy.

When the session's finished, they stand around the table in Terence's living room, chatting about music equipment. Herman wants to buy one of the latest sequencer/drum machine hybrids that nearly all hip hop is made on these days. The good ones are expensive, though: several thousand dollars each. Part of him thinks that he should buy a car if he can save enough, because a car makes life so much easier in Los Angeles. But what he really wants is the sequencer.

'MPC 2000,' he says. 'That's what I'm going to get.' He's looked at them in the music shops up in Hollywood.

'Hooey,' says Terence. 'The Akai MPC 2000. That's the bomb.' And he fetches some magazines and starts peering at them, holding them inches away from his bad eyes. 'Is that it? Read that out to me.'

And Herman reads the specifications of the machine out loud. 'That's what I'm going to get,' he says again. 'Then nothing's going to stop me.'

The starting price for the MPC 2000 he is hoping to buy is around $2500.

3

Stuff That Bad People Do

RAH

The lampposts and telegraph poles of Los Angeles are always freshly stickered with the names of hip-hop artists: bright, newly printed labels fixed from about two feet above the ground to however high a hand can reach. As far as most of South Central goes, the glorious West Coast light falls on an unrelentingly drab city. Even before I discovered who was responsible for them, I loved these illegal adverts, and the colour they add to the grey sidewalks.

Everywhere you look the name of every new single and CD has been fixed to any available surface. The record companies call this form of guerrilla marketing 'street promotion', but the street slang for stickering a neighbourhood is 'sniping'. It's a word that conveys some of the adrenalin rush that 'snipers' get, putting up the posters on a busy street, hoping the police won't catch them, because though fines are low, they're much more than most snipers can afford.

It is impossible to pinpoint exactly how or where street promotion started because, at the outset, street promoters were just fans. One minute a graffiti artist is tagging the name of his favourite artist on a freeway wall; the next a record company is giving him money for the paint. Today, though, street promotion is a huge business. There are hundreds of self-employed street promoters in every city in America. Typically they are inner-city teens trying to find a foothold in the industry. Street promotion is a sort of inner-city internship.

If wealthy CEO-rappers like Sean 'Puff Daddy' Combs of Bad Boy Entertainment and Percy Miller, a.k.a. Master P, of No Limit Records perch at the top of the hip-hop ladder, way down here at the very bottom lurk the street promoters. They are the cheapest but most cost-effective weapon the hip-hop industry has. Promoters are paid to be walking billboards for the latest hip-hop 12-inch – peer-group evangelists who are employed because, above all, they're fans. They sticker the lampposts, hang out at high schools talking up new artists, pass out clip tapes, with short samples of music on, to anyone they see wearing a Walkman, call up radio request lines, bug radio and club DJs, pester record-store owners, pass out merchandise at shows or even carry picket signs through the streets proclaiming the name of the artist who's paid them to spread their name back to the grass roots.

As hip-hop specialist companies like Tommy Boy, Def Jam, Priority, No Limit, Loud, Noo Trybe and all the others know, a new artist can prosper if word of mouth is with him, or die if it looks like he's being hyped too much by corporate advertising.

A good street team's work is like precision bombing: companies can pinpoint a neighbourhood, hire the right team and let them loose. It's a very modern working relationship. The street promoters are often high-school drop-outs, armed only with a staple gun. Those doing the grunt work are paid a pittance: they are unlikely to trouble the IRS with their tax returns. But thanks to the wonder of electronic technology, it's a particularly cost-effective relationship for the record companies who employ them. They can monitor a street team's progress with astonishing accuracy. Each week the sales of records from local shops are compiled by a national computer system, Soundscan. Companies can check the effectiveness of a team by watching sales in their neighbourhood. The team that doesn't get results won't get work.

It's cheap, but effective. 'Fifteen hundred dollars, and we'll put your stickers all over LA and we'll hit every single lamppost in your primary target area with seven or eight stickers,' boast a young mixed-race team who call themselves Platinum Plus. That's a sum that won't even buy you a single legal advertising billboard. You could probably bargain them down to half that too.

The effectiveness of street promotion means that it's not just the record companies who are using it as a sales tool. In LA, the street teams of the two local hip-hop radio stations, Power 106 and 92.3 The Beat, trawl Crenshaw at the weekends, handing out stickers and competition prizes. Clothing manufacturers like Nike, Karl Kani and Reebok have all used street promoters.

One day I drive out to Palm Springs, to a hip-hop industry convention called Urban Focus Network. These are bullish days: the independent companies are thriving. I try to squeeze my rental car in between the new Expeditions and Explorers. The conference has commandeered the whole sprawling Palm Springs Hotel complex. On loungers and tables and chairs around the pool, under the surrounding hills, the West Coast's industry figures are doing business in an ostentatiously relaxed manner. The new urban-music bourgeoisie are exchanging business cards and strategies. Others, who want their business, have come to petition them, armed with printed plastic bags, free phonecards and other sweeteners.

The street promotion teams are here today to promote themselves for a change. There is money in the air, and even the lowliest sniper wants some of it. A team called Ghetto Pass from Oakland, northern California, say that business is going through the roof. There are no limits. There is a giddy optimism among those who have found their footing. Ghetto Pass boast that they're planning on pitching their services to both the Republican and Democratic parties when the next presidential elections come around.

Poor city youths don't have much to sell, but they do have the elusive quality that the rest of America wants so badly. People think they're cool. The paradox is that the people with the least are also those who hold the greatest sway over popular taste. The ghetto bangs the drum and the suburbs follow.

Sleep, an LA promoter who runs a team called Mad Pro, carefully arranges piles of free CDs and flyers on coffee tables, cellphone pressed to his ear. He passes around his business card and adds a few more to his wallet. His real name is Anthony Wilson, but everyone calls him Sleep because his heavy-lidded eyes lend him a narcoleptic air.

In Los Angeles the main promotions companies are Lockdown, N5, Opium, Blueprint and Mad Pro. Sleep joined Mad Pro at the bottom after he was laid off from a job working in government warehouses. His first job was putting up stickers for the LA rapper Coolio and he was lucky to be clearing $150 a week, which is a lot more than most newcomers to street promotion usually earn for months. He worked his way up and now he runs the outfit. He's spent years making the right connections in the industry: now he's getting them to work for him. If some aspiring rapper wants to hang with LA radio DJs like Tha Baka Boys, Theo or Julio G from 92.3 The Beat, it's not a bad idea to make sure that Sleep is working for you, because he can make the introductions. 'I slip him my number, and he can slip me his,' says Sleep. 'I'm helping out.' Sleep has hustled himself a position as an intern on Julio G's influential *Westside Radio* show on 92.3 The Beat. Radio is a powerful medium in the music industry, and if Sleep keeps his foot in that door, some of the power will rub off on him.

Tonight the Bay Area rapper E-40 is visiting the convention with his cousin B-Legit. At some point in the evening Sleep will call up Julio G on The Beat, pass his mobile phone over and put both the rappers on air for an interview. That way the rappers receive a little extra promotion, and Julio has a couple of special guests that he hadn't bargained for on his show. Sleep doesn't get paid for doing it, but it means that he's owed a favour down the line.

The boys from Platinum Plus move through the crowd *en masse*, covering each table with glossy flyers. They move through the hotel lobby placing them on the sofas, then pass out through the car park, dropping them casually all over the tarmac, all over people's vehicles. A street promotion team must be cheeky: it must show how it's going to get your product imprinted on the consciousness of the ghettos, even if that means scattering trash all over the car park. They are ambitious: they want to save enough money to buy themselves a recording studio, and start their own record label.

Then I notice another street promoter – a thinner boy moving through the crowd on his own. He moves up to the tables more hesitantly than the bullish Platinum Plus crew, but he diligently covers the entire hotel area with his flyers. He is an olive-skinned African-American; tall, lean and good-looking. He hunches diffidently as he walks. He introduces himself to people with a mixture of shyness and fierceness. His name is Rah, short for Rasheed. His flyers are much more cheaply produced than Platinum Plus's: simply a photocopied phone number and a name: Transit Crew.

I call Rah up a few days after the convention. I tell him I'm interested in street promotion. I say I see the stickers everywhere, but never the people who put them up. Can he tell me what he does, and how he does it?

'Well,' says the boy. 'That would be all right, I guess.'

The next day Rah is already there by the time I arrive, sitting at a corner table in a bare Del Taco in one of the less glittery parts of Hollywood, south of Sunset. He hunches with his back-pack by his side on the banquette, in his big black nylon jacket. 'Coffee?' I ask.

'No thank you.'

'You want anything else? Something to eat?'

'No,' he says. 'I'm OK.' His voice is quiet; he looks past me rather than at me. It's not that he's unfriendly – just reserved. He's probably not sure why he's meeting me here in the first place. At first glance he seems too self-contained and quiet to make it in the street promotion business.

I order a coffee for myself to give us some excuse to be in the restaurant after dark and sit opposite Rah and make small talk. I ask him about the Urban Network conference; he says it was good. Just outside the glass door behind Rah, a vagrant positions himself with a soft drinks cup to beg for quarters.

'Did you always want to get into the music business?' I ask.

He looks past me. 'What I really wanted to do,' he announces, 'was play ball. I played basketball for years. I was tight.'

The girl behind the counter has overfilled my coffee: when I add the milk, stir it and then try and lift the cup, I spill some. The dark puddle inches across the table towards Rah. He says, 'I could have gone somewhere as a basketball player.' His reserve melts. He talks quietly still, but intensely.

Rah spent the early years of his life in the Crenshaw–Slauson district, south of the junction with Martin Luther King Boulevard. His dad wasn't around: he had moved away to Hawaii before Rah ever had a chance to know him. He flew back sometimes but Rah still feels that he never got to know the sort of stuff he feels he should know about his father: '. . . What he likes to do. What he doesn't like . . . He came to kick it and stuff, but I never been to no basketball game with my dad.'

His mother was beautiful: she had been a model. She moved the family from South Central to an apartment up in Hollywood. For a while there were four of them, living together as a family: Rah and his mother, his younger sister Christina and an old man that they had befriended and whom Rah took to calling his 'grandfather', in the absence of his own father. Rah had an older brother too, but he was wild. His brother was a fully-fledged gang-banger, as Americans call gang members. 'My brother,' he explains, 'was on some big shit. Crips. Real, real shit.'

But the gang life didn't appeal to Rah. He was going to be a basketball player. Maybe for USC or UCLA.

Gazing at the coffee I've spilt, Rah says: 'And then my mom had a mental breakdown. She just snapped.'

Rah was too young to know what was going on when she started falling apart. He would just watch her lying in bed all day, and listen to her talking in her little girl voice. 'She didn't do nothing. She didn't eat. I used to have to beg her just to put something in her mouth. It was really, really rough. You know what I'm saying?' The story is pouring out of Rah now. And I'm listening, nodding and tutting, with the sort of distant fascination of someone whose life has so little in common with his. 'I went through hell with her,' Rah is saying. 'And I love her and everything. I just thought: Why did it have to happen like that?'

The man Rah called his grandfather was old. He had diabetes and became bedridden, so Rah gradually slipped into the role of head of the family, doing the shopping and trying to keep everything together. Sometimes his mother would take the social security cheques, cash them, buy alcohol and head straight to the park to share it with the vagrants. Rah learned to wait for the mailman, so he could get to the cheques before her. He learned how to pay the electricity bills. 'I had to take on all these responsibilities that a father would be doing,' he says.

Rah's family slowly descended into poverty. The horror stories that LA hip hop tells usually involve crime, drug addiction or sudden violence. Rah's is grimmer for being so much less dramatic.

By 14, Rah was longing for something else, something outside the apartment where he lived with a geriatric man and a young sister and the mad woman who lay in bed, singing, 'Mmm-mmm' to herself. Rah turned to a click – or clique – who called themselves

31

the Criminals or CMA, the Criminal-Minded Assassins. The Criminals were a fledgeling gang. It is hard for outsiders from stable backgrounds to recognize the benefits a gang confers. Rah was looking for a sense of security that was absent in his family. He had seen what the 'colours' gangs were all about from his older brother's violent life. Among the African-American gangs in LA, 'colours' – Crip blue and Blood red – denote membership of the premier league of gang-banging. Rah just wanted to join one of the smaller local gangs that could provide him with the sort of companionship he didn't receive from elsewhere. But the reality fell short of the ideal.

According to the mythology of gang-banging, new members are 'jumped in' – that is, beaten viciously by other members. That's how they portray it in the movies, anyway: real Blood and Crip gangs are usually less finicky about it, but the Criminals believed that if they were going to be a gang they should do things by the book, so they jumped Rah in. 'They beat the crap out of me. Believe me,' he says ruefully.

Once he was in, all that hanging around a gang did was get him into trouble. The Criminals included one bona fide psycho: a boy who was about two years younger than Rah, but who carried a gun and wasn't afraid to shoot people. One time Rah and this boy were in Culver City when the kid went crazy and hit somebody with a bottle who he felt had disrespected him. Rah saw the man fall, and the blood start gushing, and he tried to run away from the fight but the police caught him and accused him of attempting to rob the victim of the assault. 'Which I didn't,' insists Rah.

Anyway, Rah ended up in juvenile hall and that's when he decided that this whole business was pretty pointless. Another myth about gang-banging was that members were supposed to support each other when they were in trouble. Nobody came to visit him in jail. He sat in his small room and grew increasingly despondent. Damn, he thought; there's nobody down for me. Which was true.

When he was released he decided that, from now on, if he wanted anything he was going to have to get it himself. 'Yo, man,' he told the gang. 'I ain't with you no more.'

Back at home, things were getting worse for Rah. His mother's behaviour was becoming increasingly chaotic, and she had fallen so far behind with the rent that the landlord decided it was time to evict the family. At 15, Rah found himself responsible for finding them somewhere new to live.

A girlfriend told him of an apartment going in the mid–city area, around Wilshire, so Rah went and met the landlord. 'Imagine doing that when you're 15,' he says. 'You're too young. But my mom wouldn't come up with me to fill out any applications.'

In the end he found a new apartment, but they didn't have a stick of furniture, so he scrounged three beds: one for his mother, one for his sister and one for his 'grandfather'. His grandmother gave them a couch, which Rah slept on. He still feels guilty about the lies he had to tell to the landlord to cover up for his mother, the references he had to falsify and the income he had to pretend he was making. He feels he let the landlord down. But at least he had put a roof over his family's head.

He feels guilty, too, that he didn't understand how he could help his mother. By now she was repeating herself constantly. Whatever Rah told her, she would have forgotten a minute later. She was often abusive. She was jealous of Rah's girlfriends. 'Fuck you!' she would scream at them. Looking back, Rah thinks it was probably something to do with the Thorazine and the other prescription drugs she was taking erratically, which were supposed to calm her down and make her sleep. He wishes he had gone with her to visit the doctor, so he could have watched out for her better, or taken her along to all the psychiatrists' appointments that she missed.

The old man was a mess too. Rah and his little sister would try to take him to the shower so that he could wash, but it was hard. 'He should have been in a home or something,' Rah sees now. One of his leg became infected and he had to have it amputated. 'God,' Rah remembers quietly. 'It was hectic.'

It's now pitch-black outside the Del Taco. I say, 'I need another coffee. You want one?'

'No. I'm all right,' says Rah.

That Rah had given up gang-banging didn't mean he had given up criminal activity. Instead, he realized that the only way to get things done now was on his own. A lot of it was shoplifting. Hollywood's whites have almost universally deserted the state school system. Rah went to Fairfax High, a predominantly African-American and Latino school, situated slap bang on the fashionable thoroughfare of Melrose, where all the young, oh-so-slightly-counter-cultural clothes shops are situated. Several of Rah's fellow pupils from Fairfax used to steal from the local stores. Most of what he stole he sold to other people, but if he needed a pair of Timberland boots he would simply steal them for himself.

Sometimes, he admits, he would mug people too. 'I had my little licks I did to make my money,' he says wryly. 'All the stuff that bad people do. Jacking people. Crazy stuff.'

I look at Rah. He's not a big boy: he's wiry rather than muscular, and bashful. It's hard to imagine him as a mugger.

Either way, Rah looked out for himself, still dreaming of becoming a basketball player. Even now it pains him that all through his dark adolescence there was nobody who he felt was really on his side. 'I had nobody there for me. It's the one thing that really hurt inside. I was playing ball games, and I had nobody there to sit and watch me and say, "You had a good game."'

His mother came to a couple of games, but a lot of the time she'd be in the hospital when he was playing, or she'd be too nervous to attend because being in a crowd made her condition worse, and her hands would start to shake. Rah demonstrates for me above the table. So he told her, 'It's all right if you don't come.'

But he wished he had someone who could be there to see him when he scored that last-second shot, the one that won the game.

And on Father's Day he used to fantasize about having someone he could go up to and say, 'Here, father, here's a present.'

Rah looks up. 'That's like the empty part,' he says. 'I wish I could have had someone I could share that with.'

But he grew older, and more independent, and adolescence began to be more fun. He acquired a Tommy Guerrero skateboard – one of the old-fashioned wide boards – and used to spend days in ninth grade skating on a half pipe. And he started getting into music, too. Pop music is one of the greatest consolations of a lonely adolescence: the revelation that popular culture can join you to a community you never knew existed.

Rah's moment of conversion was listening to Gang Starr's 1994 album *Hard To Earn*. That was the point at which hip hop started to take over his life.

Gang Starr are a well-respected hip-hop band who base themselves in Brooklyn, New York. There are two members: an aggressive, combative lyricist who calls himself Guru and a producer called DJ Premier, who is the master of the meticulously crafted stripped-down beat.

Enthusiastically, Rah says, 'Premier is dope. Him and RZA [of the Wu-Tang Clan] are the best producers right now.'

For the first time I notice he's wearing a T-shirt with the Gang Starr logo on it. Street promoters usually dress in free promotional items: their sartorial sandwich boards.

'*Take this for example,*' ran the track 'The Code Of The Streets':

Young brothers want rep
'Cause in the life they're living you can't half-step
It starts with the young ones doing crime for fun
And if you ain't down, you'll be played out son . . .

For middle-class hip-hop fans, the music supplies the vicarious experience of a world they don't have to live in. Teenagers like Rah experience it in a very different way. They like it because it talks about something they know already:

Tonz a gunz – everybody's ge'in' strapped
Tonz a gunz – you gotta watch the way you act
Tonz a gunz – real easy to get
Tonz a gunz bringing nothing but death . . .

Guru raps about a reality Rah recognized. But if any rapper exemplifies how complicated it can be to be a black boy in America now, and how complicated that reality is, it's Guru. His real name is Keith Elam.

I met him on a couple of occasions. The first time I had just been listening to a political commentator called Patricia Elam on America's National Public Radio on the day before: I mentioned this to Guru, because it seemed such an unusual surname.

'That would be my sister,' Guru said proudly. Both were, after all, social commentators of a kind, though they'd chosen rather different media. Guru raps about the violence in the ghettos and the code of the New York streets. In fact he comes from the other end of the social spectrum from Rah; his is a high-achieving well-to-do Boston family. His father was Boston's first black judge; his mother was director of libraries for the city's public schools.

The sixties civil-rights movement created a new black middle class in America. Guru's parents were beneficiaries of this new social openness. They gave him a good private education, but, mindful of the effect of middle-class flight from black areas, the family decided not to quit the inner-city neighbourhood they'd come up from. Dad was a disciplinarian. ' "If you don't go to school and work then get the fuck out," ' reminisced Guru, grinning. 'When we were little we just used to see his belt. He didn't even have to take it off. He just used to show you the buckle.'

But Guru was torn between the upwardly mobile, bourgeois, politically active aspirations of his family and the strong kinship he felt with the more romantic and urgent life in the neighbourhoods around him. He became the black sheep. It's a familiar story. Instead of reaping the fruits of his private education, he kept company with the hustlers, dealers and street boys.

The children of the new African–American middle class faced a new set of pressures that are only now being understood. The children of those who moved out of black communities often felt alienated. Black middle-class suicide rates jumped alarmingly in the eighties and nineties. To Guru, whose family stayed in the ghetto, the working-class street life around him seemed more vital than the aspirational lifestyle of his family. He would borrow his dad's car to drive around hookers for a pimp friend. One time his father found a gun on the car's back seat, left there by Guru's disreputable friend. The judge was not best pleased. 'We was definitely in conflict,' remembered Guru.

We were sitting in the trailer parked on 130th Street in Harlem. Gang Starr were shooting a video. Between takes, Guru was enjoying a drink with his friends and admirers. A few younger rappers burst into occasional bouts of freestyling – ad-libbing rhymes – trying to impress the star. After he'd finished the Courvoisier, someone opened a 1.75-litre bottle of Hennessy. The blunts were being rolled as if by production line.

Guru was in his late teens when the dealers who used to bring drugs from New York started to appear with mix tapes of some of the new music that was starting to come out of Brooklyn, Harlem and the Bronx. Guru and his friends were electrified by it. A friend, a small-time Boston hustler called Giovanni, encouraged Guru to take his rapping talent to New York, which back then was the only place where an MC could succeed.

Woozily clutching his plastic cup of brandy in one hand and a joint in the other, Guru reminisced happily: 'Giovanni – rest in peace – was the man. He always had the new mix tapes and the flyest gear – the waves in his hair and the Adidas sneakers. But he was quick to pull his gun out,' Guru remembered. 'He got murdered. But he did a lot of shit, so . . .'

There was a likeable transparency about Guru. He was drunk, bumptious and proud of his status as one of what the hip-hop generation call 'the old school', one of the keepers of the hip-hop faith. The single they were shooting the video for was called 'Royalty'. 'Real hip hop to me is like royalty,' he explained loudly. 'Gang Starr are royalty. People that follow our music are royalty.' He slipped on his Phat Farm jacket and held forth about today's rappers who had risen fast on the back of the million-dollar budgets old-school heroes like Gang Starr had never been offered. 'Man, the work ethic has been lost among young men in the urban environment,' he shouted at the younger rappers around him. 'A lot of artists, they can't build a career. That's what I did. A lot of artists can't even read or write,' he blared, swaying impressively, drunk, effusive and fiery. I couldn't help thinking how much like his own father he was probably sounding as he lambasted the work-shy youth of today.

And then I asked him about an incident a few months earlier in which he had been arrested at La Guardia Airport for carrying a .380 pistol – with filed-off serial numbers – in his baggage. At the time, Guru had denied the gun was his. He claimed that a friend had mistakenly placed it in his baggage. The story made headlines.

I imagined the respected Judge Elam, who had worked against the odds to get where he had, who had once found a gun in his own car, reading the newspaper reports about his son. I asked Guru what it was like when his father found out. 'It hurt' – he shook his head – ''cause my father is a great black man, and my mother is a great black woman and I felt like I failed,' he said, in a tenderly soulful, befuddled voice. ''Cause I hurt them when I was 15. When I was 15.' He was shouting again now; he seemed about to break down. 'And to hurt them again at 35 . . .' And the noisy trailer was suddenly silent, everyone watching the famous rapper, great big shiny Hennessy tears filling his eyes.

Shortly after he discovered a love for Gang Starr, Rah also discovered street promotion. It started when an acquaintance named Breck Ayres – or Cash as he's known to friends – began working for an established Los Angeles street team named Lockdown. Priority Records were paying Cash to promote the LA rapper Lil' Half Dead. Cash asked Rah to help.

Suddenly there was a chance for Rah to be part of this music. Like most of the younger street promoters, Rah worked unpaid, taking the flyers and the tapes to South Central's high schools and handing them out. He discovered that there was respect to be had from being the one with the merchandise. 'And the girls,' he smiles for the first time, 'was like, "*Yo!*" '

Sometimes Rah would get into the 21-and-over clubs to hand out clip tapes and flyers and sometimes people would pass him a drink and he was suddenly part of something. 'And it was like, cool.'

Now, instead of just being a kid with nothing going on for him, he was a street promoter. He acquired the only equipment he needed for the job: a staple gun and a camera. Every good street promoter carries a camera: usually a disposable one, so you don't have to worry about losing it at two in the morning at a nightclub.

Still no money, of course. A young street promoter is lucky to make a couple of hundred dollars a week working flat out, but Rah was working for Cash for the love of it. He still had to rely on other less legal activities for his money, like thieving. There was legitimate work too, whatever he could turn his hand to. For a while he worked at the El Capitan, a glorious 1926 South American fantasy of a cinema on Hollywood Boulevard, where Clark Gable and Rita Hayworth had once performed live. When Rah was working there, it was showing Disney's *Toy Story*.

Street promotion was just for fun. When he wasn't sniping, Rah was working the nightclubs, getting his face known around places like Ballistics, Flex, Kingston 12 and Unity. It was at Paradise 24, at Las Palmas and Santa Monica, that he first bumped into a young guy called Josiah Brocks. Josiah Brocks was a street promoter too, but he took the job really seriously. 'When I met Josiah,' says Rah, 'he just touched my life.'

The Del Taco is empty now. A bored girl stands behind the counter staring into space.

Josiah Brocks is of mixed race: part Latino, part African–American. He is good-looking, wears his hair in dreadlocks and has a big, wide smile to light up any room.

He grew up in Los Angeles. His mother was a religious woman who had worked as a gang counsellor. But like a lot of Angelenos, she had moved the family out to somewhere where the quality of life was better. Josiah never liked it in Seattle, where they settled. He and his mother had a big-bust up when he was 16 and he left home and headed straight back to the Los Angeles he missed.

Josiah first appeared on the scene back in the summer of 1996, turning up at the Inglewood office of the street promotion team N5 – Niggas To The Fifth Power – run by an old music-business hand, Mike Nixon.

Everybody in the LA music scene knows Mike. He turns up everywhere. To the young kids he's an 'old man', though in fact he's in his mid-forties. He arrives at shows and at record stores clutching his big bag full of promotion merchandise, and always wearing a Kangol hat over his dreadlocks.

Mike has been in the music industry since the sixties, and so comes from another, more civil era. He looked for promoters who would knuckle down and get the work done: in turn, they would look to him to teach them how to act professionally. Mike ran a team of between 20 and 25 boys, but good talent was always scarce.

All the 'slangin'' he heard from so many of the young boys didn't impress him. He understood why they did it, but he let them know that they weren't going to get anywhere in this business if they couldn't communicate in a businesslike fashion.

In Mike, it's partly the fustiness of the older generation talking, looking down on the young; but what he told his teams had a more serious point too. How you talk is what you are. The increasing isolation of America's underclass is not just economic and spatial: it's linguistic too. The African-American vernacular that thrives so richly in hip hop has its roots in West Indian Creole, and in the eighteenth-century speech patterns of the Irish and Scots immigrants. But linguists who have studied black English over the past few decades have noticed that instead of converging with what they call Standard American English, it is fast drifting ever further away from it. The creative, fast-evolving language that black Americans speak in the inner cities may be increasingly desirable on wax, as a cultural artefact, but it is becoming less and less like the language of the majority, the language of the classroom, of the mass media, of politics and of the workplace.

The thing that first impressed Mike about Josiah Brocks was his persistence. That first time they had made an appointment to meet, Mike had to cancel at the last moment. He called Josiah, who simply said: 'That's OK. I'll just come again.'

That sort of attitude scored points with Mike. He was tired of all the boys who expect something for nothing. All that talk talk talk that these kids like to do, thought Mike: 'I'm the best and nobody can beat me.'

Josiah quickly became his star pupil. He loved life back in Los Angeles so much that he called up his older brother, Silas, and told him to come down too.

Together the two brothers worked hard. In one day they plastered five miles of Martin Luther King Boulevard, all the way from Rodeo to Figueroa, with flyers for the hip-hop radio station Power 106.

They were good too: when the police came up and yelled, 'Hey! That's illegal!' they would blink innocently, smile and say, 'Oh. We seen another guy putting flyers up so we thought it was OK . . .'

Josiah and Rah clicked straight away. For Rah, meeting Josiah was a revelation. Both were huge hip-hop fans; both were street promoters working the same circuit. Rah dreamed of becoming a performer too. He had his own rap name: R. Shottie – a 'shottie' is a shotgun. Josiah and Silas had already formed their own hip-hop group, the Black and Brown Movement – so named because their parents were black and brown.

Right at the start of their friendship, when Rah told Josiah that he was working for Lockdown for free, Josiah was appalled. 'Hey, you don't make no money off of street promotions?' he asked. He told Rah to leave Cash and join his crew working for N5.

All his life, if Rah had wanted something he'd had to do it himself. He never expected anyone to help him. The gang hadn't helped him. His family had not been able to help him either. Now, for the first time, these two brothers were looking out for him. They went to Mike Nixon, who gladly took him on as one of N5's promoters.

But back then it was still a game to Rah: thieving was still his main hustle. Josiah had been raised to believe that theft was wrong, and kept telling Rah that whatever you do wrong will come back to you in some way. If Rah lost some money he'd made from robbing somebody, Josiah would say, 'See? It comes back to you. That's why it happened.'

One day he told Rah, 'Hey, man. Why don't you stop stealing? You'll get into trouble. If you stick to stealing, then you're going to stick to a jail cell.'

Two days later Rah was caught shoplifting and sentenced to 25 days in the county jail. It was a nightmarish time for him. He could hear people being beaten up in other cells, and there were seriously ill inmates who seemed to be getting no medical attention. I'm never coming back here, Rah thought. Never. I'm going to be positive. I'm going to listen to everything Josiah says.

Josiah has that effect on people. He's two years younger than Rah, but according to Rah, he changed his life. 'I can't take it any more,' Rah told him. 'I can't settle for hustling like this for ever. It's hard. Everything comes to an end one day.' And he gave away all the tools he used to burgle and shoplift, the razors, and pliers, to a boy called Tommy. Tommy wasn't going to stop thieving; he's in jail right now, in fact.

So the boy who thought he should have been a basketball player became a street promoter instead. Josiah, Rah and Silas became a team. They call themselves Transit Crew.

It's a private joke. When the Brocks brothers first moved to Los Angeles they didn't have anywhere to live. Sometimes they would crash over at Rah's apartment. At other times they would sleep on the Santa Monica No. 4 bus, riding back and forth until the driver threw them off and they would spend the rest of the night on the beach. They couldn't afford a car. If they needed to get to a club, or to go sniping, they travelled by bus. Hence Transit Crew. They added the name proudly to the stickers they sniped, so that people would know who they were.

4

Fire Comes Through a Forest

KOOL HERC

There are plenty of record shops here in South Central; big chains like Wherehouse and Tower in the malls, local chains like VIP and King of Music, or thriving 'mom and pop' stores like Underworld Records on Alondra Boulevard in Compton. The record racks are filled with hip hop. But a simple demographic calculation will show that the inner cities aren't what make these records turn platinum.

Early on, Jerry Heller, the white Jewish manager of NWA, recognized the essential dynamic of hip hop. 'Obviously,' he said, 'inner-city kids aren't buying the volume of rap records that sell. So when talking about those kind of albums – Public Enemy, NWA – those have captured middle-class white America, y'know, as far as the kids go.' For some hip-hoppers, that's an uncomfortable truth.

It's one of the most fascinating oddities of hip hop: it is mostly consumed in a totally different environment from that in which it is produced. White suburban boys buy rap. They don't make it. Not successfully, anyway. There are a small number of exceptions to the rule, but for most of its consumers rap ceases to have meaning when performed by white people. It is almost as if America has created a new caste system, in which only one group of people are permitted to be the musicians, or the tellers of a particular style of folk tale. By and large, the economic fact of rap is that young men who come from some of the most degraded neighbourhoods in America create it for other young people who rarely have the opportunity or desire to visit those places.

A ghetto is, by and large, an area rejected by the rest of a city, or by a whole country. So it is not surprising when that ghetto answers with a culture that shuns the aspirations of the society that has rejected it. Gangsta rap, in particular, does its best to turn liberal middle-class morality on its head. It is deliberately foul-mouthed, deliberately offensive. *''Cause that's what we try to do on our music,'* as Eazy-E explained so eloquently on the intro to NWA's 'I Ain't Tha 1':

We try and make music to piss you off. That's why we say bitch-bitch-bitch-bitch-bitch-bitch-bitch-bitch-bitch. And nigga-nigga-nigga-nigga-nigga-nigga-nigga-nigga-nigga. And fuck you if you don't like it.

Of course, for the suburban middle class, for whom rejection of their parents' values is a ritual developmental phase, the 'gangsta rap' of the early nineties was perfect. It was the new punk rock. *'And fuck you if you don't like it.'* Boys like Budman and Rah suddenly realized they had a commodity they could sell, if they were lucky and clever: their own stories and way of life.

Young people the world over are wearing their pants loose, hung around the waist, aping the fashions of the hip-hop stars, who in turn had copied the styles of gang-bangers, who had their dress sense forced upon them when the prison authorities took their belts away. Hip hop derives much of its power from the fact that America is an increasingly segregated society in which the rich and the poor are increasingly buttressed against each other, but increasingly fascinated with each other. Perhaps the obsession that white suburbia has with the culture of the black inner cities is an attempt to reach out over that divide, as much as an attempt to buy into its counter-culture. Every rap fan must wonder what it is really like in the neighbourhoods in which the stars they love grew up, and must fantasize about what it would be like to go there. In some ways, that's what I'm doing here in South Central.

This schism between consumer and producer is one of rap's most peculiar dynamics: it's not just an accident of history. You could even say it's integral to the genre. It goes right back to the origins of hip hop. This is a book about the boys of South Central Los Angeles. They are 'Westsiders', but to understand their passions I first have to go the East Coast, to where hip hop was born.

Clive Campbell is 44. He still speaks with a hint of the Jamaican accent from the country he left when he was about 13. Most of the time he works in boat-yards, Simonizing hulls. He still does the occasional show, whenever interest in the 'old school' springs up anew; but he doesn't listen to any modern hip hop: his interest in it peaked years ago.

Die-hard hip-hop fans know him as Kool Herc. Although generally acknowledged as the most pivotal figure in the creation of the music, Kool Herc didn't appear on a single contemporary recording. 'People thought it would never go anywhere,' he says flatly.

In its beginning hip hop was such an underground culture that for the first five years of its existence not one record was put out. Kool Herc remembers hearing, as a child, the Jamaican DJs 'toasting' over the 'dub plates' – the specially recorded instrumental acetates – behind the corrugated-iron fences that surrounded Kingston's dancehalls. It was Kool Herc – he called himself Herc because of his muscular physique – who put in place the two cornerstones of the music. He was the inventor of 'breakbeats': the first DJ to use two turntables to spin the rhythm parts of two records back to back, creating an instrumental backbone that could be extended for as long as the DJ wanted to continue 'mixing' between the two records. Second, he was the first to have his own crew of MCs – the artists who would later become known as 'rappers', rhyming over the beats. It was an innovation he borrowed in part from the dancehall DJs of his youth, and partly from the New York disco DJs who sometimes spat out a few brief rhymes between records. Kool Herc and the mighty Herculoids ruled the Bronx, watched by starry-eyed fans like Grandmaster Flash, Melle Mel and Afrika Bambaata, who much later transferred the ideas on to wax.

Herc had arrived in the Bronx in 1967. The Bronx was in a tailspin. America's ghettos have been at the receiving end of social policy for a long time. In the seventies, the city of New York was in financial crisis and slashing services to fend off bankruptcy. While middle-class areas were protected from the worst of the cuts, the poorest areas suffered the most. Fire Departments all over the Bronx were closed down, even though the poverty of its inhabitants made it a high-risk area, resulting in a rash of fires that made it resemble a war zone. Crime and poverty were careering out of control. By the early seventies the Bronx had become a byword for inner-city decay. For the African-American urban underclass, the promises of the civil-rights era had come to nothing. Poverty and ghetto housing effectively meant that they were more isolated, arguably even more segregated than they had been in days of slavery, when rich and poor, black and white had actually lived in far closer proximity to each other.

'The Bronx was burning down,' Herc says. 'It was in turmoil. It's like when a fire comes through a forest, you find new roots springing through. And it was in a transition period . . .'

He remembers going into the early discos of the Bronx – places like the Rathole on Claremont Avenue, where for the first time he heard the James Brown records that would form the basis of so many of his most famous beats.

'And then,' says Herc, 'the gangs started coming up strong.' As overcrowding grew, unemployment, crime and drug consumption rose, and the Bronx fell apart. Disaffected youths formed gangs. In those days the Bronx gangs initially modelled themselves on the white motorcycle gangs, wore leather jackets and gave themselves names like the Nomads, the Outlaws and the Black Spades.

With the rise of the gangs, the clubs closed down. Increasing violence meant that club owners were no longer prepared to take the risk. So if you lived in the Bronx, you had to find something else to do. And that's when the block parties and the park jams that incubated hip hop started.

Up until then disco had been the new thing. It preceded hip hop by only a few years, emerging from the same black and Latino clubs of the New York neighbourhoods. The names of the disco DJs, like Grandmaster Flowers, Pete DJ Jones, MaBoya and DJ Hollywood mean little today, but like Kool Herc, they were heroes to the generation who went on to invent hip hop. But while hip hop was to be an underground phenomenon, confining itself strictly to the neighbourhoods where it was born, disco was from the start openly cosmopolitan. It headed downtown to the glitzy discos of Manhattan as fast as it could. As violence had shut down most of the clubs in the Bronx there was nowhere for the DJs to play anyway, and the downtown clubs which welcomed them in were considerably more profitable too.

But those who remained in the Bronx weren't happy that their DJ idols had deserted them.

'Pete DJ Jones played mostly down mid-town,' recalls Herc, 'playing for *bourgeois* blacks – people who're too big for the Bronx. Can't be seen down the ghettos – so called.'

Bronx natives felt excluded from disco. Another key member of the Bronx old school was Guy Williams. As Rahiem (not to be confused with the Rahiem known as O.G. Budman), he rapped first with the Funky Four Plus One before joining Grandmaster Flash and the Furious Five. Rahiem too remembered disco as being too exclusive a scene for the Bronx's working class: 'Disco was too bourgeois for us,' he says, echoing Herc's words. 'It was for older people. We couldn't get into the disco clubs because we weren't dressed properly. And disco was against everything we represented.'

'On the flyers to the disco parties would be a little notice: "No sneakers",' agrees Fab 5 Freddy, a.k.a. Frederick Braithwaite. 'That,' he says, 'was a direct message to the more urban side of the crowd, the poorer side of the crowd, to keep away.' A young Brooklyn-born graffiti artist, Freddy used to take the young white punk élite like Blondie down to the Bronx to witness the new hip-hop scene. Blondie returned the favour by name-checking him (and Grandmaster Flash) on their 1981 hit 'Rapture'.

Shut out of the clubs, the new 'b-boys' – the 'Bronx Boys' – who made up Herc's fans embraced the down-beat sneakers that kept them off the glitterballed disco floors. Even when it started, hip hop was an attempt to reclaim a territory that the MCs and DJs felt was rightfully theirs, a rebellion against the larger bourgeois world. From the very beginning, it was about laying claim to identity.

The b-boys adopted the same slogan as the white-rock backlash that was simultaneously gathering pace: 'Disco sucks'. Disco was fake, phoney and, worse, 'bougie' – bourgeois. And because there were few clubs that would let them play their music, they hooked up their speakers in the parks, stealing electricity from the lamp-posts, and threw their own block parties, so that for the first few years of its existence hip hop remained invisible, unseen and unheard by white middle-class America. It was ghetto music.

Disco was inclusive. It was easily assimilable, so assimilable in fact that within a few short years a bearded Australian rock group called the Bee Gees could undergo a make-over and become the genre's figureheads. It *wanted* to be the music for the international jet set. Within a few years even the *haute* bougie Princess Stephanie of Monaco could – briefly, at least – attempt a career as a Euro-disco singer. In contrast, hip hop was deliberately working-class, and defiantly urban, in an American context in which urban usually meant black or Hispanic.

Disco embraced the dominant middle-class morality; hip hop rejected it. And while disco was about girls and boys, girls dancing with boys, girls singing about boys, or even boys dancing with boys, hip hop was, well, mostly about men. Even when it was about women, it was really about men. While disco was embraced early by gay culture, hip hop headed deliberately in the opposite direction and has become openly homophobic. With a small number of exceptions, MC-ing has remained a boy thing. DJ-ing has remained almost exclusively male. Girls were frozen out of dancing very early on, when the breakdancers started inventing moves that were so aggressively athletic that girls no longer felt they had a place on the floor.

Those critics who have a romantic historical view of African-American culture like to emphasize the depth of the roots of rap music, of what it shares with the ancient African griot style of storytelling. True, there are ancient African and West Indian oral traditions, but there's a sense in which trying to hitch rap to older forms underestimates how abrupt and radical the arrival of hip hop was. Hip hop was called into being because it met a desire among the young people of the Bronx to have something that was their own, that didn't belong either to the middle class, to parents who had grown up in more optimistic times, or to history.

It sounded like nothing that had preceded it. Instead of melody, it substituted the spoken word. Instead of a band, it substituted a beatbox and two turntables. And by the time gangsta had emerged, it had already distanced itself still further from what had gone before. Unlike blues, r'n'b or soul, it was not sensual; it became more often than not angry or confrontational. And it was incredibly direct:

Bitch-bitch-bitch-bitch-bitch-bitch-bitch-bitch-bitch. And nigga-nigga-nigga-nigga-nigga-nigga-nigga-nigga-nigga. And fuck you if you don't like it.

Herc quit hip hop in 1977. At the height of his success, he was running his own club, the Hevalo, on Jerome Avenue in the Bronx. One night, after performing there, Herc went to play a gig at the Police Athletic League club on Western Avenue. A fight broke out, but Herc has no idea why the man with the knife attacked him, stabbing him several times and gouging the hand he held in front of him to fend off the blows.

'I survived it,' says Herc sanguinely. 'The party people ran out and stabbed the guy who stabbed me, but he survived it too.'

But the incident demoralized him badly. He felt it was time for him to put his turntables away. New DJs like Grandmaster Flash had come up. Though Herc had led the way, Flash's turntable technique was already light-years ahead of Herc's.

This was a full two years before rap burst out of the ghetto into the *Billboard* charts in 1979. There had been a few attempts to capture hip hop on record, but none of them was successful until a couple called Joe and Sylvia Robinson turned up at a rap show at the Harlem club Harlem World, saw the reaction of the crowd and sensed that there were large profits to be made from this stuff. The idea of putting the music on record is one that the DJs and MCs had flirted with but which most people felt uneasy about. Disco had been recorded straight away, and the neighbourhoods had lost control of it.

On the Hudson River side of the Bronx an exuberant former Black Spade turned DJ who called himself Afrika Bambaata had established himself as the dominant force, competing with Flash's Furious Five. Bambaata remembers the discussions about whether the DJs and MCs should put the music on wax. 'People were very negative about records at first,' he says. 'They felt it would kill the parties, that it would change everything.'

Change everything it did. The Robinsons put together a ramshackle group they called the Sugarhill Gang, and had them recite – word for word – some of the rhymes that the best Bronx MCs had developed. It was a hit all over the world.

The single 'Rappers Delight' shocked the people of the Bronx, who had nurtured the music and were proud of the fact that it was exclusively theirs. Melvin Glover – MC Melle Mel of the Furious Five – remembers the shock he felt, hearing his own lines in someone else's mouth. 'Nobody in the Bronx really appreciated "Rappers Delight",' he says. 'We just felt it was sub-par rappers saying anything.'

The genie was suddenly out of the bottle. Hip hop no longer belonged to the underground. Grandmaster Flash was as disturbed by the record as anyone. 'That shit was haunting me because I felt we should have been the first group to do it,' he says. 'We were the first group to do this – someone took our shot. Every night I would hear this fucking record on the radio. I would hear this shit in my dreams.'

Suddenly everything had changed. 'Well, you just had to get on that train, because it was rollin',' said Melle Mel.

'I'm never the one to feel sour, or that I missed the boat,' Herc says. 'The things I've seen . . . Just the mere fact that I'm living to see it. A lot of the guys . . . they're dead. I'm living to see it.'

As hip-hop culture reaches its quarter-century, there has been a rash of old-school revival shows. A generation of earnest young middle-class hip-hoppers with a sense of history is eager to see Herc play again. 'I'm blessed. People hug me, congratulate me. "Thank you for starting this culture. Thank you for giving me something to do." I feel it. Nobody can buy that. Tears come to my eye.'

In the meantime he works at the boat-yard. 'It's all right with me,' he says.

5

The White Owl

KHOP

Killing Hoes Over Pussy. That's what Khop's name stood for when he first got it. 'Hoes', a popular corruption of 'whores', is loosely used to mean most of womankind. Khop acquired the name as student at LA's Inglewood High School. It was the same school that Inglewood heroes like Mack 10 and AllFrumTha I (i.e. Inglewood) went to. From about the tenth grade onwards, when everyone was forming clicks, any group of boys kicking it together would give themselves a name – usually a three- or four-letter acronym. They weren't gangs, exactly, though some clicks sometimes went a little further than others and crossed the line into gangsta-dom, just as Rah's click the Criminals had tried to.

Khop's friends had decided that their click was going to be called the KHOPZ. Being the shortest, he became Mr Short Khop. The name stuck. Now everyone calls him Khop.

Khop lives in Inglewood, but he travels over to the Valley regularly, the territory north of the Santa Monica hills that real-estate developers carved up after they'd started to run out of the more valuable land in the LA basin. Charlie B and Casual T run a new company called Relentless Entertainment there on Van Nuys Boulevard. It doesn't look much, just a tiny two-room office. The first room has a desk and chair, a sofa, a TV, a Sony Playstation and an answerphone. The second is a makeshift recording studio, where

Khop records his songs. Charlie B and Casual T have big plans for him, though: Khop could be a valuable asset, if everything goes to plan.

Khop loved NWA as a little boy. Everyone seemed to, when they first arrived. Khop's walls were plastered with NWA. He had group shots, and individual pictures of MC Ren, Eazy-E and Ice Cube on the walls of his bedroom. But he couldn't play the records at home much. His dad wouldn't have minded, but his mom? 'She's like a Christian-type lady.'

Khop is more fortunate than Herman or Rah. He has connections. A relative of his used to make jewellery for Ice Cube. When Khop was in junior high school the relative took an awed young Khop with him to meet Cube at the studios and offices that the rapper had invested in on Crenshaw: Cube called the place Street Knowledge.

NWA made gang-banging fashionable. If you weren't in a gang you dressed as if you were. 'If you wasn't bangin' you was going to start bangin' when you heard NWA,' laughs Khop.

But though he shared every boy's fascination with the gang life, Khop never got caught up in the whirlwind that was ripping through Los Angeles in the late eighties. He was too bright for a start; an honour student, in fact. 'A smart little nigga,' he boasts, laughing. Besides, his parents would have given him hell if he'd even ditched school, like some of the other boys used to. They are a hard-working family. His father used to be a probation officer; now he does a little bit of everything, but mainly he works as a self-employed pest exterminator. Khop sometimes used to help him out. His mother is a legal secretary. Both parents pushed him to achieve good grades.

But Khop liked to rap, too. It was his Uncle Billy who helped him get started. Billy knew a white rock band, and one night Khop went on stage with them, rapping at a little nightclub called Mancini's in Canoga Park. It was also Uncle Billy who introduced him to another relative who had a studio. Khop spent time there, recording tracks.

Charlie B first came across Khop when his business partner of the time visited the studio. He could hear Khop that had something; Khop's style is laid-back, but his delivery is confident. By now Khop's hero was Snoop Doggy Dogg, the new Death Row artist from Long Beach whose cool, witty, scurrilous drawl was setting a new standard for West Coast gangsta rap.

'Yeee-ah,' says Khop, who has a way of drawing the word 'yeah' out into two long syllables. 'I love Snoop. Snoop is the bomb. I just hope I don't sound too much like his ass.'

In rhymes Khop portrays himself as a louche ladies' man fighting off the women, a man who likes to drink Hennessy and smoke Indian bidis and the finest weed. One of the tracks he's recorded in the small back room is called 'Dollar, Dank and Drunk'. Dank means weed.

He had his sidekick, Kidub, another Inglewood boy, intone the Snoop-influenced chorus that pretty much sums up Khop's world-view:

Don't love no hoes because they full of drama
I love my weed I love my marijuana.

The image is partially true. Growing up, Khop *was* a ladies' man. He's got a fine-boned face, and his hair is braided back over his head. Khop gets into trouble with women easily. 'There's some scandalous bitches out there,' is how explains it away. At 20 he got a girl pregnant and became a father.

Khop lives at home still, with his mother and father. Trey, his three-year-old son, is raised partly by Khop and his parents; partly by his own mother.

Now the 23-year-old is more cautious when it comes to women. He says, 'Fuck the bitches. Find one cool one. Kick it with her. The only cool female right now on my team is my baby momma,' he says.

'Baby momma': the mother of my baby. The differences between black and white America run deep, but so often express themselves in tiny ways. Though single-parenthood is just as much a phenomenon in white communities, white America doesn't yet have an equivalent of this simple piece of kinship terminology, baby momma, baby poppa; as if we're still ashamed to admit that such relationships still exist.

'Me and my baby momma have this understanding that we can kick it, we can do whatever, but I'm going to have this shit here on the side. You can do what you want to do too, but don't let me catch you,' he giggles, "cause if I catch you, I ain't fuckin' with you.'

Khop is looking after Trey today, so he has brought him up to the Relentless office. Trey is a shy child. He clings to his daddy. Khop, meanwhile, is obviously nuts about Trey, holding his hand proudly.

Charlie sits at the desk. He's eating a fatburger and fries. The small office is grubby; the grey carpet on the floor is stained and worn. A notice taped to the wall pleads: 'Keep studio clean'; another reads: 'Keep doors locked at all times.' They do. There is no security in this building, and they like to know who they're letting in. When there's a loud knock at the door, Charlie shouts, 'Who is it?'

A woman's voice answers. Two buxom girls enter; friends of Charlie's, one quiet, the other loud. They are student nurses. Today is Friday. The weekend is coming and they're dressed to kill. Both have been to the hairdresser. Their hair is elaborately curled and pressed. The loud, busty one is wearing a pair of very brief cut-off denim shorts that have been slit with a razor-blade until there is little of them left. Showing through the holes are the black lace knickers she is wearing underneath. There's not much of her anatomy that you can't see. She is, it would seem, clearly on top of her own sexuality.

She plops down on the sofa and bats her eyes at Khop. Khop is good-looking: slender in a baggy plaid gangsta-style shirt, hair parted into two tight plaits. He ignores her, coolly, so she picks up a copy of *Vibe* magazine. She turns to a fashion spread. 'She's pretty, isn't she?' she says to no one in particular. Then she turns to Khop and flirts: 'You think I could become a model?' No reaction. She turns the page. 'Do you think I'm too short? I have a pretty face, though, don't I?'

Khop doesn't rise to the bait. He tells her he doesn't know anything about modelling. Holding on to his father's legs, Trey gawps at her.

'What's his name?'

'Trey,' answers Khop.

'Oh, he's so beautiful,' she gushes. 'Come here, Trey.'

Trey clutches his father's leg a little tighter.

'He's so shy,' the girl complains. 'Why's he so shy?'

Khop bristles visibly. 'His dad's shy, that's why,' he answers.

The girl cackles. 'Hell, *you* ain't shy. I know you're not. That's how you got a child. You ain't shy.' She laughs loudly. But she gives up. Khop is obviously not interested.

'Females. You know how females are, man,' says Khop, later, when Trey is playing in the room next door. 'They're full of shit. They try to get from you what they can get.' He says he doesn't let them get away with it any more. He says he's learned his lesson. 'Once I kind of ran across a situation where I got stuck and I had a little boy . . . but it's all good. Trey is where my heart is at,' he says fondly. 'I ain't mad. But that'll never happen again.'

Talent aside, Khop has a lot going for him. He has good management, and he has a family with connections, who are backing him. A little over a year ago, in 1996, the relative of his who does Ice Cube's jewellery told Cube about him and passed on a demo tape. About three weeks later Cube called to set up a meeting with the fledgeling rapper. Cube remembers thinking there was something raw about his talent: he receives a lot of demos, but there was something about Khop that he liked.

On the day of the meeting, Khop's '84 Cadillac was out of service, so he called a friend and asked if he'd drive him to Cube's office. All the way he was thinking: Damn. Ice Cube. I'm going to sit and talk with *Ice Cube*. And then, trying to stay hard: This is just another nigga. Fuck that. I'm just Khop. He's just Cube.

Cube turned out to be fine, of course. Listening to his records, you'd think that he was the angriest, most confrontational man in South Central. In person he's usually soft-spoken; he even has a habit of lifting his hand in front of his face as he talks, which suggests a shyness you'd never guess at from his furious performances.

They talked. Cube said he'd be interested in trying him out. 'I'm going to put you down,' he promised.

That was that. Khop went home and waited for the call, but nothing happened. Khop carried on making demos with Charlie and Casual.

RAH

Cash from Lockdown is not best pleased that Josiah has persuaded Rah to join him working for Mike Nixon's street promotion team, N5.

'He took it really bad,' says Josiah's brother Silas, who thinks Cash regarded Rah's departure as an act of treachery. The way Silas sees it, though, Cash was using Rah for his connections, his ability to get into clubs. It's better for Rah this way. 'Rah never had no loyalty to anybody,' Silas says. 'He was really into himself and he didn't have true friends. Everybody would use him. We kind of opened Rah up,' he says proudly.

Mike calls Josiah, Silas and Rah 'the three stooges'. The strange thing he notices is that it's the youngest boy, Josiah, who is clearly the leader of the crew. Silas is his older brother, but you would never know that.

The three stooges are always hanging around together. Like all boys they have their fights, like the time Silas got drunk and turned up at Rah's apartment. Rah was ready to punch him out. 'He was faded,' he explains. 'He was disrespecting.' They got into a big argument about nothing, then Silas said, 'Man, let's take it outside.' So they had a fist-fight out in the street, and then afterwards they hugged each other.

'It brought a respect level to our relationship,' says Silas.

'That made it like a bond,' agrees Rah.

Now, with the money coming in, the Brocks brothers can finally afford an apartment not far from Santa Monica Boulevard, where all the gay clubs and bars are. 'Freaktown' is what Silas calls it.

The summer is shaping up to be a great one. Though they are still working with N5, they are laying plans to go it alone as Transit Crew. They sticker the city for acts like EPMD, Roxanne and local heroes the Alkaholiks. They can cover the city fast. If another crew covers up their stickers they will jump right back out there and do them again. Rah has worked out his own tricks too. If other clicks are snapping at their heels, he smears his posters and stickers with baby oil. Try sticking something on top of that.

They're putting their hearts into it. They believe that the quality of work they're doing is making everyone else step up their game. There is great music around too, just as there should be in the summer, when you can sit outside with your radio on. Josiah's latest discovery is the Boot Camp Click's album, especially the passionate final track, 'Last Time', featuring Buckshot and BJ Swan –

If you read my diary it'd break your heart
'Cause I been losing like a motherfucker from the start . . .

– which he loves to play over and over. Rah didn't like the album when he first heard it, but now he's heard it so many times he's starting to love it too.

I call in on Sleep from Mad Pro, the other promoter I met at the Palm Springs conference, at his first-floor apartment in Downey. He says that competition in the street promotion game has reached a new peak. There are now so many teams out there this summer, all trying to gain a foothold, that they're starting to tread on one another's toes. 'Oh yeah,' says Sleep. 'It's tough. Like war on the streets, man.'

His walls are lined with warehouse shelves loaded with product: stickers, tapes, 12-inch singles and posters, all waiting to be handed out to his teams. Any spare space is covered in posters.

'Like, these youngsters,' says Sleep, 'they want to be in the industry, you know what I'm sayin'? They'll do *anything*. I heard of some of the guys on some of the other street teams – they don't even break 'em off [pay them]. They give 'em some albums and tapes. Man. They're getting paid, so they should give 'em something.'

Mad Pro is known as a good team, but there are always new companies springing up, trying to undercut them. Like Mike Nixon, Sleep has to constantly recruit new promoters. His best find recently is a guy called Bear. Bear used to be a gang-banger; a crack dealer who lived in motel rooms and had that don't-give-a-fuck attitude that goes with the street-corner lifestyle. But he came around to this apartment a few times and marvelled at all the records and posters that Sleep was being sent by the record companies. 'Here you go, dude,' said Sleep, handing him a few tapes to pass out.

Another time Sleep took Bear to an industry party. Bear enjoyed peering at all the hip-hop celebrities. This was something he didn't get to see standing on a street corner trying to shift cocaine. So

Sleep suggested he quit staying in motels and move into his apartment and work for Mad Pro. Now he's one of Sleep's most effective promoters.

Apart from the competing teams, there are the other routine dangers of working late hours on the streets of Los Angeles. Every promoter has his story about his brush with street gangs. If they're not objecting to the gang affiliations of the artist you're promoting, they're telling you to take the poster down because its colour offends them. The Crips can take exception to the red favoured by the opposing alliance, the Bloods; and the Bloods to the Crips' blue.

Sleep tangled with Crips who wanted to know why he was putting up posters for East Coast acts like Jay-Z. They threatened him, saying, 'Why don't you hang up some Jayo Felony, or Above The Law?' Thinking fast, Sleep told them that this Jay-Z was on the same label as Jayo anyway. That seemed to pacify them. 'I got to feed my kids, man,' says Sleep. 'I ain't tripping on that shit. And you know what? That poster stayed up for a while.'

Few young African-American men can travel with total freedom throughout South Central. Gang loyalties run throughout the region. Whether you're in a gang or not, you're affected by this situation. Just because you come from a particular neighbourhood can mean that you're associated with whatever set is in charge there. So navigating unfamiliar neighbourhoods requires subtlety. If Sleep is sure he knows which gang he's dealing with when he's confronted, he can try mentioning the name of a rapper who's affiliated with that particular gang. 'Broadway and 89th? That's where LV's from. Yeah, I know LV, I know Poppa' – which is what they call him in the neighbourhood. 'All right, man. Do your thing,' they tell him.

Sometimes, though, that's not enough. As Ice Cube said, South Central is so unpredictable. 'Man,' sighs Sleep. 'You know these

61

streets, man. I ain't going to sit here and lie to you. Sometimes I carry a gun.'

BABYBOY

Babyboy has had some good news. Budman was messing around with a girl, and this girl's uncle knew a man called Alonzo Williams who has a new record label and is saying that he wants to hear something by Ya Highness.

Lonzo, as everyone knows him, is a big, bald-headed man who wears large gold earrings that make him look a little like a pirate. Everyone in hip hop in South Central has heard of him. His claim to fame is that he used to be in a group called World Class Wreckin' Cru. By today's standards, World Class Wreckin' Cru were cheesy:

> Listen to the story as we rap to the beat
> As we educate ya 'bout life in the street . . .

ran their song 'Gang Bang', like most of their music, a tinny, unconvincing attempt at commerciality. Their claim to fame, however, was that their membership included a young Dr Dre before he left to join Eazy-E's NWA. For a few years Lonzo made a fair living out of repackaging the masters to the old songs, which sold on the boast that they featured Dr Dre, LA's most successful producer. The small, white-painted office of All Access Records on Crenshaw Boulevard has a gold disc on the wall to prove it. But Dre and Lonzo are in litigation now, and that source of income has dried, so Lonzo has dreamed up All Access Records.

The idea is simple. Since LA has been put on the hip-hop map, there are thousands of acts out there trying to attract attention. But violence has closed nearly all the hip-hop clubs, and getting on radio is almost impossible unless you have a record deal. So he's offering new acts a deal. If they pay him $300 he'll put their track on a compilation CD. That way they can attract some attention – in theory, anyway. The economics of the operation is fairly simple. If it takes off, it could be a good earner.

To start the ball rolling Lonzo decided he needed to put out a compilation which will get some attention, so he's willing to put a few acts on the first one for nothing. He already has some tracks by an act called Camp Zero which he thinks might be good.

For Babyboy, the only problem is that although Ya Highness have a couple of songs demoed, the quality of the recording is mediocre. Nevertheless, he drives over to Inglewood with the DAT containing 'Bud For Life' and 'Bud House'.

C-DOUBLE-E

The Crossroads of the World on Sunset Boulevard is a building in the 'moderne' style of the thirties. At one time an outdoor shopping mall, it was built to look like an ocean liner, complete with portholes and rails, steaming straight on to Sunset. On top of a stylized ship's mast, a neon–lit globe spins round slowly.

These days the Crossroads of the World houses mostly small offices. The Island Trax recording studio is tucked around the back. Inside the front door the white message board announces in green ink that A Nu Creation are in Studio B tonight between 7 and 11. The session is costing a remarkably cheap $170. Herman wasn't happy with the demo Terence had recorded for him. He wants to try re-recording the song in a more professional environment.

The night hasn't gone as planned, though. When Herman and his group arrived, the engineer pointed out that the vocal tracks they had were on one-inch tape but the backing tracks were on DAT. This marked them out as beginners, as the two formats were incompatible. The engineer is a long-haired white guy called Eric, one of the vast population of rock musicians whose calling is to come to Los Angeles to try to make it big. Eric tells the group that if they wanted them both on DAT, they would have to do the vocals again.

The trouble is that Diamond DX hasn't turned up. Herman has been paging him all evening, but he hasn't answered. Herman can't understand why DX and the third member, DJ RBG, never appear to be quite as enthusiastic about this whole project as he is. He shrugs resignedly. 'It's . . . unfortunate.' He has spent an hour re-recording the vocal – yet again. It doesn't seem to distress him that DX, the better rapper, hasn't bothered to turn up. Herman just records his verse too.

DJ RBG is a large, gentle, soft-spoken man. His real name is Dennis. Today he's brought along his eight-month-old son Dennis Jr, or 'Lazy-eye' as he calls him, on account of a right eye which tends to wander upwards. Dennis's wife is working tonight, so he's looking after the baby.

Eric tightens up the existing backing track as best he can and makes it sound funkier, but Herman's vocals are as awkward and jerky as ever. Herman doesn't seem to notice. He's excited just to be here in this studio.

When he's finished laying down the new tracks, Dennis sets up his turntable and starts scratching over the track, adding the rhythm of the turntables. Dennis Jr is normally in bed by this hour, but tonight he's wide awake. He leans on his father's arm, and starts whining quietly. Herman picks him up and holds him tenderly until his father is finished, when he can fish a bottle of milk out of his bag for his son and watch him fall asleep in his arms.

'What do you think, then?' Herman asks Eric as they finish up. The engineer shrugs and says, 'It's OK.' He manages to sound semi-encouraging without saying anything more. It's praise enough for Herman, who beams happily. Eric has told him that Bone, from the hit hip-hop group Bone Thugs N Harmony, uses this studio. Eric engineers for him sometimes. Herman is visibly impressed, as if his 170 bucks has bought him proximity to the big time.

As he leaves the studio he is bubbling with excitement: 'I used to go to the clubs a lot. I don't go so much now, but it seems to me that this is like a song they'd have to play. It would be, like, an anthem. They couldn't help but dance to it, could they?' He says he's on the way now, boasting, 'We get this mixed, make some CDs and put it out there so people will notice. Now we're taking this to a whole different level.'

The DAT tape costs another ten bucks, and they pay a further six for two cassettes so that Dennis and Herman have copies to listen to at home.

'Can I get your card? We need to come back and mix this. We want to work with you again. Will you do it for us?' Herman asks Eric.

'Sure.'

Dennis Jr snoozes in his baby seat.

KHOP

A few weeks ago it finally happened. Ice Cube called Khop. Cube says the reason he waited so long was that he really wanted Khop to become maturer, to gain some experience: 'And then come back and show me that he's better.'

Something else had happened too in the intervening 12 months. Though it's NWA's Dr Dre who produced some of the biggest records of the early nineties, like his own album *The Chronic* and Snoop Doggy Dogg's *Doggystyle*, Cube has proved himself to be the most adept at keeping in tune with the times, at constantly moving his style along. He was in search of a new direction. For the last few years his main project had been Westside Connection. As the name suggests, this group's agenda was doggedly territorial. They became major players in the rivalry that became known in the hip-hop press as the East Coast versus West Coast war. This was a very public battle. It was to lay bare the territoriality of hip hop.

Until outright hostility broke out between the coasts, most fans were only dimly aware of the importance of hip hop's geography. Before the arrival on the scene of Los Angeles-based rappers like Ice-T, NWA and Cube – and later Snoop and Tupac Shakur – New York ruled. It was the culture's unchallenged epicentre. Its tastes were the tastes of the entire movement, and had the monopoly of the hip-hop media too: the most influential radio shows and magazines were all based in New York. Even after LA acts started to emerge, New York radio was slow to acknowledge them, and critics on the city's influential hip-hop magazines took a long time to recognize what was happening on the other side of the country. With little idea of the effect NWA's records were having on the local West Coast fan base, they dismissed the music as crudely recorded, vulgar and violent. Which it was, but that was always the point.

Later, when Dr Dre's 'G-Funk' sound emerged, writers raised on James Brown samples were equally slow to catch on to his use of Funkadelic and Parliament licks.

As New York's hegemony was finally overthrown, some local Eastside artists reacted badly to the popularity of the new territorial chest-beating of albums like NWA's *Straight Outta Compton*, Compton's Most Wanted's *It's A Compton Thang* or DJ Quik's single 'Born And Raised In Compton'. The reaction of Queens rapper Tim Dogg was a musical raised finger: he released a single called 'Fuck Compton'. Initially the battle was a verbal one. Snoop's protégés Tha Dogg Pound released the taunt 'New York, New York'; Mobb Deep retaliated with 'LA, LA'.

Cube has always been adept at playing to the gallery. He soaked up the bellicose jingoism of the moment and launched Westside Connection with LA rap veterans Mack 10 and WC. Westside Connection posed in photographs almost invariably throwing up 'Westside' signs with their hands. Hand signs have always been a territorial code in LA: every gang has its own signal. As the East–West rivalry deepened, the 'Westside' hand sign became commonplace: middle and ring fingers crossed, and index and little fingers splayed out to form the letter 'W'.

In 1996 Westside Connection launched the album *Bow Down*; its title was directed at all the East Coast artists who failed to give respect to the West:

> *Bow down when you come to my town*
> *Bow down when you westward bound*
> *'Cause we ain't no haters like you*
> *Bow down to some niggas that's greater than you . . .*

Another track, 'All the Critics In New York', declared simply: 'Fuck all the critics in NYC . . .' But *Bow Down* was mistimed. By the time Cube released the album the battle between the coastal rivals had become more than just banter. Adoptive Westsider Tupac Shakur had publicly blamed the East's Christopher 'Biggie Smalls' Wallace for a gun attack made on him in November 1994. The accusation was almost certainly unfounded, but it was a serious one. On top of this, Death Row CEO Suge Knight publicly blamed Sean 'Puff Daddy' Combs, the head of Biggie Smalls's label Bad Boy, for being involved in the murder of a friend of his in an Atlanta club. A poisonous atmosphere of suspicion spread. Fearing retaliations, rap groups from each coast began to fear for their lives when visiting the opposite side of America. Promoters became wary of putting on shows for East Coast bands out in the West.

It was no longer such a smart commercial move, shouting loudly for the Westside. Partly as a result of the industry's fear of what was happening there, Los Angeles' turn as hip hop's mecca was drawing to a close. The first omen had come in March 1995, when Eazy-E died.

Eazy, the king of LA hip hop until Suge Knight stomped on his empire, died of AIDS-related illnesses in Cedar-Sinai hospital. A chronic womanizer raised in a culture that still believed that AIDS was a gay affliction, Eazy refused to believe that there was anything wrong with him until he was officially diagnosed with the disease shortly before his death.

Then, on 7 September 1996, the LA-based rapper Tupac Shakur was shot and killed after attending the Tyson–Seldon fight in Las Vegas. Six months later Tupac's former friend turned arch-rival Christopher 'Biggie Smalls' Wallace was assassinated in his GMC Suburban at the junction of Wilshire Boulevard and Fairfax in Los Angeles by an unidentified killer's 9mm gun. The New York rapper had been visiting LA to accept an award from the TV show *Soul Train* for being rap's Best Lyricist. At first it was assumed to be a revenge killing. Tupac had venomously attacked Biggie in the press over the last two years of his life, claiming in song that he had fucked Biggie's wife, Faith Evans, and accusing him of anything, from plotting his own death in a 1994 gun attack to 'biting' his rap style; Tupac's bile stirred the East Coast–West Coast war still more. The police, however, found no evidence to support any idea that the shooting was a reprisal for Tupac's death.

Eazy-E's Ruthless label had been pushed aside by Suge Knight's Death Row. But Death Row's turn on top didn't last for ever. After her son's death, Tupac's mother, Afeni Shakur, learned that despite Tupac's platinum hits for Death Row, his bank account contained only a few hundred dollars. She commenced court proceedings and was granted control of Tupac's tapes. Talent began to flee the label.

Now in New York the hip-hop press were writing editorials saying that the West Coast gangsta scene was dead. Magazines which had detailed each new rivalry in the conflict were now adopting a haughty 'told you so' tone.

Suddenly Westside Connection's belligerence was out of place: the album's reception was lukewarm. The industry was nervous of any project that appeared to increase the tension between the rival camps. It was time for Cube to move on.

After his success in John Singleton's *Boyz In Tha Hood* Cube had been given a production deal with the Hollywood movie company New Line. His latest project was something he'd written and planned to direct himself – *The Players Club*, a film set in a Southern strip joint. *The Players Club* was to be a film that's about sex, dancing and living large. With it, Cube was toying with a new musical direction too. Enough of fighting: now it was time to party.

Cube remembered Khop, the boy with a lascivious drawl and the demo whose style could fit Cube's new mood perfectly. He called him up and said: 'You want to do a hit record?'

'Hell yeee-ah.' So a year after he'd told him, 'I'm gonna put you down,' Cube was finally inviting Khop to the studio. The first recording that Khop took part in didn't amount to much. All Cube needed him for was to add a few lines to a song whose title was going to be either 'Get Your Club On' or 'We Be Clubbin''. The track was a declaration of intent, not just for the soundtrack but also as an announcement of Cube's new direction.

All Khop had to do was shout, 'Y'all in for the night?', to add another voice to Cube's and Mack 10's, but it was a start. Besides, he felt happy enough to be on it because it was an obvious club hit. Then Cube gave him a real test. The former NWA rapper was working on a track entitled 'Dreamin'' for a band called Emmage that he was going to put on the soundtrack. He suggested that Khop lay down a verse at the start of the song.

Aware that it was important that he impress Cube, Khop walked straight into the booth and started rhyming. Cube was won over then and and there. 'He's a pro,' he decided.

The studio didn't intimidate Khop, and he didn't stand around asking what anyone wanted. He just got on with the job. Cube liked that.

Now Cube is working frenetically. His new direction seems to have unleashed a wave of creativity. It's been four years since his last solo album: currently he's working on the soundtrack for *The Players Club* and also planning a solo double CD.

He calls Khop regularly, booking him for recording sessions: 'Khop, I got an idea for this song. Come on down to the studio.' Cube doesn't tell him what the idea is, just that he has to make it to Larrabee West – a studio in West Hollywood – at such and such a time. Only when Khop gets there does he find out what he's supposed to be doing; if he's just doing some background vocals, or whether he has to write some verses to fit with what Cube does.

Khop watches the older rapper closely. Cube is, he discovers, a perfectionist. Cube always finishes a verse then asks, 'How does that shit sound?' If nothing is said in the next two seconds he says, 'We doin' it over.'

Damn, thinks Khop. He wants his shit tight.

RAH

Transit Crew are developing their own style. They like to work at night, at around two or three o'clock, when the city is quiet. There are parts of the city that they regard as rightfully their own. One of them is the section of La Brea Boulevard that sweeps up into the Baldwin Hills. The road becomes a dual carriageway here and cars travel faster, but in the rush hour it slows to a crawl, giving drivers plenty of time to look at the stickers the team have put on the central divider or stapled to the telegraph poles on the west side of the road.

The top of the hill here has been left to grow wild. There are oilfields just to the south, on Stocker Street, right in the middle of the city: rusty grey pumps that nod slowly up and down all through the night. The scrubland around them is left untouched. After dark it's an eerie landscape.

One night, stickering for the rapper A/Z, Rah looks up and sees a white owl floating overhead. He points it out to Josiah. They stop work and stand there, watching the bird in the moonlight. Rah carries a camera with him in his backpack, but the bird is too far away, and it's too dark to take a shot of it. He wishes he could, though. It's something special. He's lived in this city all his life, but until he became a street promoter, ducking down the wide, dark streets after the clubs closed with his friend Josiah, Rah never knew there were owls in South Central.

6

Vapours of Lies and Deception

BIG AL

Last night Big Al – '300lb of funk' – won second place in the Independent Artists' Showcase talent show at A Hip Hop Unified Nation IV. Today he wanders around the wide corridors of the hotel dressed in his trademark white denim jacket, short dreadlocks sprouting from the top of his head. 'Three hundred pounds of funk' is no idle boast. Though only 26, Al is immense. You'd never believe that a man could burn as much energy as Al does in his wild, flailing performances and still be so fat. Offstage, too, he cuts an unmistakable figure. Delegates wander up to 'the big man on campus', as he calls himself, to shake his hand. 'Congratulations,' says a young Latino rapper, dressed in grey fatigues. 'You deserved to win, man.'

'Thank you,' says the big man graciously. There are several South Central acts who are dogged regulars on the LA talent-show scene. Al is one of them. He has competed in dozens of such competitions in the 13 years he's been rapping. He usually comes somewhere in the top three.

Over long years Al has learned that winning talent shows doesn't mean much unless someone with the right connections actually sees you win it. Every time he hopes this will be the one. Ten years ago, when Allen Stephens was 16 and his waist size was smaller, he used to rap with a group called the LA Boys. They were friends from his neighbourhood, Inglewood, and from his school, Morningside High. When Chuck Barris's famously tacky talent contest *The Gong Show* was revived on NBC, the LA Boys responded to its famous invitation: 'If you have a good or unusual act and want to be on *The Gong Show*, why not call . . .'

They auditioned, passed, went on the show and won with a song called 'Give Me A DJ'. Al was the group's 'human beatbox', passing for a DJ, grunting out rhythms in the vocal style invented by the early hip-hoppers, who were too young and poor to afford a real drum machine. The prize was a fat $701, split three ways.

Back then, Al assumed that after winning a nationally syndicated talent contest, record companies would be lining up to invite them straight into the recording studio. Ten years on, still trying, he knows that things aren't really that simple. All LA labels seemed to be interested in during the first half of the nineties was gangsta rap. Al thought his luck had changed when a successful New York independent label called Warlock Records signed him up and flew him to the East to record an EP called *Neva Doubt (The Big One)*. The East Coast was never as obsessed with gangsta rap as the West was. When at last Warlock said they were putting out the record, Al, excited at having his first solo record out after all these years, started calling local record stores: 'Have you got *Neva Doubt* by Big Al?'

No one had heard of it. Doggedly, he kept doing shows to boost the EP, handing out promo copies at his shows, but it felt like the record didn't really exist. He wrote a letter to Warlock pleading with them to do a video. They wrote back saying they were waiting to see how the record performed first. Al wondered how they expected it to perform without any promotion. He knew they were losing confidence in him. In the spring of 1997, Warlock wrote to say they were releasing him from his contract.

Al keeps plugging away at it. He's come to this four-day convention in the hope of picking up a deal with one of the big labels that the event's pre-publicity promised would be in attendance. A Hip Hop Unified Nation is the ambitious title given to the annual convention held by the hip-hop magazine *Rap Sheet*. The magazine is a minor player in the increasingly glitzy hip-hop publishing industry. Each month in editorials, publisher and editor Daryl James boasts that it's 'the only Black-owned major Hip Hop publication', but it struggles to find big-league hip-hop names to grace its covers, and is clearly outpaced by *Rap Pages*, the other Los Angeles hip-hop publication, owned by pornographer-celebrity Larry Flynt.

This year's annual convention, held at the Red Lion Hotel near Los Angeles airport, known as LAX, is something of a damp squib too. These music conventions are potential money-spinners for the struggling magazine. They attract hip-hop wannabes: young artists with demo tapes pay an entrance fee to attend, believing that if only they can persuade the right A&R man to listen to their music, the prize will be theirs.

For all his success at the talent show last night, Al is having no luck here. He's resigned to it by now. He turns up to these events hoping that he will hook up with some influential A&R man who's going to sign him up, but despite the enthusiasm of the other convention-goers for his performance last night, he's still waiting for someone to offer him a deal. 'I've had some response,' he says, trying to stay enthusiastic. 'I've been given a few business cards.' Mostly that's all he ends up with: some business cards.

There have been demo listening panels, as promised in the pre-convention publicity, but they're not packed with the heavyweights that Al hoped for. He played his song 'Freez Up' to a few people, including Lonzo Williams, who's here touting his new enterprise, All Access Records, and received the same polite enthusiasm he always does. 'It's tight,' they always nod.

Lonzo isn't here to sign acts – he has his own product to plug.

He's wearing the 'ALL ACCESS RECORDS' T-shirt; and when-ever he has a chance, he holds up a copy of the label's first CD and reminds the delegates, 'It's out this month.' The CD has a rough painting on the front of a bare-chested man in dark glasses who looks suspiciously like Lonzo. He has called it *HOMEGROWN: The First Inner City Harvest.* Lonzo has recorded the introduction himself: 'Yo. This is Lonzo, the World Class Grandmaster, and what you're about to hear are some of the phattest unsigned acts to come across my desk in the summer of 1997. Check it out . . .'

For Budman and Babyboy, the news is particularly good. The very first track on the album is 'Bud House', Ya Highness's most straightforward marijuana anthem, rhymed over a version of the Commodores' 'Brick House'. Babyboy himself has a verse on the track too, about dealing bags of grass to party-goers, a subject that he knows a little about:

Bailin' through the party with a pound of bud
All sacked up in straight dimes and dubs . . .

For delegates like Al, though, the panels are a let down. A meagre smattering of representatives from labels like Sony and Death Row have shown their faces, but only briefly.

He visits a panel on promotion. There a young street promoter called Cash listens patiently to Al as he relates the problems he has with Warlock records. Cash is sympathetic: releasing a record without promotion is like throwing money down the drain. Cash takes time to tell him how you have to work all the record stores, to let them know your record is out there. Al takes heart: each time he learns a little more about the business. It has to pay off in the end.

Things are going well for Cash, the man from the Lockdown Crew who first introduced Rah to street promotion. Recently Loud Records took him on full-time on their team. It's a great job. Right now, Loud are one of the coolest record companies to work for, and also one of the shrewdest when it comes to promoting.

Outside the main hall, Al greets a guy called T–Bob from a rap click called Camp Zero: they exchange hugs. Camp Zero were also among the runners–up in last night's show, and they have three tracks on Lonzo's *Inner City Harvest* CD, including one that people are calling the best on the album: 'Whoop Whoop', by a girl from the Camp Zero Click named Kimmie G.

A disheartened Al wanders into the Pacifica Room to hear today's keynote speech by the Oakland rapper MC Hammer. Once Hammer was the most bankable star in hip hop. 'U Can't Touch This,' he boasted, but Hammer's run of huge pop hits dried up after the eighties. In the aftermath, he tried everything. The once Pepsi–sponsored, clean–cut hip–hop poster–boy even signed to Suge Knight's Death Row for a while and tried dressing up in black leather and affecting a hard–core gangsta–rap image. The episode proved that not everything Death Row touched turned to gold. The album was a miserable flop, and in 1996 Hammer filed for bankruptcy. Now, like *Rap Sheet*, he is a little down on his luck, though you'd never know it from the way he's talking.

About 250 people are gathered to hear what Hammer has to say. He is working on a gospel–rap album now. He has now recast himself yet again, this time as the prophet of doom: 'Rap,' he lectures, 'is sick. It's in a state of denial. But all you got to do is look at the symptoms. Have you ever seen someone walking all bent over and they all skinny? You know they on crack.'

The audience laughs.

'They can say what they want but you know they smoking. Rap is the golden goose. It's the only other thing, other than moving keys, that we have been able to make big money in a quick way. Now, it's dying a slow death, and my question is, who killed the golden goose?'

Rap, he browbeats the young audience, is too full of lies. It needs a rebirth, he tells them, like a preacher calling from the pulpit. 'I ain't seen one rapper where you can go and see his rap sheet and he's got attempted murder on there. Not one. There might be someone who hasn't got hit records, and he's mad for real. But rap fans will believe anything if the beat is right. "I killed six niggas last week." "Oh he *cold*. He *down*," ' he mocks. And the audience laughs again.

The hall is large: the chairs are laid out in neat rows. The carpets have the sort of brown and orange pattern you find only in hotel convention rooms. Large, square, cut-glass chandeliers hang from the ceiling.

'On Madison Avenue the stockholders say, "I'm not investing my money in people who are killing each other and putting out negativity." This is a cold game,' he says. 'For real.'

Irritated, a young man dressed in black gets to his feet. 'You're trying to tell us about hip hop,' he protests, shouting to be heard. 'As a businessman and a person, I respect you, brother. But what did *you* do for hip hop?'

The critic receives a smattering of applause. 'You just talking about the industry. Hip hop has nothing to do with the industry,' the young man continues. 'It started before the industry, bringing the word to the people. What you're saying is totally wrong. You're saying *I* should work with these major labels . . .'

Flustered, Hammer tries to defend himself: 'I didn't say we should work with nothing.'

But the young hip-hopper is almost hysterical with rage. He believes in hip hop as a pure grail: Hammer was one of those who corrupt it with commercialism. 'You *did*. About how we should work *with* them.' He's full of burning, self-righteous indignation. 'We shouldn't be talking about that. We should be talkin' about . . .'

'Brother, brother, brother,' Hammer cuts in, magisterially. 'I know you're emotional, but please have a seat.'

'We should be talkin' about . . .' the man screams.

'. . . I'm going to take questions from the crowd later, but please have a seat . . .'

'Hey, man,' the protester shouts in bitter derision. 'You would *dance* for chicken . . .'

'I would dance for who?' Hammer shouts back angrily. A few of the audience are laughing and clapping now. When he was a big star, Hammer famously promoted Kentucky Fried Chicken, along with Pepsi. He argues, 'I would dance for *money*.'

Things are spinning out of control.

'Yeah, that's why *true* hip hop is almost *gone* right now.'

A representative from *Rap Sheet* finally intervenes: 'Now listen, black man. If you can't respect him and respect me and everyone else in here, you gonna have to get out.'

Aggrieved, the young guy objects: 'But this brother don't know nothing about hip hop.' Security have now grabbed him and are pushing and dragging him out of the hall, saying, 'Please step outside.'

'So,' says Hammer, when the man has been hustled out through the double doors, 'I maybe I killed off a couple of dreams.' For the most part, the crowd nervously applaud his departure, but it's an ungainly scene. MC Hammer, former hip-hop star, wishing the golden goose which once danced to his innocent, unthreatening pop hits would do it all over again. Hip hop has moved on. In fact the golden goose has never been healthier – at least as far as the industry is concerned. Despite Hammer's cries of doom, business booms. Each year hip hop seems to penetrate the mainstream market even further. Nineteen ninety-seven is proving to be yet another sensational year for the young New York entrepreneur Sean 'Puff Daddy' Combs and his Bad Boy label. Huge new markets in the South are being won by a young New Orleans upstart who calls himself Master P, whose platinum album *Ghetto D* has just spent ten weeks in the top ten of the *Billboard* Hot 100.

But that's not the way it feels at A Hip Hop Unified Nation IV.

On the West Coast there is a sense of frustration that, somehow, people here are missing out on their turn once again. Things have gone awry here: in Los Angeles, where the glory days of NWA and Ruthless, Tupac and Death Row are gone, there is anxiety that the limelight seems to have already passed on elsewhere before they've all had their turn.

Al goes home to Inglewood, deflated by the *Rap Sheet* convention. He locks the metal screen door of the house behind him.

He lives with his parents, close to the 105 freeway. Despite his imposing size, he's a gentle guy. It has been a frustrating ten years for him. Though others made money during the gangsta heyday, it was hard for a straight lyrical rapper like Al to get any attention. 'I think I'm as much of a man as any of them,' he complains. 'Or as macho, or whatever they want to call it.'

The sideboard is full of family photos, and there are fresh roses in the middle of the table. At the Federal Building in Downtown LA Al works as a computer operator, inputting data. He has a steady girlfriend, Latonja; he thinks it's love.

'It doesn't make me any less of a man, just because I don't carry a Glock, or smoke weed, or drink 40s,' he insists. He has a song called 'Lyrical High', all about that. Lyrics, it says, are his drug, not weed. Optimistically, he booms:

What you fail to realize is that your gangsta mentality
Is a played out mentality . . .

So he continues to hope, anyway.

At all those showcases and talent shows, the people from the record companies always told him it sounded good, but they wanted *bad* stuff. Sometimes it seems that it would make sense to cuss and talk about gangs and violence on his records. Al doesn't want to do that. It's just not him. He's never hung out with gang-bangers.

Peter Cohen, a white A&R man from the Sony dance label 550, was at the convention too. Like Al, he was disappointed in the whole event; he thought it was tacky. Apart from him, there really weren't any representatives of major companies there, he realized. But he heard Al's tape and was encouraged. It was a little too rough, and his material needed work, but it had something. Cohen passed Al's number on, and told him to stay in touch. He believes that it's worth watching how an artist develops. Al wasn't the sort of act he could sign, but he encouraged him. Told him to stick at it.

C-DOUBLE-E

There is a sense of excitement. Around the room, little groups form. Above the DJ's beats, rings of rappers in backpacks and cargo pants are earnestly practising their flows before the competition.

Friday night, and *Rap Sheet* is co-sponsoring a freestyle rap competition at the Proud Bird, a nightclub on Aviation Boulevard in Inglewood, right under the wingtips landing at LAX. Al comes, but just to watch. Herman Collins, the gawky rapper from A Nu Creation, turns up. He's put his name down to compete.

Battling is the root of rap. Almost every rapper started this way, trading rhymes in front of a crowd at junior high school or on a street corner. It's a gladiatorial contest, a verbal wrestling match.

A good rap battle is great entertainment. The rules are simple. In a formal competition like this contestants are paired off and given 30 seconds each to improvise rhymes, then another 30 in which to reply and try and quash the insults that have just been flung. Rhymes must be spontaneous. Anyone relying too obviously on prepared words will be booed off. The idea is to put your opponent off by trashing him as coolly, as brutally and as deftly as you can: the way he looks, the way he talks, the way he raps . . . anything goes. But anyone who just insults crudely, without wit, will also be booed. A panel of judges mark each round, judging who's landed the most blows, as if they were adjudicating at a boxing match.

Just out of Rykers I'm a lyrical sniper
Everytime you rhyme I just get hyper . . .

The crowd, leaning forward to catch each word, cheer any insult that's sharp, or anyone that's obviously improvised to meet the situation. The insult about the guy's brown suede shoes gets a roar of approval.

Tonight's main event has been organized by Wendy Day. She's a minor legend in the hip-hop industry. A white woman with a master's degree, she was vice-president of a liquor company until she gave it all up in 1992 and ploughed $500,000 into an organization she calls the Rap Coalition. As a long-time rap fan she was tired of hearing stories about how inequitably young black rap acts were being treated by the industry. 'For the most part,' she says, 'the music industry just sees rappers as a "bunch of dumb niggers". You can tell by the deals that they offer. The record companies front-load all their deals, which means they dangle money in your face. They say: "Here's $150,000," but they don't talk about what you're going to get down the road. Which is usually nothing or less than nothing.'

With the Rap Coalition she lends her corporate skills to new rappers, putting them in touch with attorneys, and helping to set up events like this. 'White folk have been robbing black folk since time began,' she says, 'and I wanted to do something as a white person to sort of balance out that injustice.'

Lonzo Williams invites me to sit at his table. Yella from NWA drifts magisterially through the crowd. A couple of A&R men from the rap label Interscope, which has acted as a distributor both to Suge Knight's Death Row and now to Dr Dre's new company, Aftermath, sit nearby.

For me, when the rap is live and full throttle like this, I sometimes feel like a schoolboy sitting at an unfamiliar Shakespeare play, straining to catch the words. The crowd whoop long before I've figured out exactly what they're cheering, if I ever do.

The crowd is applauding each verbal twist.

Yo' hoe is my hoe
She give me head, though.

A big roar goes up. Or:

I react so fast
I get in your ass
While you're still sittin' . . .

There's a white rapper competing tonight: he has given his name as Eminem. He looks about 20, and has short hair. White rappers who're good enough to compete in MC battles are thin on the ground, so when he starts efficiently cutting his opponents down to size, a ripple of interest goes through the room. The young boy's rhymes are full of great wisecracks.

What you need to do,

he was sneering:

Is practice your freestyle
'Cause you come up missin' more than Snoop Doggy Dogg's police file.

Eminem cruises through the first two rounds, beating his opponents easily. He's conspicuous as the only white rapper in the whole competition. Yet, watching the crowd react to him, no one is marking him down for his whiteness. 'He's cold!' someone shouts approvingly as beats drop and the round finishes.

I had imagined there would be a hostility, some resentment perhaps, about this white boy muscling his way into this arena. I don't see any, though. He now stands, waiting his turn to be lambasted by his opponent. Usually the rappers will stand toe to toe, face to stony face. Eminem's opponent starts his reply. Suddenly the crowd is booing the other rapper. I couldn't catch the line, but it's clearly some off-colour reference to Eminem's whiteness. Whatever my own assumptions about how the crowd would react were, the black audience seem no happier to hear a racial remark from a black than they are from a white. Instead, the rapper ended up playing into the white rapper's hands. The young boy responds with:

> Everybody in this place I miss you
> If you try and turn my facial tissue
> Into a racial issue . . .

The crowd cheers him again.

Afterwards, though, the young white guy, Eminem, is furious. He had made it into the final, but was knocked out in the last round by an unknown. The white boy drifts around the room sullenly. When the A&R men from Interscope ask him for one of his tapes he thrusts it at them moodily. 'All right, man.' He doesn't know who they are.

The boy's real name is Marshall. Wendy Day had heard him rhyme at another convention in Detroit and offered him a free flight to come and compete here today. He grew up in the black middle-class ghetto of East Detroit, brought up by a single mother on welfare.

Last night Marshall was homeless in Detroit. He had to break into an old house where he used to live. There was no heating or electricity on in the empty house, but at least he had somewhere to sleep. All the way over, on the plane, he had been sure he was going to win. He was coming to Los Angeles – home of Ice-T, whose rhymes had first turned him on to rap. He had to, because he needed that $500 prize money so badly. He's flat broke, doesn't have a job and he has recently split up from the mother of his infant daughter. He had pinned everything on winning this. He had convinced himself he was going to get a record deal over here.

He knew the other big names on the bill and knew that the only other serious competition in the line-up was a rapper called Kwest The Mad Lad. All the way through the contest he had been preparing rhymes in his head which he could fling at Kwest. But when it came to the finals, Kwest had been knocked out and Marshall didn't recognize the guy who made it into the finals with him.

Marshall thinks he was robbed. The rapper he was up against didn't even stand toe to toe with him, but wandered off and stood behind a film projection screen that had been set up on stage to show the seminal rap movie *Wild Style*, so that he couldn't even rhyme in his face.

'He was garbage,' complains Marshall bitterly. 'He was fuckin' garbage.'

Herman, meanwhile, only reached the second round of his competition, but he's pleased enough to have survived that far. 'I got some respect,' he says. 'It's all good.'

BIG AL

Al doesn't bother to turn up for the last day of A Hip Hop Unified Nation IV.

The closing keynote speaker in the Pacifica Room is Keidi Obi Awadu, a reggae musician turned conspiracy theorist and activist. Awadu, a lean man who wears a black combat jacket and dreadlocks that reach his waist, is the author of a self-published book, *Rap, Hip Hop and The New World Order*. He believes that the deaths of Eazy-E, Biggie and Tupac are all linked. He believes that gangsta rap is part of a vast conspiracy. Fertility and birth rates are plummeting in white society. The race that has dominated America threatens to be overwhelmed by the population growth of the minorities.

Now, Awadu believes, the shadowy National Security Council has established its own secret Population Taskforce to try to hamper the natural growth of the black, Asian and Latino populations. The AIDS epidemic is part of this vast conspiracy, persuading fertile blacks to wear condoms. Eazy-E, he believes, did not die of AIDS. 'Murdered,' he declares.

Meanwhile liberal whites favour easy access to abortion. 'Everybody's mad at the Ku Klux Klan,' Awadu says, 'but they didn't do in 200 years what those white lesbian abortion mills done last year – takin' out 400,000 of you.'

But his subject today is gangsta rap, the mutant musical form created in a laboratory by the white Department of Defense and the National Security Council ('that august body that works secretly in the basement of the White House') as a way of fomenting high mortality rates among breeding-age males. Gangsta rap is part of a vast and sophisticated mind-control scheme. The whole East Coast-West Coast war was engineered by the evil forces who control our lives.

Rap icons like Eazy, Suge Knight, Tupac, Snoop and Biggie sold their souls for success, Awadu says. A criminal justice ('not justice, just-us,' decodes Awadu) system embroiled these young men in the legal system, and then offered them fame and fortune in return for co-operation.

'Look at Tupac. About six or eight convictions. Biggie? About the same. Suge Knight? A whole *bunch* of them,' notes Awadu. 'You don't have rappers initiating these contacts. The legal profession initiate these rappers into a network of control.'

Flashing up CD covers and magazine adverts and decoding them like an eager post-structuralist academic proudly deconstructing a text, Awadu unveils the subtle language of mind control. Everywhere he sees a hidden language, designed to send the black youth mad.

The screen shows an advert for Biggie's last album, *Life After Death,* taken from *Vibe* magazine. Biggie was killed a fortnight before this CD was due to be released. Unfortunately the cover showed the rapper leaning up against a hearse. 'Excuse *me*, Biggie,' says Awadu sardonically, 'but you shouldn't have done that. Don't let nobody take your picture *next to a friggin' casket!* "You want a record deal? OK. Stand next to that hearse and we'll take your picture,"' mocks Awadu. "*Duh!* You don't want to do it. Well, drink a 40 first, you'll wanna do it."'

He sings, mockingly:

Biggie Biggie Biggie, can't you see?

It's a line from Smalls's hit 'Hypnotize'. The audience laughs. At least, as conspiracy theorists go, Awadu is more entertaining than most. 'Be careful of the music you listen to,' he warns and flips to another photo of the dead rapper, this time sitting in a carved wooden chair.

'Well, I had to take it to my laboratory and blow this up,' says Awadu. He points to a shadowy section under his legs: a vague dark shape. 'Beneath his legs, what do you see?'

It's a trick of the light, a shadow that looks like a face if you squint at it. 'A devil?' suggests a voice from the crowd.

'A demon!' declares Awadu. 'And what is coming out of the demon's mouth?' It looks as if the demon is spewing something out. 'The vapours of lies and deception. And what comes out of a gangsta rapper's mouth? The vapours of lies and deception.'

Conspiracy theory is the faith of the dispossessed and the powerless: it thrives in America's black ghettos. In recent years rumours have spread that a certain brand of fried chicken, or a particular new tropical fruit drink, was being doctored with chemicals that render black men sterile. There are powers out there that fear the black man, that contrive to keep him down. These ugly forces are given a shape in these arcane conspiracies.

At the heart of the new religious movements which have become popular among young urban blacks, in particular the Nation of Islam and its less disciplinarian, new-age offshoot the Five Percent Nation, are mythologies of the white supremacist 'white devils' who have schemed to thwart the black race. The Five Percent Nation is particularly popular among rappers. The mystical rapper RZA, the leader of the Wu-Tang Clan, discovered the creed when he was a teenager and changed his name from Robert Diggs to Rakim Allah. According to the Five Percenters, five per cent of the world's population are the poor, righteous teachers, 85 per cent are the ignorant oppressed. 'Then you got the ten per cent,' RZA once told me. 'The rich slave-makers. They know the truth, but they keep everybody blind to it, so they can master them and use them as they want.' With the coming millennium, the battle between the ten per cent and the five per cent will come to a head, RZA believes. Exploitation and inequality viewed as a titanic spiritual struggle.

The scrolls of the Brooklyn-born mystic Dwight York, who currently calls himself Malachi Z. York, are enjoying a new popularity among the 'conscious' hip-hoppers. York's teachings mix *X-Files* sci-fi paranoia with Revelations end-time theology. He prophesies that the elect of Revelations, the righteous 144,000, are due to be raised up by 2880 space ships on 5 May 2003. The ships, he says, were due to arrive in 2000, but the warp of time was distorted by a bungled wartime scientific experiment to render American warships invisible, known to sci-fi geeks as the Philadelphia Experiment.

Now Hip hop's own recent history is being viewed through the dark lens of conspiracy too. Awadu isn't the only one who believes Tupac's death was not a straightforward murder. According to street rumour, he was assassinated because his potential as a black revolutionary leader was becoming too great, or he was killed simply to increase the value of his back catalogue. Many – including Public Enemy's agitprop rapper, Chuck D – actually believed that he wasn't dead; that the shooting was an elaborate smokescreen.

To many young black men, unable to share in the greater American vision, the conspiracy of white supremacy makes a lot of sense. After all, what Awadu's saying contains a sort of truth. For all its genius, there is something toxic about the way hip hop can endorse the image of the black man as criminal, as sexual predator, and as outsider. During the height of the gangsta era, that is precisely what suburbia wanted to hear, subsidizing the underclass's culture of exclusion.

The audience for the last day of the convention has thinned down to only about 80 people, but they are listening respectfully enough.

'It gets deep,' insists Awadu. He tells them how the entertainment industry entraps young black men with promises of riches and forces them to disseminate the subliminal messages that are turning black against black. ' "Look, mom," ' says Awadu acidly. ' "I got a record deal. Look at my new Lexus." ' And if the rappers try to turn against their controllers, they are eliminated. 'Nineteen ninety-five,' he says. 'Eazy-E. Murdered in cold blood. In 1996 they murdered Tupac. Cold blood. In 1997 they murdered Biggie. 1998 is coming,' he warns.

'So,' implores Awadu. 'Do we want a record deal? Hell no. We want power! What do we want?'

'Power,' a few uncertain voices in the auditorium respond. After all, like Al, what they really came here for was a record deal. Awadu's what-do-we-want? call to arms recalls that moment in the sixties when there was a real possibility of black youths forming a political coalition in America. It sounds anachronistic now, in an era in which it looks like the only way to have power is to have money.

'How much power?' Awadu continues to implore.

'All of it,' they reply.

'Yeah,' says Awadu. 'We want all of it.'

KHOP

Khop becomes used to receiving calls from Ice Cube. One time, when he's out with his dad, Cube calls his pager. When Khop returns the call, it's a message from Cube, who wants him to come to Seattle to do a show. 'Can you get to the airport in 15 minutes?'

They're a long way from LAX. He asks his father, 'Can we do it?'

They drive fast as they can, first to Inglewood to pack a bag and then to the airport. Khop makes the plane. It turns out the show never happens. Instead, they take in a basketball game, then hang out at a club.

By now Cube is simultaneously finishing up the soundtrack for *The Players Club* soundtrack and starting work on his own solo record. He asks Khop to record a track called 'If I Was Fuckin' You' for the new CD, which he plans to release once *The Players Club* has created a buzz. Khop pulls out the stops, with a scurrilous, smut-raking verse:

> *The only way dick gettin' laid is for chips*
> *Bitch, I'm tryin' to make rich*
> *Hangin' with the Trojan pack of six and the gin 'n' juice mix*
> *No time to pause*
> *Gots to drop drawers . . .*

Khop takes Trey with him if he's visiting the Relentless studio, but he doesn't like him being around when it comes to Cube's sessions. He loves to be there himself, drinking and smoking with

Cube's crew, but he doesn't think it's the right environment for his son. 'I'm not for all that. I don't want my son to be around all that.' Khop doesn't drink or smoke if Trey is with him.

'I don't know what I'm going to do with my baby boy,' he says. 'He's going to have to go and stay with my dad and my mom. They work too, but he can stay with my grandmother too. 'Cause I don't trust my little boy with *nobody*.'

But he thinks he can make it work. In a way, he says, it's Trey that makes him want to do this. So he can earn enough money to make sure that he can really take care of him.

'You don't see a lot of fathers that, you know . . . bring it down for their son,' he says. 'I'm going to make sure that I represent to the fullest.' Becoming a hip-hop star will mean touring, and travelling out of town regularly with Cube. He promises himself that he will find a way of keeping in touch with Trey when he leaves town, even if it means phoning him all the time.

Khop adores Trey. He loves spoiling the three-year-old, taking him to the beach, or to the adventure-playground chain Chuck E. Cheese. That's his favourite. 'Where you want to go?' asks Khop. 'Chuck E. Cheese,' says Trey.

'That's my heart, right there,' is the phrase Khop always uses when he talks about him.

Cube invites Khop down to Larrabee West studios to add a verse to a track called 'Limos, Demos and Bimbos'. It's one of those sessions when the studio is full of hangers-on. Khop keeps himself to himself because he hardly knows anyone there, apart from Cube.

In the booth, he finishes his verse. Afterwards, he looks into the control room and everyone in there is jumping up and down, looking like they're whooping and hollering and throwing up the W's for Westside.

When Cube throws his hands up, he knows he must be doing something right. Khop thinks: He's a big hitter in the game. If I can make him feel it, I know I'm cracking.

Sometimes Cube tells him he's fresh. Other times he calls him a guppy. 'You ain't a fish yet. You a *guppy*.'

And then John McLean from Cube's management company, The Firm, hears the tracks Khop has been doing with Cube, and agrees that Khop has talent. Cube has recently won a new deal with A&M records to set up a label to develop new artists. McLean thinks Khop would be ideal.

Do we want a record deal? Hell yeee-ah.

RAH

Cash needs a sharp promoter to join him at Loud Records. He can offer a salary, now. He approaches Rah, not to employ him, but just to ask him a little about Josiah Brocks and his background.

Rah mentions how Josiah's brother Silas sometimes drinks a little – like he did the day of their fist-fight. This is something he will later regret ever telling Cash, because Cash repeats to Josiah what Rah said.

Josiah is furious that he could say that about his brother. Josiah, with Cash along with him, comes to confront Rah about what he has said.

'Did you say it?' he shouts. Rah looks at him and realizes that Josiah is really angry. Rah is confused. He feels that Cash must have twisted what he said; told Josiah that he said Silas was a total lush or exaggerated it in some way.

'Did you *say* it?' Josiah demands again. This is all about loyalty, and from where he stands it looks as if Rah been disloyal to his brother. Rah's friend, whom he admires so much, is angry with him. He panics. 'No,' he answers. He tries to deny outright that he said anything about Silas drinking, but it's obvious to everyone that he is lying.

In Detroit, Marshall gets a message that a big producer from LA is interested in talking to him. The young white rapper who failed to win first prize at the Rap Olympics cannot believe what he's hearing. His stomach drops. His mind starts racking. For the next minutes he's shouting, excitedly, 'Don't fuckin' lie to me, man, don't fuckin' lie to me.'

Dr Dre, increasingly ill at ease with the thuggish goings-on at Suge Knight's Death Row, had quit the label earlier in the year to set up Aftermath. The men from Interscope had passed Dre the tape, and Dre had been won over by the idea of signing this white-trash Detroit boy.

Breaks happen. Some are serendipitously in the right place at the right time. Others await their turn, believing it must happen to them in the end.

7

The Red Car

RAH

Josiah takes the work at Loud Records; he stops kicking it with Rah.

Rah tries to plead with him. 'Josiah, man. What's up with our company? You're always rolling with Cash. You're making a name for him – what about making a name for us?' But Josiah doesn't want to know.

Mike Nixon – the man who gave Josiah his break in the street promotion business – wonders about the rift between Rah and Josiah. He suspects that what set it off was that Rah was jealous about the prospect of Josiah being offered a salaried job at one of the hottest record companies in hip hop, and that maybe Rah was trying to put Cash off from splitting up the three stooges when he told him about Silas drinking. Rah says that it was nothing of the sort. He wasn't jealous of Josiah. He was pleased for him. It was just a stupid mistake.

Whatever lay behind the row, the friendship is wrecked – for the moment, at least. Rah takes the rejection badly: he wishes he had told Josiah the truth, admitted that he had spoken out of turn about Silas and asked for his friend's forgiveness. 'Cash made Josiah look at me in a different way,' says Rah. 'And I was really hurt because I'm not that type of person. I wanted to tell him I was wrong, that I shouldn't have said it. But I didn't say all that,' he says sadly.

It's the week before Halloween. A couple of music industry reps are in town, so Mike Nixon is entertaining them. He decides to take them to a psychic on 3rd Street.

Mike is a very spiritual person. 'I'm a Buddhist,' he says. He invented the name N5 back in the sixties: it stands for 'Niggas to the Fifth Power', because the number five has special meanings for him. There are five letters in his name; he is fifth-generation American; and his son was born on 5 November. He believes that there are signs and significances lurking everywhere for those who are sensitive to them.

That day the psychic tells him, 'I see an accident with a red car.'

Mike doesn't take such warnings lightly. 'I can't tell you when or how this will happen,' the psychic says, 'but I see it in your realm.'

Her words put Mike on edge, especially when he remembers that his nephew has just been in a smash in New York. This is big shit, he thinks.

When he got home, he called his sister: 'What colour was the car he was hit by?'

'Grey and blue.'

So he lost a little faith in the psychic.

BABYBOY

HOMEGROWN: The First Inner City Harvest dies. It never even makes it into the record stores. It turns out that Lonzo only pressed up a few boxes of CDs, and most of them still sit in his office. His reputation as World Class Grandmaster doesn't seem to have convinced either the A&R men or the DJs. If there had been some interest, he would have pressed up more.

Babyboy feels let down. He had imagined that Lonzo would be

promoting the CD seriously. It's true that Lonzo had arranged a show to promote it at Underworld Records. Each part of South Central has a record store which acts as a magnet for local talent. In Long Beach it's the branch of VIP on Pacific Coast Highway: that's where Snoop and Warren G used to hang out before they became famous. In South Compton it's Underworld. It doesn't look much: it's just a small store set back off the road in a scruffy mini-mall, but all the stars pass through there at some point. Unfortunately, Underworld Records also has a reputation as a hang-out for some members of the the South Side Compton Crip street gang, and that part of Alondra has a reputation as one of the roughest neighbourhoods. Though Babyboy and Budman grew up in a Crip area themselves – the dub, at Wilton and King, is Rollin' 30s Harlem Crip turf – they're not gang-bangers. Budman doesn't like the notion of going to that part of Compton and sticking his neck out by performing there. At the last minute Budman and Payback tell Babyboy they don't want to do it: they are worried there will be too many gang-bangers in the audience.

To outsiders, the harm gang culture does is usually only reported or measured in terms of the number of gang-related killings in a neighbourhood. To those who live there, the effect is more profound. Everyone knows where the turfs are, where their demarcation lines run. Insidiously, the whole population finds themselves navigating the unwritten rules.

Babyboy feels he has lost face in front of Lonzo and the people who run Underworld. 'Budman let me down,' he says. 'He ain't professional, you know.'

KHOP

There's a small mention of Khop in *Rap Sheet's* monthly 'Representing' column. It calls him 'the Inglewood, California-based Khop (pronounced Chop)'. His managers, Charlie B and Casual

T, have sent a tape of 'Dollar, Drink and Dank' to the magazine. 'Representing' offers a demo service that readers can phone. For Khop's track, dial the number shown then enter '*102'.

Charlie B and Casual T are checking who else out there is interested in Mr Short Khop; it is part of their strategy to manoeuvre him into the right place. If Ice Cube wants to sign Khop to Heavyweight, they must make sure they find the best possible deal for him. The track is attracting some attention: some companies have called up to offer Khop independent record deals, but his managers are not taking these seriously as long as someone with as much weight as Ice Cube is interested in their artist. But it also means they can tell Heavyweight that it's not the only company that is interested in Khop.

They're being careful not to jump in too quickly. Negotiating the right deal with Cube is crucial, because signing up with a big hitter is no guarantee of success. The careers of other Cube protégés, like the female rapper Yo Yo and the group Da Lench Mob, fizzled and died. 'Of all the people Ice Cube has worked with,' Casual T says, 'Mack 10 is the only one who has come up. We got to make sure we don't drop the ball.'

RAH

The sea change in hip hop that Ice Cube has sensed is gathering pace. The new mood is for sexually explicit party records. Power 106 keeps playing a record titled 'I'm Not A Player (I Just F____ A Lot)' by a South Bronx-raised Puerto Rican called Big Punisher.

This is the type of music record companies have been longing for, a respite from the darkness of gangsta rap. Something that means they hold their head up as they sell to the rest of America. Like sex. The thug *Zeitgeist* is giving way to a less threatening type of hedonism.

Big Punisher's record is pure, raucous, exhilarating smut. He's a talented rhymer, but his records are for the most part deliberately light, with strong, poppy hooks. 'Big' refers to his size: the Punisher verges on obesity. On 'I'm Not A Player' he portrays himself as an irresistible love God. Not that he is exactly a latter-day Barry White, schmoozing romantically to the sound of violins:

Yo – I ain't a player, I just fuck a lot,

he raps, graphically.

Jump on top of my dick and work them hips until I bust a shot.

The radio edit is filled with blank spaces where the expletives have been removed.

It's an exciting time for the Bronx rapper. Big Punisher is one of Loud's main priorities. Only a few weeks ago he was practically unheard of to all but the underground fans, but now the label is pushing him hard. Cash and his street team, which now includes Josiah Brocks, have been sniping the city with yellow and black stickers that announce simply: 'Big Pun'. By the time he arrives to promote the record in Los Angeles, at the end of October, with his rhyming partner Cuban Link, he finds an overwhelmingly positive response for his music. The huge man talks in a deep, scratchy, voice. 'I love LA,' he announces.

On the night of the 31st, he and Cuban Link drive to KSCR – a college radio station at the University of Southern California campus on Jefferson, in South Central's north side. Cash and Josiah go with him.

In the studio, Pun sits at the mike and there are some young hip-hop fans present who want him to freestyle, so he just starts rhyming to the beats they've put down for him, and it's fun. The rhymes flow and the night has that sense of camaraderie and purpose that comes when several rap fans get together, broadcasting through the college radio system. At the time Pun thinks: This is wonderful. This is special. Only later will he decide: 'Maybe if I didn't freestyle so long, we would have gone home earlier, and then . . .' But the first hour comes and goes, then the second.

It's long after midnight when Pun leaves the studio. Finally Cash and Josiah can go home. They get into Cash's old Honda Civic and travel east along Jefferson to the 110 freeway, taking it north up to the 101, so Cash can drop Josiah back at his Hollywood apartment.

The Hollywood freeway is normally busy all hours. Tonight, Detective Pelt of the LAPD will note, it is surprisingly quiet. Cash is the only witness who comes forward to say what happened next. This is the version he will later tell the detectives: as Cash and Josiah's car approaches the Vermont exit, another Honda, a maroon or red two-door, drives up alongside. There are four Hispanic men inside. For no reason, one of them points a gun out of the window and fires.

Josiah may even have been asleep when the bullet entered his head: he could sleep anywhere.

Los Angeles has given the twentieth century many new words and phrases: one of them is 'drive-by'. Cash left the freeway at the next exit on the northbound lane, on Melrose, with Josiah lying across him, unconscious from his head wound.

Around two in the morning on Halloween eve, Mike Nixon's phone rings; he answers it from his bed. It's a guy called Minus, Cash's partner in Lockdown. Minus is trying to get hold of Josiah's brother, Silas, to pass on the terrible news, but he doesn't have his number. The only person they can think of who will have it is their competitor, Mike Nixon, Josiah's old boss.

'What happened?' asks Mike.

'He was shot in the head – but he's still alive.'

The emptiness fills Mike. His sixth sense is telling him that Josiah is already dead. He knows he is gone.

Mike hears the description of the killers. Four men in a red

Honda. For all his grief, he is impressed by the prescience of the 3rd Street psychic. He remembers how she told him, 'I see an accident with a red car.'

Minus hangs up and calls Josiah and Silas's apartment in Freaktown. Silas, fast asleep, stirs when the phone rings. Minus tells him that they've taken his brother back to University of Southern California Hospital.

Tonight, Rah is out, as he so often is, 'sniping' poles at the junction of La Brea and Rodeo. When his pager goes off, he recognizes Mike Nixon's home number, finds a phone booth and deposits his 35 cents.

'Man,' Mike tells him. 'You know what happened? Josiah got shot on the 101 freeway.'

'Oh God.'

Rah doesn't believe it. He thinks they must have made some kind of mistake, that maybe Josiah has just been shot in the arm or something. There are some poles he hasn't done yet. All he can think of to do is just carry on stickering them. When he finishes, he heads back to his own apartment.

But back at home, the phone is ringing. It's Silas. He's at USC Hospital. He says: 'You should come up here.'

In the ICU, Rah looks at the young man, lying there with a single bullet in his head, surrounded by tubes and wires. It doesn't even look like Josiah. The doctors are pessimistic.

Rah is still thinking: I can't believe this. He wishes that Transit Crew had never split up. If they had stayed together, this would never have happened.

'Man,' he says to him, in his head. 'I wish you had listened to me. But the reason why you weren't listening to me is because I betrayed you.'

He reruns the events of the past few months over and over in his mind, trying to pinpoint the moment which dictated that Josiah would end up here, dying, instead of remaining his best friend. If only Lockdown had treated him a little better, then he wouldn't have split from Cash, and there would never have been any argument between him and Josiah and then maybe Cash wouldn't have felt like he had to split up Transit Crew, and all this would never have happened.

It's daytime now. Josiah and Silas's parents arrive from Seattle. The doctors have been waiting for them. They advise the couple to withdraw life support from Josiah.

On his show *Westside Radio* on 92.3 The Beat, the DJ Julio G waits for a record to finish, then tells the listeners about a street promoter called Josiah who was shot last night. He tells the listeners, 'I send my condolences to his family, and to all the other brothers out there on the streets.' He barely knew Josiah. He had met him just once, but Julio believes in the idea of the hip-hop community: that they are somehow all in this together. He likes to make sure that people are recognized; that their names are not forgotten. He says, 'Just be careful, 'cause this stuff is getting crazy out there.'

It's a routine nowadays, saying things like this. So many people in the industry have died since Julio first became involved in hip hop. He remembers other street promoters who have been killed, like Al, and Squeaky, who was killed in another drive-by, outside his own house. A good kid. Just something that happened. Being in the wrong place at the wrong time.

Julio is a man of some influence: a DJ with one of the few shows left on LA radio to regularly play new acts. If you're a new young street promoter like Rah or Josiah, Julio is exactly the sort of person you dream of getting to know.

Julio goes way back on the LA hip-hop scene. He grew up in Lynwood – the neighbourhood between Compton and Watts – and remembers the excitement he felt listening to the mix tapes coming in from New York. He was a hanger-on with Uncle Jamm's Army, the collective of DJs and dancers who used to put on the best parties in the early eighties, and he followed them to all the events that they used to put on. He knew all the first wave of LA hip-hoppers, like Egyptian Lover and groups like LA Dream Team and World Class Wreckin' Cru.

Julio used to be a DJ on KDAY — the first trail-blazing hip-hop station in Los Angeles. He remembers how he was DJ-ing on a show called *Friday Night Live*, broadcast that night from Bell High School, when this finely dressed young street hustler, with a gang-style leather jacket and slicked-back hair, came up to him with a white-label single and asked, 'Will you play that for me?'

'What is it?' asked Julio.

'Some new stuff from Compton,' said the man.

Julio looked him over. 'Man, it ain't got no cussing in it?' he asked. The hustler shook his head. The young man stood by the turntables, watching Julio until he finally caved in and cued up the record. It was 'Boyz In Tha Hood'. He and Eazy-E became close friends; they remained so right up to Eazy's death from AIDS. 'I guess, growing up in LA I've been surrounded by death,' he says. So many of the people he grew up with have died. 'I've almost become immune to it.'

Over the past ten or so years a generation of urban youth has witnessed carnage. The kill-rate is high among the Latino population, but if you're a black man it's far higher. You are at least six times more likely to be a homicide victim than your white equivalent and almost five times more likely to die of AIDS. In 1993 the American Psychological Association estimated that young African-American males were 11 times more likely to die from homicide than non-African-Americans. Homicide is the leading cause of death for young African-Americans of both sexes. Juvenile murder rates have almost doubled since 1980. In California, around 950 African-Americans are murdered each year, compared to about

800 whites, even though blacks only make up about 10 per cent of the state's population.

Every young person I meet in South Central seems to know at least one person who has died violently, often a school friend or a relation. Many have witnessed the violence themselves. There is something truly horrifying about this, yet it has been a fact of inner-city life in America for at least ten years. In the late eighties researchers at the University of Maryland School of Medicine, in Baltimore, questioned 168 teenagers who visited an inner-city clinic for routine medical care. Twenty-four per cent had witnessed a murder. Seventy-two per cent knew someone who had been shot. Twenty per cent had had their lives threatened. On average, each of them had been the victim of assault one and a half times. If those figures appeared shocking, the doctors who had compiled them pointed out that around 80 per cent of the respondents were female. The figures, they speculated, would probably have been much worse if more young males had been included.

These are no ordinary childhoods; they are hardly childhoods at all. The trauma is immense, and all the greater for being largely unrecognized and unacknowledged by the rest of the American community. A sense of grief, confusion and numbness festers.

Compare this with the only other cull of American males in living memory – the Vietnam war – and the true horror emerges. The annual figure for homicides among the African-American community in 1995–6 – when homicide rates across America were already dropping – was between 150 and 200 per cent higher than the average annual number of deaths in Vietnam of the *whole* American population. But this kill-rate is being endured by a minority population.

There are no facts that illustrate as clearly as this the yawning gulf in understanding between white and black America, between middle-aged blacks and their children, between those who live in the hoods and those outside them. It is as if they are living in entirely different countries. As celebrity ex-gangster and journalist Sanyika Shakur, at one time known as Monster Kody Scott and formerly of the Eight Tray Crips, once boasted darkly: 'Where I lived, we lived, we grew and died in dog years.' After ten and more years in the hip-hop industry, Julio G says: 'I'm not even scared of death any more.' Like so many of the young men of his age and background, he shares that fatalism which comes to those who are too familiar with premature death. 'When my time has come, that's it,' he says.

Those days after the killing are awful. Rah talks about how bad he feels to his friends, and they try to comfort him, telling stories of their own, about their own friends who were killed, giving him advice about how they learned to cope with the pain. But that doesn't stop him from thinking that really it's all his own fault. All his life he has been looking for loyalty of some kind. When he finally found it in the shape of Josiah's friendship, he betrayed it by talking to Cash about Silas the way he did. 'I blame myself,' he says. 'All of us could have been like a unit.'

Cash, too, has a hard time in the days following the death. He sells his Honda. He can't bear to drive the car that Josiah was shot in any more.

The sheer pointlessness – the bloody and apparent randomness of the murder – makes it hard for the community to cope with. Apart from Cash, the police have no witness to the shooting.

Maybe it's because it's hard to imagine why anyone would want to shoot Josiah, but from the moment Minus called him up on the night of the killing, Mike Nixon has been convinced that the murder couldn't just have been random. In his mind, he reruns how he thinks the night must have gone: Cash leaves the radio station with Josiah. He's taking him back home to his apartment on Santa Monica. These *cholos* ride up in the red car and start throwing gang signs and shit. The best thing would be to look ahead and ignore them, but knowing Cash, he would probably go: 'Fuck you, motherfucker! Westside! Fuck you!'

The *cholos* react. They say, 'Who is that motherfucker? Fuck you!' They pull out a gun and shoot.

Mike is so convinced that it must have happened that way, that he tells other promoters about it, spreading his imagined version of events through the music industry. For a long while after the murder, Cash won't speak to him, even though they meet each other in record company offices. One day Cash finally confronts him. He says angrily, 'You're putting it out on the streets that I'm responsible for getting Josiah killed.' Of course, Mike can't deny it.

Cash insists, 'No, no, it wasn't like that . . .'

'Whatever you say,' Mike says, and it's obvious he doesn't believe him. There is little love lost between them now.

Rah also thinks that maybe something happened before, something that Cash doesn't want to talk about, though he's less certain than Mike of it. 'I don't know. I can't believe that they just rode up on him and shot him.' In a way, it doesn't matter, because Josiah is dead and nothing is going to bring him back.

And yet everyone – even Mike – feels sorry for Cash, for what he went through: the boy bleeding on his lap, waiting under the street lights on Melrose for the police and the paramedics to arrive.

But however much it's hurting him, Rah thinks that Cash is probably hurting even more. Imagine that, he reflects: he had to see that. He had to sit and watch another person shot in the head. That's with you for life.

On the Wednesday after the shooting Josiah's funeral is held at the Bible Enrichment Fellowship International Church, on the corner of Kelso and Spruce in Inglewood, a low, modern building in a pleasant neighbourhood, opposite the United Methodist Church.

The mourners all receive a printed order of service: 'Homegoing Celebration for Josiah Elijah Brocks. Sunrise July 14 1976 – Sunset

October 30 1997'. Josiah's father helps carry the coffin into the church. The other pallbearers are Silas, Mike and Breck 'Cash' Ayres. Loud Records pay for everything.

Rah has never been to a funeral before. He cries the whole way through; he can't help it. He keeps thinking about all the times they went out sniping together. The pastor – everyone calls him Bam – keeps introducing new friends and relatives who stand and say their piece about what a good person Josiah was, and how he never drank, and how he helped people, and how much they loved him. When it's Rah's turn he stands up and says, 'If it wasn't for him, I wouldn't be here now.' And then they play the Boot Camp Click's 'Last Time', with its weary gospel chorus:

This is the last time I will ever struggle
This is the last time I will ever fall.

Some time after Josiah's death I am talking to the rapper Xzibit from the LA rap group the Alkaholiks. He was a friend of Josiah's too. 'He was my boy,' Xzibit says. He tells me there is a special mention of Josiah on his solo album *40 Dayz & 40 Nightz*: 'All my people in the struggle move on. This is dedicated to the memory of Josiah Brocks . . .' His name is included on a list, the 'Special R.I.P. Shout', that he has had printed on the CD's sleeve, along with two other friends who died recently.

Where I live, art is something far abstracted from the day-to-day. There is nothing so indirect, so circuitous about hip hop. Hip hop is full of *memento mori*, recollections of the violence that has been perpetrated, of the friends that have been lost. Its kill-count and the music's brutality seemed theatrical from a distance. Close up, it's easier to see why it is so full of stories of death and violence.

Later Josiah's family take his body back to Seattle. It lies in a cemetery on Vashon Island.

PART TWO

'Los Angeles is overcrowded, tense and tawdry. But in spite of all this the people up and down Central Avenue feel very happy and boast just as hard for their city and feel just as superior toward the East as do the white Los Angelinos.'

'The Ten Best Cities for Negroes',
The Negro Digest, 1914

8

The Rain

KHOP

This time Cube wants Khop to travel to Houston. Khop's not sure why. He has been performing some shows with Westside Connection and he assumed this would be another of those, but last night he was in the studio with Mack 10, and Mack 10 wasn't travelling, so Khop wonders if it's for a Cube solo show, or something.

Things are becoming hectic. Khop knows he's on the way. He's in as good a situation as any aspiring rapper could hope for. He's on the verge of starting his own solo career, and he should be excited about everything that's going on around him, but right now things are becoming very stressful. 'And I ain't even out there yet . . .' he laughs.

Khop's attorney has had the contract from Heavyweight for a few weeks now. She's dealing with it, but it's all going slowly. Then again, that's pretty much the way Charlie B and Casual T want it. Khop is on somewhere around eight tracks with Cube now, but no contracts have been signed. Effectively, Charlie and Tyronne – Casual's real name – have created a roadblock. They're playing a careful game of brinkmanship. Cube's people have a release schedule they have to keep to. They need to start putting out tracks to publicize Cube's new movie soon. The tightness of the schedule leaves Relentless with a strong hand in negotiations. If

Cube's people want to put out one of the tracks with Khop, then they're going to have to persuade Relentless to come to the table.

'It's kind of a touchy situation,' is how Khop sees it. 'I'm already on so many songs, but there's no paperwork yet.' He knows that just being on those songs means he could be worth millions, because Cube has the power to sell platinum. But until the papers are signed, Khop is worth nothing at all.

As he said on 'Dollar, Dank and Drunk':

It's going down like this,
one shot, so I can't miss . . .

'I don't have a plan. This is it, right here. If it don't happen, I don't know what I'm going to do. I'm not going to go back to school, you know what I'm sayin'?'

And while Charlie and Tyronne are playing hardball with Cube's people, Khop is the one who has to work alongside Cube.

In the Relentless office, they're playing a waiting game, watching the afternoon soap *As The World Turns*. Cube's office calls up. Anxious about how long this whole contract negotiation is taking, they're trying to move things along.

Charlie puts the call on to the speakerphone so Tyronne can hear too. 'Tell me this,' the voice is saying. 'Exactly when is your attorney going to get back to me with her points?'

'There's a couple of things she's still checking out,' Charlie fluffs. 'I'm sure she'll get right back to you any minute.' Tyronne grins at him.

The voice on the line sighs, and tries to put pressure on. 'Look, guys, I'm not trying to tell you how to do your business, but this woman is dragging her feet.'

Charlie says innocently, 'Well, if you needed her to move, you should have got back in touch with us earlier.'

'Come on! She's your attorney. She does what you tell her to do. If you really want things to move forward, you can.'

'OK,' Charlie mollifies him. 'Now we know your concerns, we'll talk to her.'

'We need to finish this.'

Tyronne, too, makes conciliatory noises: 'Let's work as a team on this, OK?'

The moment Charlie puts the phone down, he and Tyronne start laughing. 'He's sweating, man! He's sweating! We got eight tracks and he ain't got a contract,' Tyronne says, rubbing his hands together happily.

'You hear him? He was stuttering,' beams Charlie.

Simultaneously the fax starts spurting out an itinerary for Khop. Cube wants him to be at LAX tonight to catch the 12.55 a.m. Continental flight to Houston, Texas. Things are going fine.

Cube is observing Khop. From a distance, he's pleased with the way things are coming along: 'I always look at these rookies coming into the NBA,' he says. 'You come in with that talent, but this business can overwhelm you.'

RAH

For Rah the funeral didn't seem like enough to remember Josiah by. 'All fine and dandy,' he say. 'But I think they should have done a little bit more.'

Josiah lived on the streets and should be commemorated there. Rah begins to write his name on the bottom of the posters, or on the pieces of cardboard he fixes the stickers on: 'Josiah Brocks R.I.P'.

He starts adding messages to the greeting on his answerphone: 'Yeah. Rest in peace Josiah Brocks. One love. We'll never forget you. We're always keeping your spirit alive.'

He talks about Josiah all the time, writes his name wherever he goes. It is his way of making restitution. He has a baseball cap made up. Embroidered on the side, it says 'Transit Crew' and on the other 'R.I.P. Josiah Brocks'.

One day Sleep from Mad Pro is visiting the Virgin Records office in Beverly Hills. He meets Rah in the reception area, a wide, wood-floored expanse with a single sofa and a small stack of old copies of *Billboard*. Rah is also along for a meeting with the promotions department. Sleep notices the baseball cap that Rah's wearing.

Sleep has heard about Josiah getting killed, but it's been bugging him that though he knows that Josiah ran with Mike Nixon's crew, he can't figure out which one Josiah was. So he approaches Rah. 'Man,' he says, 'I heard so much about Josiah, but I can't picture his face.'

Rah is happy to oblige. He wants everyone to know about his dead friend, so he opens up his bag and pulls out his photo album. He has it with him whenever he goes to a record company so he can show off pictures of his handiwork as a street promoter.

Even before he's seen the photograph, Sleep suddenly remembers Josiah's face. He looks at the photograph Rah is showing him, Josiah proudly standing next to the rapper Common Sense, and thinks: Oh no. Sleep, the big man, ex-army, with a vicious-looking tattoo on his right shoulder of a gang-banger clutching a semi-automatic, turns away from the photographs. He can't look. He hardly knew Josiah, but he finds himself crying.

KHOP

In Houston Khop discovers that Cube has a recording session booked at Atomic Dogg Studios. He wants Khop to add backing vocals to a couple of tracks, and lay a few verses of his own.

Khop is having a great time. To him it seems like the studio's in the middle of nowhere, but Houston is just far more spread out than LA. They work on five songs out there, with Cube urging him to write more of his own lyrics on the spot.

One is 'Pushin' Weight', a play on the idea of the rapper as drug dealer, pushing illegal substances. Khop raps:

I keep a firm grip on my shit when in transit,
Uncandid, it's the young bandit
Fresh out the trenches – the wood work
City of Champions
Where the hoods lurk
In search of rich blocks to lick spots and kick rocks . . .

He's on a roll now. His laid-back Snoop-isms have disappeared. Partly that's because some of Cube's muscular style has rubbed off on him, but Khop is also sounding more confident, more arrogant than he has done before. His voice is triumphant, his style fired up. As he says, he is the young bandit, come to show everyone the way it should be.

Cube is winding up his solo album, *War And Peace (Vol. I)* now. He's going to hold its release until some time next year, after *The Players Club* and its soundtrack album have been out for a while. 'I'm on half the motherfuckin' album,' Khop realizes, happily.

Cube says: 'We going to start working on Khop's album as soon as I finished mine.'

'I'm the new nigga on the block. Y'all have to pass me the baton because I'm going to be the biggest shit,' Khop tells everyone, only half in jest. 'I'm really going to put it down like that. My shit is going to be the tightest.'

They even cook up a track called 'Mr Short Khop', Cube supplying the choruses and Khop taking the verses. 'The shit,' says Khop happily, 'is beautiful.'

He calls home. His baby momma tells him Trey is sick, he's missing his daddy so much.

RAH

It's now three weeks after Josiah Brocks was murdered, and Rah is out working again. At the end of November it's still dark at five in the morning.

Mike has asked him to put up some 'P5s'; that's his own word for blocks of five posters, sniped so they're all in a row.

He's on Rodeo and La Brea, just close to where he was the night when he first heard the news about Josiah getting shot. The posters look good, so he decides to take a photo of them, so that Mike will have something to show the record company.

So he pulls the camera out of his backpack, then he moves back so that he can get all the posters in one shot, and as he turns his head to check that it's clear behind him, he catches something moving behind him.

They're about half a block away: four or five young boys, just about 11 or 12 years old. At this time of night it's wise to be careful of any boys that age out on the street. And sure enough, when he focuses on them, Rah sees that one of them is clutching a handgun – not a particularly big one, but a gun all the same – and he realizes he is about to be mugged.

The boy who has the gun is wearing a Wu-Tang Clan T-shirt bearing their slogan 'C.R.E.A.M.'. The irony of it sticks in his head. 'C.R.E.A.M.' is the title of a song by the Wu-Tang Clan. Of all the groups on the East Coast, the Wu-Tang Clan were the one who most vividly documented the emergent crack epidemic in New York and the deadly effect that it had on the young boys that they were before they escaped out of Staten Island's Stapleton and Park Hill Projects and into the rap game. Early Wu-Tang Clan songs mix childlike, shoot-'em-up video-game imagery with real tales of murder and brutality. As a result they sound authentically like they're coming from the inside of a traumatized teenager's head. 'C.R.E.A.M.' – which has become a nineties hip-hop standard –

recounts the story of their own flagitious childhoods as dealers, gang-bangers and muggers:

Rollin' with this one and that one
Pullin' out gats for fun
But it was just a dream
For the teen who was just a fiend . . .

In the pounding chorus, the smoke-voiced rapper Method Man announces:

Cash Rules Everything Around Me
C.R.E.A.M.
Get the money
Dollar dollar bill y'all . . .

The boy is running towards Rah, yelling, 'Give me your money.' Rah turns and runs down the sidewalk away from them. He knows that if you're close to someone with a gun, running away isn't going to help you at all, but if you have the advantage of distance it's important to use it. He's older than these boys and calculates he can outrun them to reach the all-night Ralph's 24-hour supermarket on the other side of La Brea, where he'll be safe.

He zigzags side to side, his heart pounding. Running straight makes you an easy target. He makes it across the road without looking back and bursts into the supermarket, panting. The store carries on calmly with its business around him. A check-out boy looks at him, startled. 'Somebody tried to shoot me just now,' Rah explains.

That night Rah wonders if he should give this whole game up: first Josiah, and now this. When finally he feels it's safe enough to go back out, he walks back to the car he's borrowed for the evening, and then drives slowly around the streets. He sees a group of early-morning joggers, leans out of the window and says, 'You guys should leave, 'cause there's some guys out here with a gun.'

Later, when Rah tells me about this, I ask him how he knows how to react when he's approached by a gunman.

'I just been in many predicaments like that,' he shrugs. 'Not that I wanted to.'

When Rah hung out with his gang, the Criminals, he was never a shooter, but he watched other people use guns. Other times, he says, he has been with people when they've been shot. He thinks it quickly becomes an automatic reaction, knowing when to duck for cover under a car, or to high-tail it across the street.

For him, it started when he was around eight years old, hanging around with his older brother, the Crip. He remembers drive-bys where other Crips would grab him and throw him down on to the ground to protect him from the bullets. They would show him how you're supposed to act when the guns start popping.

'It's just being around those people who know what to do,' Rah tells me.

KHOP

Back in LA, Cube is shooting the video for what's now called 'We Be Clubbin'' in a warehouse in Burbank. The track is being released in advance to drum up awareness for *The Players Club*. Khop has hung around on all sorts of video sets for other bands he knows, even taken part in them as an extra, but this is the first time he's ever been a star in one. This one is directed by the famous hip-hop video-maker Paul Hunter. Hunter, like Hype Williams, is one of the new African-American video directors whose careers have blossomed as mainstream TV networks like MTV have expanded their hip-hop coverage. Khop is standing right next to Hunter and Cube, telling the director what he thinks of the shots. He only has three lines in his first song, but it's fun. 'I am loving this shit,' he says.

The next day Khop switches on 92.3 The Beat, where, for the first time, he hears the single being previewed on air, his voice broadcast all over LA.

'That,' he pronounces, 'is cool stuff.'

C-DOUBLE-E

The forecasters have been predicting that El Niño will bring storms rolling in from the Pacific. When the first one breaks, LA descends into chaos. The rain ends a long dry season and turns the oily freeways into skid-pans. Sybaritic Californians, too used to the easy driving of the roads here, are thrown by the conditions. KNX 1070AM broadcasts an item that claims there are 6000 car accidents in Los Angeles County on the first weekend of the downpour.

Herman Collins, C–Double–E, loves it like this. He can turn El Niño into money. Every day he gets up around five or six and makes his way to the corner of La Cienega and Pico, in West LA, to sell umbrellas.

He has to be careful working an area outside his usual pitch. 'It's, like, real scrutinizing. You have to keep looking.' But selling umbrellas means money, and he needs it to pay for his demos and to save up for the equipment he wants to buy.

His father has been calling him up from Florida. It's unusual for his dad to get in touch like this. The first time Herman ever remembers seeing him was when he was 18 years old. Propped up on the window ledge in his room he has a faded three-inch by five-inch photograph of his father when he was in the military. Under the neat army cap, the young man, about to go and serve in Vietnam, looks uncannily like his son.

Herman's father has telling him that he should move to Florida: life is safer there, the standard of living higher. And he says he also needs his son to help out with his landscaping business. From what Herman says, it sounds like his father has also come to a time in his life when he, too, wants to rebuild some bridges.

Herman is torn. He hasn't seem him for years, and he feels it's his duty to go. But his dreams of a music career are important to him. And business is good right now. He has sold 40 umbrellas already today. He buys them for five dollars each and resells them for ten. That means he's cleared $200 in a single day. 'I just thank God, you know, for the rain,' he says.

BABYBOY

For Babyboy, things aren't so much fun. In the first storm, two tyres on his silver Mercury Cougar blew and he had to spend an hour out in the wet trying to fix them. He has had a shitty day. Now it's evening he wants to have some fun.

'I got to go on a ride,' Babyboy asks me. 'You coming?' We walk down to the car and he asks, 'Oh, you got change for a dollar?'

I pull out my wallet and look for four quarters.

'No,' he says, ostentatiously flicking a new $100 note in front of my face. 'A dollar.' Like I knew.

'I'm on a bud run,' he explains; he's going to buy weed.

Babyboy feels that something has to break for him soon. Ya Highness led nowhere, but he is always thinking up grandiose new schemes to try and put his name out there. Today's idea involves persuading two rappers with a track record to let him try to get a deal for them so they can relaunch their careers. Both of these men used to be big on the Los Angeles scene, but have since fallen on hard times.

One is called Kokane. In his heyday he appeared on albums like NWA's multi-platinum *Efil4Zaggin'* and the benchmark *Deep Cover* soundtrack that put Suge Knight's Death Row on the map. His own solo album sold respectably too. The other calls himself Lil' Half Dead: like Snoop Doggy Dogg, he's a former member of the Long Beach Crips and became famous riding the same wave that swept Snoop up. But these days he's broke and desperate for a deal. Lil' Half Dead needs money to get his car fixed. Babyboy reckons that if he can get an advance from a record company for Lil' Half Dead, he'll be able to become his full-time manager. It's a plan of sorts, but Lil' Half Dead and Kokane will need persuading that Babyboy is a big enough hitter to manage them. All he has is his enthusiasm: he has no track record to speak of.

Babyboy drives one-handed, his seat tipped so far back it's a wonder he can see out of the windscreen. In thick rain he has to set the wipers on their highest speed. 'Like I told you, I'm going to be big,' he promises. 'Lil' Half Dead is going to be the money-maker, 'cause he's Snoop's partner, you know what I'm saying? I'm gonna have money.'

The rain gets heavier as we drive east up Stocker Street. 'You know, my dad was a millionaire from drug money? I used to watch him count it. He would take it out of the safe at my great-grandmother's house and count it. Sometimes he used to let me count it too.'

'So it's in the blood?' I joke.

'That's right.'

Babyboy remembers seeing his father only maybe six times in his whole life, but he talks about him all the time. The presence of his dead father seeps into everything he does.

Teenage boys in Los Angeles swap stories about the O.G.s. The acronym is the respectful name for the 'Original Gangstas', the hard men of the seventies, who fought in the early days of the escalating gang wars between Bloods and Crips. In the retelling, the O.G.s have become legends, just as the psychopathic gunmen of the Wild

West became heroes to white boys. Ice Cube once told me about it: 'All niggas do is reminisce. "Damn, man . . . I remember T-Bone. He went to such and such a place and shot it up." That's the whole language.' And I asked him if he used to idolize the gangstas too. 'Did I? Hell, yeah. When I was in seventh grade, it was all about that.'

Gregory Wayne 'Baby' Daniels was a hustler and drug dealer. His family were Southern migrants from Louisiana, Arkansas and Texas, but Baby Daniels was born and raised in LA. He was a wild child. At 17, he fathered Kimeyo, his only son, by a girl a year younger than him. Everyone called the child Babyboy, because he was Baby's boy.

According to Babyboy's version, which grows a little larger each time he tells it, his father was a drug kingpin. He wasn't around much when Babyboy was growing up. He was either in prison, hustling out of town, or just simply not around, but his presence was everywhere. As the son of a local big-time dealer, Babyboy automatically received attention. 'Everywhere I went I got a lot of respect,' Babyboy says proudly. 'I used to go to church as a little kid and come home with 15, 20 bucks.'

When he started school, he always felt he deserved to be what he calls 'the COA' – the centre of attention. He became the class clown, and has been performing ever since.

Babyboy often repeats stories about Baby Daniels, with a sort of grim passion in his voice. He wants everyone to know who his father was, what his own roots are. The details of his father's life may become a little polished in the retelling, but that's only because Babyboy wants everyone to know what a big man he is descended from.

Baby Daniels was eventually arrested in Milwaukee on a drug charge, stood trial and served six years in prison. He went to jail a successful dealer, with $8 million still owing to him – so Babyboy says. When he came out he went looking for the man who was supposed to be holding the money for him. He found him, but the man didn't have the money, so Baby Daniels pulled out a gun and shot him three times with a .57. Says Babyboy, 'But the guy didn't die.'

Babyboy was hundreds of miles away, training with the Marines in San Diego, when this drama was unfolding. He tells the story that one night he spoke to his father on the phone. 'I ain't seen him for six years,' he said. 'Tomorrow we have a furlough. I was going to come on down there and see you,' Babyboy remembers telling his father.

'The next day I woke up and went for my PT. I was running down the side of a mountain, and the First Sergeant pulled up alongside us in a car and said, "Please come down to the company office." Down at the company office they asked me, "Do you know Gregory Wayne Daniels?" I said, "Yeah, that's my dad." They said, "Well, he was murdered last night."'

Babyboy shrugs. His sense of destiny comes so plainly from his father, and from the absence of his father. 'There you go. That's how I found out that my daddy was murdered.'

'Who do you think killed him? The man he shot with the .57?'

'Yep. He got someone to shoot my daddy in the back of the head with a .45,' he said. 'It blew the left side of my daddy's head off.'

The police, he added, knew who arranged the murder, but didn't have enough evidence to arrest him.

We are stopped at an intersection. 'I tell you, though, if I see him . . .' Babyboy says. He raises his arms, clasps his hands together and makes a gun with the fingers of his right hand. '. . . *Duh-Duh-Duh!*'

Babyboy dreams of becoming as big a man as he remembers his dad was. He wants to find some way to step into his shoes. His father had no other male children. 'I'm the last one,' says Babyboy. 'I'm the last Daniels. I don't have no brothers with my last name.

That's probably why I want a son so bad.' Babyboy has two daughters but no son. ''Cause if I leave, my daddy's blood-line leaves. That's what I want to keep from happening.'

Babyboy drives across South Central back to the area he grew up in. 'The hood,' he says ostentatiously. We drive down 39th, and he points out Volume 10's house, as if it's some important landmark, and I'm a tourist and he's the guide. Volume 10 is one of Babyboy's friends, a rapper from the hood who made it briefly with a single called 'Pistol Grip Pump' and an album called *Hiphopera*, but who's now back again struggling to find another deal.

Babyboy pulls the car up outside a house nearby and runs inside, leaving the wipers swishing and the heater blasting. He returns five minutes later, hunched up in the rain, with two large bags of grass.

On Western he pulls up at a liquor store, buys a half bottle of Hennessy, a can of Coke and a bag of ice, then chooses four cigars.

There's a small girl in a short sun-dress at the counter, buying a packet of Kools cigarettes. 'What's your name?' he says. 'I'm Babyboy Delatorres.'

'Renée,' she replies, looking him up and down.

'I'm just on my way to a recording session,' he says ostentatiously. 'You want to go out later?'

'I'm married,' she flirts. She walks towards the door, but slowly enough for Babyboy to catch up with her.

'You're married?'

'Yeah, I'm married. But I'm not saying I'm happy.'

'Uh, hon? OK. Give me your number,' smiles Babyboy. 'I'll be finished after midnight. Maybe we'll hook up.'

He writes her number on a scrap of paper and puts it in his pocket, then drives off back to the studio saying, 'I started the evening with $100. I buy the Hennessy, the blunts and the bud.

Maybe a motel room later on,' he says, thinking wishfully of Renée. 'By the end of tonight it will all be gone.'

The Edge in Inglewood is at 6814 La Cienega, by the corner of Centinela. It's a small studio, but most of South Central's hip-hop artists, from Tupac to Cube, have made demos here.

Kokane is here tonight: right now he sits on the old grey sofa downstairs, watching the Lakers, who are 61–51 up against the Clippers. 'This track is called "Penal Code 9350 Possession of Kokane",' explains Kokane. He's 26, has penetrating hazel eyes and his real name is Jerry Long Jr. 'Kokane, that's my rap name,' he explains, 'which is specifically talking about dope lyrics, ah . . . we using that gimmick as far as the name is concerned.'

Kokane is trying to record an album that will put him back on the map and get him some money. For any rapper trying to get on, it's not just a question of having good material; you also have to get noticed. The best way to get noticed is to have some impressive credits on your record. For 'Possession of Kokane', Kokane has enlisted the rapper Spice 1 to record a verse, which raises the value of the track. They've been on the scene together for years. Spice 1's track record is solid: he had a number-one album on the *Billboard* r'n'b charts back in 1993 with *187 He Wrote*.

Kokane leaves the game and dashes up to the studio through the rain via the outside staircase. It is easing up now. A guitarist called Overdose is there, clutching a white Fender copy. Overdose is a session musician whose biggest credit so far is an appearance on the Dogg Pound's album. He is actually the son-in-law of the outsize king of disco, Barry White: he used to tour all over the world with White, playing funk guitar. Now he's struggling to make his name as a hip-hop producer. He sits on a stool, eyes shut, carefully adding blues riffs to Kokane's track.

'That's *tight*,' shouts Kokane enthusiastically.

'I'm just feeling it,' shrugs Overdose shyly.

There's a chance that Priority records might be interested in the resulting album, which Kokane plans to call *Slangin' On Wax*, and if so, Kokane can finally make it back into the big boys' team.

Babyboy bursts through the door with his bags of dope, his Hennessy and his Garcia Y Vega coronas, and demands loudly, 'Anyone know how to roll a blunt?'

And while it looks like Babyboy is just squandering his 100 bucks on drugs and alcohol, it's more than that. His purchases tonight are a sort of investment. Of all the rappers I'm hanging around with, it's Babyboy who understands this particular dynamic of the game the best. He doesn't have a relation who is close to Ice Cube, but he's determined to create connections wherever he can. He spends a lot of time late at night hanging around, keeping close to the people who may just be able to help him. It's all about making friends for when his chance comes.

C-DOUBLE-E

The second big El Niño storm breaks a few days later.

Los Angeles does metaphors of the last days of Sodom so well. The last decade of the twentieth century has proved particularly adept at throwing up suitably apocalyptic imagery: it has had fires, riots and earthquakes. What LA lacks in grand buildings or monuments, it makes up for in symbolism.

The heavens open around 11 a.m. Tarmac laid on desert soil can't begin to absorb the inches of water that fall. The torrent quickly overwhelms the storm drainage system.

I'm driving slowly down La Brea: the road slopes gently downwards from the Hollywood Hills and the water quickly reaches a foot in depth on either side. Adding to the spectacle, it's trash collection day. All the plastic bins, carefully placed by the sidewalk earlier this morning, are swept away. They drift down to the intersections, making their own barricades of blue and black plastic, blocking up the road with floating trash bags.

South of Santa Monica Boulevard, the drains are so full that a manhole cover has popped up and water is jetting in a four-foot-high column in the middle of the road.

Some people run quickly from one storefront shelter to the next. The homeless, on the other hand, move far more slowly or lurk quietly in office doorways. They're suddenly more conspicuous because the shopping carts they normally push from place to place are covered in brightly coloured plastic in an effort to keep their worldly goods try. The tired figures who push them are wrapped up likewise, in capes or plastic trash bags strapped at the waist.

Drivers hate the cart people, who inch across intersections, holding up the flow of cars. The police carry out regular swoops, alleging that the trolleys are used to transport drugs, or as stepladders to break into buildings. The Central City East station picks up as many as 60 carts a week. Homelessness campaigners accuse the police of harassing the vagrants and dumping their possessions on the sidewalk.

Stuck in the rain in my car, I remember Herman and his umbrellas. I turn west and drive carefully to La Cienega, and then southwards to his new pitch. Sure enough, there he is, standing on the corner by the Shell gas station, dressed in thick black and yellow waterproofs, spinning a black umbrella in a circle around him in a wide arc like he's Gene Kelly, to attract the attention of drivers. I park up next to him.

He waves. 'I made $300 already today,' he says happily. 'Run out of umbrellas once.'

He offers me one at cost price: $5. He lets the people who work at the gas station and at the Bank of America across the street have umbrellas at the same reduced price. That way he keeps everyone happy, and no one moves him on. His pitch is neat: a large bucket full of umbrellas, which he positions as far back on the sidewalk as he can so he doesn't get in anyone's way.

Underneath his overalls, he's wearing a goose-down jacket for warmth. The rain is easing up now, but he doesn't care. 'It's all good,' he says. It's his favourite expression. He spends his days working the streets with his bucket of merchandise and nothing ever seems to get him down. 'It's all good.'

He tells me he's decided to visit his father in Florida some time in the next few days. It's something he feels obliged to do. He'd much rather stay in town as long as the weather's like this; and he'd much rather save his El Niño windfall for the MPC 2000 sequencer he wants to buy than spend it on a plane fare.

'You heard a weather forecast?' he asks.

'More rain this afternoon. And another big storm coming through on Tuesday.'

'Wooo,' he grins. 'Maybe I'll stay in town a few more days.'

RAH

A month or so after Rah was nearly mugged, Mike Nixon decides it's time to let him go. It's a business thing. Rah has outgrown his time at N5. He is doing too much of his own work now and he thinks Mike's probably tired of seeing Transit Crew's written name up there alongside posters that he's been putting up for N5.

Rah is hurt by Mike's decision, of course. Mike has looked after him well. He's like a father to his crews. Rah had wanted to continue taking the N5 work alongside his own new accounts, but he always understood that this situation could arise.

Transit Crew is just one person now. Josiah is gone and Silas left for San Francisco after the funeral and he doesn't want to come back. 'I just chose not to live there. Because of my brother. LA's kind of' – Silas sighs – 'really fucked up, if you ask me.'

Now Rah is going to have to make it on his own. In a way, it's what he's used to. He's had to do things for himself for so much of his life. It's going to be tough, though. It's harder in winter, now that the nights are cold. This winter there has been so much rain, and there's no point going out when it's too wet.

The work trickles in for Transit Crew, though. Big Wes, head of the street promotion team at Priority, calls Rah up to ask him to help with a campaign stickering for Ice Cube's new single, 'We Be Clubbin''. At the bottom of the posters and the stickers is written, in big letters: 'Introducing KHOP'.

9

Dirty Records

TIBU

Famously, Dorothy Parker once called Los Angeles 'seventy-two suburbs in search of a city'. LA was much smaller then, of course.

This modern sprawl goes on for ever. Once-new neighbourhoods decline and those who can move still further out. To the south-east of Compton and north of Long Beach, Bellflower flourished in the sixties, but it has had its day now. It is well beyond the area that was traditionally thought of as South Central. Until recently it was clearly a white community, but the money went elsewhere, and working-class Latinos and African-Americans are moving in. The centre of the city is Bellflower Boulevard, a brief, anonymous strip of shops and restaurants, built in the area's mid-century heyday, that runs southwards to the 91 freeway.

Eucalyptus runs parallel to Bellflower, a block to the east. On the corner where Eucalyptus crosses Alondra Boulevard is the HQ of the 706s, Bellflower's own street gang.

Taking their name from Bellflower's zip code, 90706, they are the sort of click you can find almost anywhere in the city: an independent outfit, without allegiance to either Blood or Crip. Many of these smaller sets are usually short-lived, but apart from occasional minor disputes with bigger affiliated groups like the Hoovers, the 706s have managed to survive since 1989 without becoming involved in any major turf wars. They say they're about hustling, not gang-banging. When the police aren't cruising slowly past, they sell drugs here, on the corner.

Caleb Candler is a huge boy. He wears large, plain, baggy T-shirts which conceal his overweight belly. His head, with close-cropped hair, is also disproportionately massive; an underbite forces out his lower jaw, giving his bottom lip a petulant-looking, downward curl.

Caleb's rap name is Mr Tibu – taken from the Swahili middle name his mother gave him. For the past few months he's been the leader of the 706s' own rap outfit, which he has christened the Vietnam click. 'Spelt with an "o",' says Tibu. 'It stands for "Victory Is Everything To Niggas On My Side". How we live is like Vietnam,' he adds proudly. 'We droppin' bombs on motherfuckers.'

Tibu used to be in another outfit called Mercenary Click; but they were from the city of Los Angeles, and they used to mock Tibu because he came from Bellflower, a suburb with no history of hard-core gang activity and no reputation for producing rappers. So he said, 'Fuck 'em' and set about forming his own click here in Bellflower.

Montrie 'Sneak' Ledford is there too. In the Vietnam click they call him Sergeant Cavi. In contrast to Tibu's humungous frame, Sneak is small, with a delicate face. His hair is neatly braided back on his head. Sneak's a year older than Tibu. It was Sneak who introduced Tibu to dealing drugs back when he was 16, homeless and broke. Sneak was sick of his school friend always trying to borrow five bucks from him, so he introduced him to life on the corner here at Eucalyptus and Alondra, and Tibu, who's now 18, seems to have spent most of the intervening two and a half years hanging out right here.

Tibu's living with Sneak right now, a couple of blocks up Eucalyptus. It's mid-afternoon, and nothing is happening, so he and Sneak wander up towards Sneak's home, a sixties craftsman-style house set back from the road.

It's dark inside, and musty-smelling. The blinds in the front room are always drawn. Someone has been playing the game *Parapper the Rapper* on a Playstation plugged into the big old TV. Sneak sits on the old couch to roll a joint. Behind him there's an old glass dining table surrounded by Z-shaped metal chairs that at one time probably looked the height of modernity. Now the stuffing is coming out of their seats.

Tibu wanders into the bedroom that Sneak's family are lending him and riffles through a pile of tapes. The room is bare save for an unmade bed, a wardrobe and a chest with a sound system on it: a tape deck and CD player. Wires trail everywhere. A sub-woofer sits on the floor: it's home-made. With admirable economy, the loudspeaker has been set in the cardboard box it was bought in.

Tibu presses 'Play'. A slow G-funk rhythm crackles out of the improvised system:

S'all for my niggas in Belltown, California,
Seven-oh-six way, what you say?

He adjusts the volume. It's a track that the Vietnom click have recorded called 'Bunnies', a straight-down-the-line gangsta rap, full of tub-thumping bravado, about 'Terrible Tibu, illegal/with his Desert Eagle' – a prestigious brand of Magnum handgun – hanging out with Sneak on 'Euccy' – Eucalyptus.

Used to smack niggas up – this is Belltown
When I take your cash, this is melt down . . .

boasts Tibu.
'You's a b-u-n-n-y,' taunts Sneak in the chorus:

Why you bunnies scheme and try
To fuck with hustlers from this side?
Who love to ride, love to ride . . .

In song, anyway, the 706s are the bravest, boldest, baddest click on earth, and their opponents are weak and cowardly. 'They're all bunnies out there,' Mr Tibu scowls. 'They're soft.'

Outside, in the living room, Sneak's grandmother sighs. 'Well,' she says, 'I hope they do make it soon. I'm sick of hearing it all the time. That noise.'

South Central is a state of mind. That's just as true to the white fans who have never been here as it is to its young African-American, Latino and Asian inhabitants. To come from South Central is to come from somewhere: from a landscape in which true manhood is validated. In Tibu's mind, he's as much a part of South Central as anyone from Watts, even though he comes from the satellite of Bellflower – Belltown, as the 706s call it. Of course, anyone from Watts would probably regard such a claim as ridiculous. South Central has become a relative concept.

These days the term generally refers to a 40-square-mile stretch of land between Downtown in the north and Long Beach in the south, bounded on its sides by Gardena and Torrence. The population of this area is somewhere over half a million, though, as in Bellflower, the youth of dozens of other surrounding LA County communities want to count themselves in.

Originally South Central was just a narrow strip of land, running north to south, where African-Americans clustered around the southern end of Central Avenue. On a rare bright day in December, I decide to take a drive down Central, starting in the Downtown area, the financial and administrative heart of the city and also the oldest part. I have my Thomas Cityguide and other guide books laid out beside me on the passenger seat.

This wild, unstoppable, dysfunctional conurbation was originally the eighteenth-century dream of Felipe De Neve, Governor of California within the territory known then as New Spain. Travelling to the then Californian capital, Monterrey, De Neve came across the coastal plain of the Los Angeles River and decided it was an ideal place to establish a *pueblo*, a village. Los Angeles was founded on 4 September 1781. Its 44 founding inhabitants included nine Indians, two Spaniards, seven 'mulattos', one 'Chino', one 'half-breed' and two 'Negroes'.

There was a river – more of a stream, really, except when it flooded – but little else. The sea was miles away, there was little in the way of natural shelter, or trees for fuel and timber, and it was isolated by the mountains and deserts that surrounded it. It was an unlikely place for what was to become one of the most influential cities in the world. As a consequence, for 100 years it remained a backward, violent cow town. The poorest and most desperate street on the south side of the town was christened 'Nigger Alley' – in 'honour' of its African-American residents, despite being populated largely by poor American Indians and Chinese labourers. It was a lousy, disreputable neighbourhood full of brothels, bars and drug dens, just parallel to Main Street. 'By four o'clock,' reminisced one farmer who passed through in the 1850s, 'Nigger Alley would be crowded with a mass of drunken Indians, yelling and fighting. Men and women, boys and girls, tooth and toe nail, sometimes, and frequently with knives, but always in a manner that would strike the beholder with awe and horror.'

The black population remained insignificant until the 1887 land boom, when the number of African-American surged abruptly from 102 to 1285, as unskilled migrant labourers started to arrive from the rural South. The city was a magnet for others too. From the 1880s to the 1920s, Los Angeles exploded rapidly from the obscure village De Neve had founded to a significant city.

The black community began to coalesce at the junction of First and Los Angeles, close to the start of my journey down Central Avenue, where City Hall sits now. The African-Americans spread southwards to Second and San Pedro, where they began to establish their own businesses, catering to the growing population. From there the black enclave began to edge southwards along South Central Avenue.

The new city dwellers exuded an optimism about what they were achieving. Those African-Americans who had made it to Los Angeles reckoned themselves much better off than those who had stayed down South. Black newspapers sprang up, full of a sense of pride in the growing community. Locals noted, with a sense of accomplishment, that they were not being forced to live in 'black-only' areas.

Migrants were looking for the best place to move to. Black Angelenos believed they had found the best option. J. B. Loving, of the city's black newspaper the *Liberator*, wrote gushingly in the early years of the twentieth century: 'The Negroes of this city have prudently refused to segregate themselves into any locality, but have scattered and produced homes in sections occupied by wealthy, cultured white people, thus not only securing the best fire, water and police protection, but also more important benefits that accrue from refined and cultured surroundings.'

During the century's first two decades, distinct African-American communities sprang up in several locations in the Downtown area. Some moved into properties on Temple Street, others along Jefferson, between Normandie and Western, well to the west of Central Avenue. Some set up house in the Boyle Heights area, in the business district to the east of the Los Angeles River.

Some couldn't afford the 'refined and cultured surroundings'. To the south, the Furlong Tract had sprung up in 1905, after an Irish farmer named James Furlong started selling off lots of his land between today's 50th and 55th Streets and Long Beach Avenue and Alameda. Black working-class families moved in and the area quickly became a healthy community, boasting three churches and the first all-black school in Los Angeles.

Further south still, around 103rd Street, even poorer migrant African-Americans moved into the beet-farming community known as Watts. During the first two decades of the century Watts Town had been a working-class community of Germans, Scots, Mexicans, Italians, Greeks, Jews, Japanese and some African-Americans. That its first black community was known as 'Mudtown' probably says something about the esteem their neighbours held for the incomers, but the upside was that Watts offered plenty of good opportunities for black labourers. It was also an important rail junction. The Pacific Electric's Long Beach–Santa Ana line ran through the middle, and the company soaked up arriving labourers.

Watts grew fast. By the twenties, Pacific Electric was building houses for its African-American employees south of Watts rail station. These were the heady days of the trolley car, before the automobile took over Los Angeles. The Southern Pacific Railroad Company was also a big employer in Watts, taking on blacks as porters and waiters for its Pullman carriages.

To Southerners, this was a land of opportunity, a place where they could finally sidestep the discrimination they had suffered elsewhere. Though they were optimistic, they don't appear to have been downright naïve. It wasn't that they had any illusion that there was a more enlightened breed of Caucasian living here on the West Coast, just that there were others here who were even further down the scale of prejudice than they were: in particular, the Chinese.

The 'Chinos' had come to California mostly from the poor region of Kwantung, in south-east China, lured like so many others by the Gold Rush. After 1850, the Chinese 'coolie slaves' began to drift down from the northern part of the state to arrive in Los Angeles by the thousand, some as road builders, others as labourers for Southern Pacific. Many whites panicked at the sudden influx. Communities in Norwalk, Vernon, Burbank and Pasadena drew up special legislation to exclude the Chinese from their neighbourhoods. Many Chinese settled near the ramshackle, despised, 40-foot-wide 'Nigger Alley', and this became LA's first

'Chinatown'. Here, in 1871, a mob of 500 whites went on the rampage after a Chinese man shot and killed a white policeman who had tried to intervene in a fight between two Chinese factions. Within five hours whites had lynched and murdered 19 Chinese men and boys – just under a tenth of all the Chinese in the area.

Suspicion, hatred and fear of the Chinese persisted. When the black sociologist Charles S. Johnson carried out his *Industrial Survey of the Negro Population of Los Angeles* almost 50 years later, he confirmed that among the reasons why local African-Americans regarded themselves as better off in Los Angeles was that here they longer represented the most despised of races. 'The focussing of racial interest on the Oriental has in large measure overlooked the Negro,' he wrote, 'and the city, accordingly, has been regarded by them, from a distance, as desirable and likely to yield for them important opportunities for living and earning a living.'

This wasn't one-upmanship: this was 1926, when the dreams of the Southern migrants were turning sour elsewhere. In 1921 the flourishing segregated black community that had grown up in Tulsa, Oklahoma, had been violently razed to the ground by white lynch mobs, inspired by the 'rape' of a white woman which almost certainly never took place. The destruction was so ferocious that the exact number of dead is unknown.

Los Angeles in the boom of the twenties seemed like a picnic in comparison. On top of that, it was a land of opportunity. There was oil here, and the movie industry was flourishing too, adding a splash of glamour to the city. The real-estate men were making fortunes portraying the city as a balmy, fertile paradise. In 1923 alone, 25,000 one- and two-bedroom family dwellings were completed. Buy a house and watch its value soar.

But the giddy boosterism of the speculators had an ugly downside that turned out to be disastrous for non-whites. Those who wanted to buy and sell Shangri-La wanted a perfect, unsullied product.

In 1915, the Ku Klux Klan arrived on the West Coast, not just as an organization, but also as a myth, ennobled by the movie industry. That was the year that D. W. Griffith completed his historical masterpiece *The Birth of a Nation*. Technically and artistically, the film was visionary. In one movie Griffith laid down the syntax of modern film-making. Awkwardly for his film-historian admirers, it was also a film inspired by the fears of white Northerners about the African-American populations that were straying northwards; an eloquent piece of pro-KKK propaganda. The hooded men were depicted as the saviours of white women from black marauders (actually white actors in face paint), careering on horseback around the hills of what was in fact the new suburb of Hollywood.

In the twenties and thirties, the KKK thrived on the new white fear of blacks moving into their neighbourhoods, working to thwart the early dream of commentators like J. B. Loving that in Los Angeles blacks would live in integrated neighbourhoods.

During the housing boom of the twenties, racist attacks on blacks who had dared stray out of their areas became commonplace. The politically progressive black newspaper the *California Eagle* diligently reported each atrocity. 'P. Reynolds, red cap porter at Union Station, returned home to find his wife beaten and the letter "K" branded in blood on her cheek,' it noted on 29 October 1921. 'On the door by her bed chamber upstairs where Mrs Reynolds had been attacked was pinned the following note: "*Show this to s'more of you that wants to be white. Get out of this neighborhood. KKK*".' 'This neighborhood' was the predominantly white Highland Park district.

The message was clear. Stay in your own part of town. The KKK reacted with particular horror to the rapid growth of the African-American population in Watts. Fearing that the number of blacks was now enough to form a political majority there, the Klan organized a secret political campaign. In 1926 the politicians successfully moved to annex Watts to Los Angeles, ensuring that the town continued to be white-run.

But the Klan and their burn-'em-out tactics were a relatively crude instrument. There was a far more subtle and effective enemy of new black aspirations. Speculators and property owners didn't even have to be doggedly racist themselves to fear minorities moving into their neighbourhoods: the fear that those minorities could affect values was enough. Property prices could only hold up if confidence was maintained. The mechanism by which the real-estate industry sustained that confidence was a legal one. Newly built houses were sold with 'deed restrictions', restrictive covenants which decreed that only Caucasians could occupy them. Asians and African-Americans were welcome too – but only as domestic labour. Once these properties were sold, housing associations sprang up to oversee these covenants. Some of the names they gave themselves betray their purpose – for example, the Southwest Wilshire Protective Association. One can hazard a guess that the good members of the White Home Owners' Protective Association were not trying to dictate the colour that houses were painted. They policed the racial purity of the massive area that now lies between Martin Luther King Boulevard and Main and Vermont. The arrival of a single black household in the East Budlong area inspired the formation of the Anti-African Housing Association.

By the 1920s a 'colour line' had been drawn around the South Central community, making 95 per cent of the city off-limits to Asians and African-Americans. Apartheid on this scale was a new phenomenon. Until the twentieth century, blacks and whites had lived in relatively close proximity in cities in both North and South. But the social, economic and technological changes brought by industrialization were changing all that.

The demographic facts were already operating against the new minority community. Though there were black enclaves in places like Pasadena, Santa Monica and Long Beach, by 1930 70 per cent of the black population was concentrated in that remaining five per cent of LA's residential space. 'Jim Crow legislation' – named after a grotesque, bumbling black stage character played by white actors in the nineteenth century – had proved remarkably effective in that burgeoning city.

As the colour line was being strengthened, the industries which were profiting from black labour were simultaneously gobbling up much of what little land there was within the Central Avenue corridor. Meanwhile, any concerted attempt to provide subsidized housing for the poorer incomers was vigorously opposed by the politically dominant white real-estate men, who argued that government interference would undermine the health of the property market. When the Los Angeles City Housing Authority did construct new houses only 10 per cent were allocated to blacks under a quota system that continued until 1943.

The migrants flocked to LA for a better life, but before most arrived, the apparatus to blunt their aspirations was already in place. All the conditions were there to create a modern ghetto.

Los Angeles often seems rather like those ageing pop stars who insist on discussing their latest dreary album, even though their past is far more fascinating. It has become a cliché now to remark that it's a city with little sense of its own history, a city in which the present and the future are the only things that count; but that doesn't stop the observation being true.

What is remarkable about Central Avenue now is the resounding absence of almost any sign of what used to exist here, of any of the excitement that this street used to generate. There was a time when the road on which I am driving southwards was probably the liveliest in the whole city. In its clubs you could hear the finest musicians in the country. In its meeting rooms, some of the greatest members of the black intelligentsia lectured and agitated. The African-American community has almost entirely deserted it: the north end is predominantly Hispanic territory now.

Looming absurdly on my left on 14th Street is the Coca-Cola bottling plant, one of the few survivals from the days when burgeoning industries colonized the area. It was, my guide to local architecture announces, built in 1936 in the 'streamline moderne' style, designed to look like a swish ocean liner, complete with round portholes and a ship's bridge and railings.

The Coca-Cola Company maintains its old plant beautifully; but the environs have crashed, and it looks as if some drunken captain has beached his luxury cruise ship among the surrounding deserted warehouses.

The first black-owned nightclubs started to appear around this section of Central Avenue during the First World War. Pianist Jelly Roll Morton settled in Los Angeles, playing regularly at places like the Cadillac Café at 553 Central and the Penny Dance Hall on 9th Street and Central, and even at the brothels that then thrived on 'Nigger Alley'. Between performances, he pimped for some of the whores there.

Central Avenue quickly established itself as the centre of the black entertainment industry. As early as 10 March 1916, the Angelus Motion Picture Theater was advertising in the *California Eagle* as the 'Only Show House Owned by Colored Men in the Entire West'. Clarinettist and saxophonist Reb Spikes opened his music shop, Spikes Brothers Music Store, on 12th Street and Central in 1919, selling sheet music, instruments and recordings. It became a centre of the South Central music scene, and white fans would venture there to buy jazz and ragtime records. From its earliest days on record, black music provided something of a daring thrill for white suburbanites. Reb Spikes, himself of mixed African, Norwegian, Irish and American-Indian origin, remembered how Hollywood's brightest young things would 'drive up in long limousines and send their chauffeurs in to ask for "dirty records"'. The dirty records of LA's South Central will continue to appeal to the young and white through the century.

Meanwhile, just as the black middle classes today look down on some of South Central's cultural output, the redoubtable *California Eagle*, while eager to foster the advancement of the African-American cause, was not altogether sure that the black entertainment industry was developing in quite the way it believed it should be. One editorial harrumphed: 'The question has been asked of us what are we going to do about the conditions on Central Avenue. It is claimed that gambling is flourishing on this thoroughfare like the proverbial Green Bay tree, but we surmise that the anti dice-shaking ordinance will now at least put a quietus on the crap games and reduce the pernicious practice to a minimum.'

Local bands flourished. In the early twenties you could catch trombonist Kid Ory's Creole Jazz Band playing on bills alongside their arch-rivals the Black and Tan Jazz Band. Just like today's rappers, bands would vie to outdo one another. Back in those days, these battles were known as 'cutting contests'.

Central Avenue exploded into life. Some clubs, like the One-Eleven dance hall at 3rd Street and Main, offered pretty girls, who would dance with you for ten cents a minute. They were known as 'taxi dance halls'; the girls, presumably, always kept the meter running. By the late twenties the region between 19th and 41st Streets became the 'Brown Broadway'. It was packed with night-clubs and beer gardens, and at weekends crammed with revellers.

Before he became famous as a vibraphone player, Lionel Hampton was the drummer with Paul Howard's Quality Serenaders, who, as one of the best black dance bands in the city in the late twenties, performed regularly at the Kentucky Club Café at 2200 Central Avenue.

At the southern end of what was the Brown Broadway, on my right as I drive down towards Watts, sits a large, five-storey building. An old metal sign outside proclaims: 'Dunbar Hotel'.

Once this was the grandest black-owned hotel in Los Angeles. It was named in honour of the great Harlem poet and former slave Paul Laurence Dunbar, as if to announce that this Central Avenue meeting place was worthy of being equated to the East Coast's Harlem renaissance. The seminal African-American sociologist and activist W. E. B. DuBois stayed here, and held meetings of his National Association for the Advancement of Colored People (NAACP) in its rooms. Duke Ellington, Count Basie and Bill 'Bojangles' Robinson were among the guests. Jazz guitarist Gene Phillips, who lived in a room here in the forties, recalled nostalgically in the liner notes of one of his albums: 'All the cats hung out at the bar there 'cause that's where all the chorus girls hung out. Any night you could find Nat ['King'] Cole, Duke [Ellington], Cab [Calloway], Basie here. Everyone who was anybody ended up at the Dunbar bar.'

The strip around the Dunbar, which boasted the very best night-life Central had to offer, was known as 'the Stem'. Next door to the Dunbar was the famous Club Alabam, which was long ago demolished. The Dunbar escaped destruction in the sixties thanks to a redevelopment committee who wanted to reinvigorate the local African-American community here. Although they saved the hotel, the community they saved it for has disappeared.

I pull over and peer at the old hotel. It is now a sad, dusty-looking building. There is, rather appropriately, what looks like a thriving funeral home on the opposite corner. A sign on the hotel entrance reads: 'Private property. Door locked at all times.' These days the hotel is rented out by the room as small dwellings. The only sign of its former greatness is a small wall plaque which says: 'Dunbar Hotel 1928. Honoring Black Achievement.' Around the corner there is a large mural depicting the glory days of 'the Stem', depicting W. E. B. DuBois and Duke Ellington side by side. 'Don't move, improve,' pleads the slogan at the bottom. 'Don't buy where you can't work.' Despite the mural's imprecations the African-American community has all but deserted the neighbourhood. Poor Latin-American immigrants have taken over instead.

I get back in my car and continue southwards, past the Supermercado, the Carneceria Latina and Iglesia Pentecostes Lucero De Jesu Christu, past the advert for the Latino pop radio station 105.5 ('Más Música! Más Excitos! Que Buena! Norteñas, Mariachis, Bandas') and past Teresa's Liquor Store, where the saint is painted on the walls, arms clasped, halo shining on her head. 'Anything is possible in the State of Courvoisier,' reads the advert above her.

KHOP

On the day that the 'We Be Clubbin'' video is added to the selection on the cable channel The Box, Khop's father calls in to punch in the number and request it. The Box operates like a jukebox: you phone up on a premium line and choose the number of the song you want to see. Though Khop has seen rough cuts, this will be the first time he sees himself performing on the TV.

The selection finally comes up. Instead of Khop and Cube's video, The Box plays comedian Chris Rock's single 'Champagne', a skit that pokes fun at Sean 'Puff Daddy' Combs.

Khop's sidekick Kidub is so incensed he calls up The Box. As an apology, they give Kidub two free plays.

BABYBOY

Babyboy's neighbourhood is in the west side of South Central. The west side's geographic proximity to Hollywood sometimes means that it has closer connections to the entertainment industry than do areas like Compton or Watts.

Babyboy has a friend who used to be road manager for LA hip-hoppers the Pharcyde. This friend suggests that he sign up with a casting agency, Mega Large, which routinely casts for hip-hop videos.

That's how he gets a call one day to drive over to a set on Central Avenue, where a group called Beats By The Pound are shooting a video. Beats By The Pound are one of Master P's production crews, but they're putting out their own record for P's No Limit label. They want Babyboy to act the part of a criminal.

He arrives and introduces himself. Everyone in the group seems to be called Something Dog, like Lil' Dog or Hound Dog, but they're friendly enough. The group invite him into their trailer and offer him a big blunt stuffed full of chronic and he takes a deep pull on it. This is Babyboy heaven. The band are happy, because they're going to be successful, and he's happy just being around them, soaking up the optimism of the moment. 'It's a beautiful thing,' he decides. 'It's a beautiful thing.'

There is work to be done too, of course. Babyboy has to run around a little, while a car chases him, and then someone shoots a gun at him and he has to play dead. But he notices that in the crowd of people who have turned up to stare at what's going on, the girls are all paying him attention, because, he thinks, they believe he's some kind of star.

He gets only $100 for hanging around all day, but it feels like a million to him.

I bump into Babyboy a few days afterwards.

'Where was the shoot?' I ask.

'Right around Central Avenue and 40th.'

I tell him how that part of Central Avenue where he was working was once the centre of South Central, the heart of African-American California.

'Central?' he says incredulously.

'That's where all the clubs were, all the dancing. All the gambling.'

'Central?' he says again, disbelievingly.

As the population and its spending power increased, the clubs and bars spread southwards. Raymond Chandler's 1940 thriller *Farewell, My Lovely* opens in one of the blocks south of 'the Stem', 'one of the mixed blocks, the blocks that are not yet all Negro'. When Chandler's hero Philip Marlow enters a bar that five years previously was white-run, he is told, 'No white folks, brother. Jes' fo' the coloured people. I's sorry.' There goes the neighbourhood.

Chandler's thriller was part of a white vision of Los Angeles that was already starting to depict South Central as an encroaching, murderous environment in which the usual rules no longer applied. The inauthenticity of the scene betrays itself in more than the bartender's awful 'I's sorry' accent. Chandler also reversed the reality. In fact, despite the fact that blacks were banned from clubs and bars in white districts, the opposite was seldom true. Whites flocked to indulge themselves in South Central's night-life, at the Kentucky and the Alabam.

Music has always been regarded as the most dangerous of all the arts. Middle-class society imagined jazz, in particular, as possessing some primitive quality which could persuade even the well-bred to forget themselves. Though most Central Avenue Clubs allowed both whites and blacks to dance, they did so on condition that they were not allowed to dance together.

Blacks, however, were routinely excluded from white venues. At the earliest white jazz clubs, like Baron Long's (later the Plantation and then Jazzland) at 108th Street and Central in Watts, black musicians would play to a crowd that included Charlie Chaplin and Fatty Arbuckle but no African-Americans. Many clubs remained reluctant to employ black musicians at all. During the twenties and thirties, the *California Eagle* diligently celebrated each new venue that reversed its policy and started employing African-American musicians. They might have been welcome as players in some of the clubs, but the musicians were often unwelcome to stay on after they'd finished their set. Police cars would sometimes escort musicians from Pasadena, or from the nightclubs springing up along Sunset and Hollywood, back to their turf, south of Pico Boulevard. Black audiences remained largely restricted to the clubs around Central.

When, in 1940, the Casa Mañana – formerly the New Cotton Club – in Culver City started to allow mixed-race dancing and an open-door policy, it was the exception rather than the rule. That was the year the Benny Goodman Orchestra were booked to play a dance for the La Fiesta Club at the Shrine Auditorium on Jefferson. However, the Los Angeles Police Department refused a permit for the show, for fear that whites, blacks, Filipinos and Mexicans might dance together.

War was good for Los Angeles. By 1942, the weapons industry was booming, transforming it into a major industrial city. Howard Hughes's Hughes Aircraft Company in Westchester, Lockheed in Burbank and the Douglas Aircraft Company in Long Beach all accelerated their production. The shipyards in Long Beach, Terminal Island, Wilmington and San Pedro all rushed to take on workers. Steel manufacturers like Henry J. Kaiser grasped the opportunities too, Kaiser himself setting up a massive steel plant in Fontana. Skilled positions were largely reserved for whites, but basic wages rose, and migration from the South soared.

The transport system struggled to meet the new demands industry placed on it. The Southern Pacific Railroad Company actively recruited workers from the South. At the height of its growth in 1942, it was bringing between 300 and 400 new people to the city every day. The following year was even crazier. In June 1943 alone, up to 12,000 African-Americans arrived in the city.

July and August saw that figure rise to a peak of 15,000 new black incomers a month.

The Central Avenue corridor was swamped. Fenced in by restrictive housing policies, families were squeezed into districts that couldn't possibly accommodate them. Housing was only one part of the catastrophe. Key elements of the infrastructure, like sanitation, along with the education system, could not cope, and the 1940s economic boom turned ghetto to slum.

Relocation from the rural South had a profound effect on some families. Relationships which had endured in farming communities fell apart in this screaming, barely regulated new world. 'We came to Watts in 1942 by car from Texas,' one female migrant recalled years later. 'The adjustment or change in environment was hard on us. Whereas the entire family used to go to work in the fields together, we now worked in different places at different times; whereas I used to make one large lunch for the entire family, during the war my husband and my two sons were able to buy their lunch on the job; whereas we used to be paid at the end of the year, we were paid for two weeks; whereas we used to be paid with groceries or with chickens or pigs, during World War II we were paid by check; whereas we used to work from sun up to sun down, during World War II we worked eight hours and were often paid over-time; whereas we used to take the baby to the field with us, we had to find a babysitter. So you see, our whole lives changed when we moved to the city; after a while we didn't seem to be as close somehow. We didn't seem to have time to talk.'

Existing residents, who saw their standard of living decline as the ghetto filled to bursting point, viewed the poor, unsophisticated, under-educated rural newcomers with almost as much hostility as did their white neighbours. Middle-class African-Americans saw their social privileges eroded. The writer Chester Himes arrived in LA in 1941 after the poet Langston Hughes advised him to come here to seek work as a script writer, but he ended up labouring in the shipyards instead. His novel *If He Hollers Let Him Go* is one of the bitterest memoirs of the period. In it he created one memorable character, a sniffy, poisonous doctor's wife, who declares: 'A lot of our people are not worthy. They just don't deserve any more than they're getting. And they make it so hard for the rest of us. Just the other day the doctor went into a Downtown restaurant where he's been eating for years and they didn't want to serve him. Southern Negroes are coming in here and making it hard for us . . .'

Inevitably, when the war ended, production dropped. Though African-Americans had, while the times were good, enjoyed considerably higher wages in Los Angeles than they had in the South, now their standards of living crashed. The overall unemployment rate in California soared higher than throughout the rest of America. Poverty increased dramatically along the old South Central corridor.

The shape of South Central began to change rapidly after the war. The insidious legal framework that supported the deed restrictions that had dominated the pattern of housing occupancy in Los Angeles had already begun to crumble. In 1943 the West Adams Improvement Association had tried to force out 30 black property owners – including the black Hollywood star Hattie McDaniel – from the Sugar Hill District, but the judge in the case ruled that deed restrictions broke the 14th Amendment. The US Supreme Court finally demolished their legal basis in 1948. When wealthier African-Americans now gradually moved westwards, towards Crenshaw, leaving the slum housing of the Central Avenue corridor behind them, the name South Central followed them.

Moving into areas which whites had once so jealously protected, they extended the borders of the vaguely named region towards La Cienega, and also southwards into Lynwood and Compton. Even though deed restrictions had been abolished, there were still barriers to overcome. Mortgages were routinely harder to obtain and more expensive for African-Americans than they were for white home-buyers. As blacks moved in, the whites moved out. Between 1950 and 1960 the white population of Compton declined by 18.5 per cent, while the non-white population surged by 165 per cent. As whites retreated, the values of houses that African-Americans had paid over-the-odds prices for often slumped.

Meanwhile the poorer African-Americans remained in the areas that had been wrecked by the pressure of the forties boom, creating a tension between the east side and the west side, the middle class and the lower class. The problems of those left on the east side were worsened by the flight of their wealthier black neighbours. Money drained out of the older neighbourhoods. Local infrastructure collapsed. By 1950 32 per cent of housing in Watts was in need of major repairs, while on Central the figure rose to 41 per cent. The move to the modern American metropolitan phenomenon of 'chocolate city, vanilla suburbs' had been completed. Inner cities were poor, occupied by racial minorities, and dependent on the tax dollars of the outer-city dwellers, who increasingly viewed the centre with suspicion, as a drain on their purse.

In a decade, a whole generation of urban dwellers had had their futures dented and seen their neighbourhoods turned into over-crowded slums. A simple calculation will tell you that many of the young black men who burned down Watts in 1965 were the children of those who moved to Los Angeles during the brief optimism of the forties.

'The only thing that surprised me about the race riots in Watts in 1965,' said Chester Himes, 'was that they waited so long to happen. We are a very patient people.'

10

The Man With a Million Friends

KOKANE

Fontana is a city about 50 miles from Downtown LA, out along Interstate 10, on the eastern edge of the metropolis's massive sprawl.

Jerry 'Kokane' Long lives there, with his wife and four children, in a small brown and white trailer in Lot 47 of the Aetna Trailer Park. Outside on the tarmac, someone has scrawled '5mph' angrily in orange fluorescent paint.

When I met Kokane at the Edge recording studio with Babyboy, I had taken down his home number, and later I asked if I could visit him. I knock on the screen door of Kokane's trailer. 'Hold up,' comes a voice from inside. I can hear someone tidying up inside.

When he opens the door, Kokane apologizes for the mess. He hasn't had a chance yet to wash up last night's meal: the plates and chicken bones still sit on the table of the kitchen/living room. He's at home looking after his two-year-old daughter Allyssa, who sits on the drab brown carpet, her hair in tidy bunches, dressed only in her nappy. The TV shows an empty blue screen. Apart from the children's toys, there aren't many possessions in the trailer. It has all the feel of a temporary home: things have not been going well for Kokane.

He almost made the big time five years ago. There was a moment when he was really in the middle of things. He grew up in Pomona, a few miles west of Fontana. His father, Jerry Long Snr, worked for Motown; Kokane claims he helped Norman Whitfield write 'Just My Imagination'. But the pressure of the music business was too much for his father, and he suffered from bouts of mental illness.

Kokane left home at 17. He was having fun with drugs, going wild, hanging around with gang-bangers. He started trying to rap, too. Those were exciting times. If you were a Westside rapper in those days, you were a pioneer: you were finally putting the LA ghettos on the map.

Kokane's cousin is Gregory Hutchinson, who performs under the name of Cold 187. One-eight-seven is a popular piece of hip-hop numerology; it's the police code for homicide. Cold 187 was in a local Pomona group called Above The Law, who took the baton from NWA, who pioneered explicit West Coast gangsta rap. Gregory encouraged Jerry to join in the fun, even christening him with the typically gangsta-rap name Kokane. Above The Law were signed by Eric 'Eazy-E' Wright to his label Ruthless, and though their name is remembered reverently by gangsta hip-hop fans, they were never able to cash in on their reputation in the way NWA were. Above The Law were the group who evolved the archetypal West Coast gangsta musical style, mixing old Parliament-style funk hooks with hard-core rap; the style which Dr Dre later made famous as 'G-Funk'. Kokane also joined the Ruthless stable, at a time when it was the most prestigious label in the West. 'You know, for good or bad financially, I can't be mad at Eric, because if there weren't no Eazy, there wouldn't be no Kokane. He definitely brought me out of the woodwork,' he says.

Allyssa is toddling around the trailer looking for something to do. She wanders up to the video player and starts fiddling with the buttons. 'Don't do that, sweetie. Play with your castle. I'll change you in a minute.' Allyssa wanders obediently over to a plastic toy castle on the far side of the room, and starts messing around with it instead.

'I was an 18-year-old kid, just coming into the music industry, and it was just, like, exciting for me to go out there and do shows . . . making tens of thousands of people feel good about the music. I mean, that was a very exciting time.'

In those days everyone was dizzy with the realization that it was finally the West Coast's turn. Above The Law and Kokane were local heroes. Young would-be rappers like Snoop Dogg and Warren G used to come and sleep on their floors. 'But at the same time, being so early in the game . . . it has a price to pay with it,' Kokane says. We're sitting on a couple of chairs at a small table on one side of the living area. There are no other chairs in the room. 'You come into the music industry, and you're just happy doing tracks. You don't really want to know about the publishing side, and recouping, and all those little words that mess you up.'

I say, 'You're telling me a sad story.'

He smiles. 'Yeah. Somewhat.'

Kokane was a victim of the civil war that broke out between Eazy-E and Suge Knight, Crip and Blood. He was caught between the two camps. Though Kokane appeared on Dre's debut for Death Row, the hugely successful *Deep Cover* soundtrack, which launched Snoop Doggy Dogg, by the time his own solo album, *Funk Upon A Rhyme*, came out on Ruthless, the animosity had become ingrained. Kokane, showing his loyalty to Eazy, also took part in the label's attacks on Dre on the record. It was a bad miscalculation. Dre and Death Row emerged as by far the stronger of the two labels. Kokane had nailed his colours to the wrong mast.

'I kind of fell under that sacrificial lamb thing,' he says. 'The sacrificial lamb for the higher powers that be. There was a lot of bullshit, man. There was so much turmoil in the air . . .'

A bad situation became catastrophic when it became obvious that Eazy was seriously unwell. Kokane remembers attending a meeting at the House of Blues on Sunset Boulevard to discuss the shoot for a video for a song called 'California' which Above The

Law were due to film, with Eazy-E and Jada Pinkett, the actress and girlfriend of actor Will Smith. He noticed that the permanent snuffle that Eazy had had turned into a retching cough. To demonstrate, he makes a throaty, retching noise. Allyssa looks up from her castle for a second, startled.

'I was like, "Man, you got to get that shit fixed." He just handed me a bag of weed. He always had a bag of weed on him,' Kokane laughs.

A few days later, when they were shooting the video, the news came through: Eazy was in hospital, dying of AIDS.

'That really put me on the spot,' says Kokane. Without Eazy, he had no record deal. He's been trying to rebuild his career ever since.

'You didn't make any money out of your early records, then?' I ask him.

'Not really. Not really. But I'm still here living to tell the story.'

He's still hoping that the Priority label will take on his new album and put him back where he belongs. On his lap he holds Allyssa, who has picked up a plastic model of the Creature from the Black Lagoon and plays with it silently.

His wife works in an architect's office, but money is obviously tight. Sometimes he talks about giving up trying to get back into the rap business. When he does, she tells him that Michael Jordan wasn't Jordan when he first came out. It takes work and persistence to succeed. She says, 'When you come out, make sure you come out right.'

'I just love her to death,' says Kokane. 'She just really, really helped me through the shit . . . I have a wife and she understands. I make the best of it. In life, it's best not to cry over spilt milk.'

Kokane has changed a lot from the wild Pomona teenager he was. 'Kids . . . Oh man. That will make you change. If you're gang-banging, and you don't have kids, you think: Oh, that nigga shot at me. I got to go kill him. I got to go kill his whole family. It ain't like that any more. I know what it is to have a family.'

He stands up and pulls down the big brown Dickie trousers that have been hanging low off his hips, exposing the waistband of his Basic Equipment underpants, and there, on his right thigh, is a neat, cherry-red round hole, about a quarter of an inch deep. A bullet wound from the days when everything was crazy, when boys like him would shoot at other boys and they'd shoot back.

'Man,' he says. 'You get involved in the game and you get involved.'

The other night Kokane had a dream in which he was performing on stage at Lollapalooza, the touring rock festival which has helped many hip-hop acts cross over to acceptance by the lucrative white audience. LA's Ice-T played on the first Lollapalooza tour in 1991 with his band Body Count, helping to open the door for gangsta rap to market itself directly to white suburbia. The tour also put Ice-T face to face for the first time with the sort of white boys who loved his music, and that was an eye-opener for him too. 'You don't know that people on the Metallica bus are listening to NWA until you do a tour like that,' he once told me.

That night, Kokane dreamed about following in Ice-T's footsteps, being on stage in front of that cross-over audience. 'I will be up there,' promises Kokane. 'This time next year I will be up there.'

Kokane lives among truck parks and vacant warehouses. Fontana is a product of the war boom of the forties. Industrialist Henry J. Kaiser was given the contract to build a massive steel-plate factory there by the government. Sleepy citrus farms were supplanted by a huge factory complex that needed 5000 men to run it. Black newcomers and others hoping to escape the congestion of the Los Angeles ghetto were among the recruits. But in some ways conditions in Fontana turned out to be just as bad as they were on Central Avenue at that time. African-Americans were again segregated by deed restrictions, and found that the only areas where they were permitted to live were to the north of Fontana, above Baseline Avenue, amid the steel plant's coke ovens.

The Kaiser Steel plant in Fontana finally went belly-up in 1983, leaving the heart of Fontana with a giant derelict industrial zone and a reputation for being one of the poorest satellite suburbs of Los Angeles. Since the collapse of Kaiser, Fontana now boasts the lowest property-tax base of the whole Los Angeles conurbation. In Beverly Hills in 1994, the average property was valued at $594,634 for tax purposes. Fontana scrapes in at an average of $55,240, less than a third of the region's average. Not surprisingly, in the early years of this decade Fontana gained a reputation for being a haven for crack gangs.

TIBU

A few days later I'm driving in my car with Tibu, the 19-year-old rapper from Bellflower. I tell him that I went to visit Kokane and that he was broke, living in a trailer in Fontana. Tibu looks shocked. Kokane used to be a big name in the LA hip-hop scene. 'For real?' he says. He is silent for a minute, then says, 'I ain't going to do that. When I blow up, I'm going to take care of my business.'

I'm driving Tibu and Cavi to a recording studio. Tibu seems a little shocked that I'm driving an old 1984 Subaru that I picked up for $900. He expects me to drive something a little classier.

Tibu commandeers the car stereo, turning up 92.3 The Beat as loud as it can go: the elderly speakers sound like they're going to rip themselves apart. Tibu likes to assert himself like this.

The floor of the car is littered with demo tapes I've acquired on my travels. He picks up a couple. The first he plays is A Nu Creation's earliest demo of 'Nine Times Out Of Ten'. Tibu plays about 20 seconds of Herman's nervy rhyming, not even getting as far as the first chorus, then Cavi shouts, 'That shit is so wack.' Even without Herman's awkward delivery, the rhymes are not hard-core enough for Tibu. He and Cavi laugh, and Tibu yanks the tape out of the player and makes to throw it out of the window.

Poor Herman, I think. There's a demo tape by a Los Angeles hip-hop crew called NX. 'Hey,' says Cavi, picking up the tape. 'I know them.'

'How?' asks Tibu.

'I sell these guys weed.'

'Serious?'

'Yeah.'

They nod their heads to the tape. They listen to Khop's demo all the way through, and more intently. Khop's delivery is so much cooler than Herman's. His voice drips with attitude. 'He got skills,' pronounces Tibu, impressed.

We stop by a house to pick up a third rapper, a teenage girl who calls herself Ms Chevius. She's good-looking, her hair is tightly braided at the front and straightened at the back into a pony-tail and she wears a sharp Nautica jacket and a brand-new pair of XXIII Air Jordans. Even Tibu is impressed. He gazes longingly at her shoes and asks, 'You have to queue up to get those?'

Cavi is looking pretty smooth himself today, dressed up for the holiday in a blue T-shirt, blue corduroy trousers, blue suede Lugz shoes, even a blue Tommy Hilfiger watch on his wrist. The only thing he's wearing that's not blue is the black Tommy Gear gangsta stocking cap that covers his braids. 'Hell, I'm all dressed in blue. I look like a super-Crip, don't I?' he laughs.

The studio is a couple of miles away in a classier neighbourhood in Cerritos. Dave Watkin is a white, pony-tailed, goateed musician who runs a small studio in his home. 'You ever heard of Electric Booty Mob?' he asks me. I shake my head. 'That was me,' he says, slightly disappointed that I had never heard of them.

His house is full of his paintings; it is light and bohemian. A glass of half-finished wine sits on the table downstairs, left over from his lunch.

Dave's home studio is upstairs, in one of the bedrooms. Tibu commandeers it, just like he commandeered my car tape machine. Within a few minutes he has put together a four-bar loop. He works instinctively, punching the keyboard like a two-finger typist. Time is money.

Tibu quickly moves on to the vocals. The track is to be called 'Belltown Niggas'. It's a typical Tibu hook, and goes:

You're losing, losing good company
'Cause you never had a nigga like me
Belltown niggas know how to fuck
Will you tell that bitch to shut the fuck up.

After he's laid down the chorus he explains: 'I'm on some gangsta shit. That's what makes the . . .' He clicks his fingers. The money.

Having decided that the Vietnom click are going to represent for Bellflower, he's intent on blowing up the myth of the Belltown *übermensch*, not only replacing the 'flower' with a less effeminate suffix, but depicting 706 manhood as doughtier than any other in South Central.

The 706 hangout is on Eucalyptus and Alondra. If you take Alondra a few miles west, you're on Compton's south side, right by where Tibu grew up as a boy. It's notoriously rough there: that's the neighbourhood Budman and Payback were so apprehensive about that they refused to turn up to promote Lonzo's CD *Homegrown: The First Inner City Harvest* in the neighbourhood that belongs to the South Side Crips – where Orlando Anderson, the suspect in Tupac's murder, hails from. Tibu's mother, a hospital clerk, moved out of Compton when he was a boy, settling in the better neighbourhood of Bellflower. Bellflower is a less credible neighbourhood, though, if you're a working-class teenage boy. He's been trying to construct Belltown in Compton's image ever since.

The irony is that Tibu's desire to come from the roughest and toughest neighbourhood may soon come true. The nineties has seen Belltown's decline outpace even Compton's. If the property-tax revenue is an index of the health of a community, it's worth noting that Bellflower's is about 53 per cent of the LA district's average, a full 10 per cent lower than Compton's.

After Tibu's turn in the padded closet that serves for a vocal booth, Cavi takes over. Though he's older than Tibu, and it was Cavi who introduced Tibu to dealing drugs, it's Tibu who's the dominant partner when it comes to rap music:

I'm fuckin' bitches for the cause
– Broads taking off they bras
Scratchin' me with they claws . . .

Cavi stumbles over the rhyme. 'Take your time,' Tibu counsels. 'If you're not happy with it, do it again.'

Cavi tries his verse again, but stumbles again. 'It's my throat, 'ler,' he shouts from the booth.

Tibu says, 'That's why you shouldn't smoke that weed before you go into the studio, 'ler.'

'Shut up, 'ler,' Cavi shouts back. ''Ler' is short for hustler. It's a favourite piece of 706 slang. Tibu is trying to put together tracks to make a whole album of material. He can have 300 cassettes duplicated by a company called Diskmakers for $555, a price that includes a printed black and white cover. Tibu figures he'll be able to sell 300 cassettes pretty quickly at the local high schools, and with the money he raises from that, he'll be able to press up more.

Ms Chevius is here to sing on the chorus. She sits quietly waiting for her turn in the closet. All the time, Cavi is eyeing her up, making passes at her. 'You got a boyfriend?'

She ignores him.

' "Belltown niggas know how to fuck . . ." You play that around your house and your momma will beat you,' he tells her.

'My momma don't beat me!'

'How old are you?'

'I'm 18.'

'Eighteen? No you're not. You're 16.'

He's right: she's 16.

Cavi sings:

Ms Chevius, she's so devious . . .

She looks at him sourly. Dave, the hippie studio owner, looks up apologetically from his keyboards and sequencers and announces hesitantly that something has gone wrong. The memory of the Roland MC505 Groovebox he's working with has just somehow wiped itself. Tibu's song has vanished.

'It's a trip,' says Dave goofily. 'The machine just tripped out. It's brand-new, man.'

Dave wanders out of the room to take a leak. When his back is turned, Tibu snarls angrily: 'This man is wasting time.' He says, 'I could fuck him up,' he declares, and he means it. 'I got this street mentality. I could just fuck him up.' Tibu has a vicious streak that can emerge suddenly. He is frustrated and furious.

But Dave returns, and Tibu calms down enough to start the process again from scratch.

BABYBOY

Babyboy has decided he's going to call me West Side. 'I just figured out, your initials are W.S. – West Side. You don't mind if I call you West Side, do you, West Side?' he laughs.

He leaves me messages like: 'Hey, West Side, if you're in pick up. If you're not page me.' Pause. 'Then again, my pager's in disguise right now, so you can't page me. You know how it is.'

Babyboy is broke. His pager is 'in disguise'. Not working. Disconnected. I soon learn that his personal economy follows the usual boom-bust cycle of the drug dealer. You can always tell when he's down, because his pager is disconnected.

The brakes in the Cougar look like they need replacing too. Babyboy might have to sell the car. He's depressed. He says that Lil' Half Dead doesn't want to sign any piece of paper about management. He claims Lil' Half Dead says he'll sign something after he's got a deal. 'He's bullshitting me, man,' says Babyboy, though his attempt to manage Kokane and Lil' Half Dead had always seemed like a long shot. Nothing is working out for him.

He's no further along than he was when we first met six months earlier. The *Inner City Harvest* album sank without a trace: nobody has picked up on his group Ya Highness. 'I don't know,' he says. 'Something's got to bust soon.'

His relationship with Marlene is on the verge of falling apart. He says he doesn't love her any more. He wants to feel what it's like to fall in love again. He sounds bleak. I offer to take him out to lunch in a restaurant called Birds, on Franklin, under the Hollywood Hills. As usual, he's flat broke. Any money he earns from dealing weed comes sporadically, and goes just as quickly. He pulls up in front of the restaurant in his silver Cougar, baby seat in the back, and orders lemonade and a chicken burger.

'What side-dish do you want, sir?'

'I'll have fries,' Babyboy says, pulling up the hood of his grey Fubu sweatshirt, to cover up the tattoo on the back of his neck, as if he's uncomfortable looking too much like a street hustler from south of Wilshire in this Hollywood restaurant.

'Fries come with the burger, sir. They're not a side-dish.'

'OK, I'll have baked beans.'

Within an instant, Babyboy's black mood has gone. Being in Hollywood makes things look so much better. 'Nice place,' he says, looking around the restaurant. Already he's hatching new schemes. His desire to succeed is almost painfully intense. His latest plan is to abandon Ya Highness and form a duo with Budman. 'I know we're going to make it.'

Meanwhile he's also caught the movie bug. Last year the New Orleans rapper Master P and CEO had a massive underground hit with his movie *I'm Bout It*. The movie distributors turned the film down flat. They had looked at its appalling production values, inaudible dialogue and wayward plotting and quite reasonably assumed it was a loser, only to watch horrified as Master P's straight-to-video release turned multi-platinum, climbing to number seven on video sales charts, right up there with all the Hollywood greats. Now it seems like every rapper in America wants to make a 'hood movie' – a film about where they grew up.

'I got this script,' says Babyboy. 'I want you to look at it and tell me what you think about it. Be honest.'

He opens the black briefcase he carries everywhere and pulls out a grey envelope. On the back he has doodled the logo he's invented for the entertainment corporation he dreams of running one day, N Entertainment; it's an asymmetrical letter 'N' enclosed in a circle. I open the envelope and pull out a notebook. On the front he's written the title: 'Young Hustlas'. There are seven pages of neat handwritten script.

There is no real story-line, just an opening. A cool gangsta called Antonio Duke Delgado is found not guilty by the Federal Court, and instead of being locked up in jail is reunited with his son Lil' Duke and the boy's mother. When the verdict is read, the three hug in an embrace 'so warm the bailiff opened the window for air,' writes Babyboy.

Reunited, the family go for chicken wings: 'After about sixty ['fifty' crossed out] chiccen wings and two ckicn' breast sandwiches fries sodas & cakes its time for the Dukes post-meal chronic blunt. Lil Duke being the best blunt roller on the west [coast] and Big

Duke being the man with a million friends keeps the best of the best when it comes to smoking weed with his son. "Blaze it up," Big Duke orders his son.'

The plot fizzles out after that. Nothing really happens. 'It's based on your own father?' I ask.

'Kind of,' says Babyboy.

I start talking in a vague sort of way about how he should introduce some conflict into the story to make it interesting, but as I do so I'm thinking this is exactly how he wants his life to be. Conflict is what you want in your movies, not in your life. Babyboy has probably had enough of that already. He has written about a big-time drug boss and his son, and about their sharing the sort of intimacy that Babyboy never really had a chance to have with his father. He has written about a father-figure who is noble, who escaped the prison system and, above all, who is alive, rather than one who was a common criminal, who was incarcerated for a large part of Babyboy's life and then brutally murdered.

So many of the people I meet carry some tragedy with them: an event like Josiah's death. These are catastrophes that happened largely unwitnessed, largely unnoticed; they leave an unresolved, unaccounted trauma. Newspapers like the *LA Times* no longer pay much attention to violent death in South Central, unless the killing has some special twist to it. There are simply too many deaths. They have a single-page section that's called, somewhat ironically, 'Community News', in which only a few of the killings are noted, in terse paragraphs. Josiah's death never made it there. It is unrecognized. It is not a surprise that so many people I meet have a need to tell their story about their own dead friend or relative. It's as if they feel that because the American media pays so little mind to the passing of their loved ones, they must take on the task themselves.

Master P's *I'm Bout It* was the heavily fictionalized story of his own brother's murder. He had left the violent, neglected Caliope housing project in New Orleans to make his fortune in the record industry, and at about 21 had just set up his own shop in the Bay Area of northern California when the phone call came through, telling him his younger brother, Kevin, had been murdered.

'For, like, about $400. He was shot about eight or nine times by a guy he knew,' Master P told me about his brother's killing. 'One of his friends killed him because they were on heroin and he didn't know it. And they needed a fix so they killed him,' he explained baldly. He told me he had made the film for his dead brother. It gave him the chance to try to make some sense of the murder. In the days afterwards, returning to Caliope, he had dreamed of taking revenge on his brother's killers himself. 'Something like that can take you and drag you right into the hurricane,' he said. But by the time he arrived home, the two men who he believes killed his brother had already been murdered themselves.

Only in the movie, in which P finally gets to shoot his brother's killers, does he achieve his revenge.

Over the years Master P had believed himself pretty immune to the tragedy of Caliope. He had seen his first murder at around the age of four, he reckons, close to the crammed three-bedroom apartment where he and 11 other children grew up with his grandmother. In his song 'Goin' Thru Some Things' he described going on 'a ghetto ride' with some gang-banger cousins aged five, and watching them shoot someone. 'Was the guy killed?' I asked.

'I don't know if someone was killed, or just shot,' he said. 'I think seeing that can ruin a child.'

'Did it ruin you?' I asked him.

He paused. He was sitting on a sofa in the CNN building on Sunset Boulevard where the Priority record company has its offices. His back was to the window that looked out over South Central. Up here it's another world.

'It made me look at life different,' he answered.

162

What the film distributors failed to recognize was that for people who share Master P's background, the quality of the movie didn't appear to matter. Its value was perhaps just as much as a shared testament, a mutual experience. Of the teenage click that Master P used to hang out with at school, five are in jail, one of them for murder.

The most sorrowful part of the movie was the re-creation of his brother's funeral, when mourners lined up wearing T-shirts on which photos of the dead boy had been printed – a growing ghetto tradition for the fallen young. Master P reckoned that he had been to about 30 or 40 funerals of people he'd known. 'But it wasn't really in my house, so it didn't matter,' he said. 'You never know how it feels until then. You feel sorry for people, but nobody knows how it feels until it gets into their house . . .'

Birds is in a strip of restaurants. Most people who live in this part of Hollywood are young and white – either something to do with movies or to trying to be. Next door is a coffee bar called the Bourgeois Pig, a self-conscious stab at bohemia where young Hollywood – all bleached hair, tattoos and pet pit bulls – smoke American Spirit cigarettes, drink mochas and tinker endlessly with their scripts. There are sockets for computers, and always two or three people clicking away at keyboards. The walls are painted red; red gel covers the windows. Large gilt-framed pictures decorate the walls; candelabras with flickering candle bulbs hang from the ceiling.

'Great place,' says Babyboy enthusiastically as we go inside and find a couple of chairs. He drops his voice. 'You figure they'll mind if I fire up a blunt in here?'

'What do you want to drink?' I ask.

'What? You mean liquor?'

'No. This is just a coffee bar.'

'Oh. I'll have a cappuccino.'

I order two large cappuccinos. It comes to $7.40. Babyboy sits down staring at the milk froth on top of his cup. 'This is a cappuccino? I never had one before.'

One of the most contradictory things about Los Angeles is that it is the most multicultural city in the world, but at the same time, the least. North and south of Wilshire Boulevard you could be in different countries. Few of the people in this coffee bar would have been anywhere near Babyboy's neighbourhood; here he acts like a tourist, fascinated by the exotica of the local lifestyle.

'What's this made of?' he asks, poking at the white froth with his spoon.

And I find myself trying to explain a cappuccino.

The following Thursday Babyboy calls me. 'That cappuccino was cool,' he says. 'We got to do that again some time.'

11

A Quarter of a Cent

BABYBOY

Saturday is Valentine's Day.

This morning Marlene gave her fiancé a diamond ear-stud set in gold for his Valentine's gift, to match the one he wears in his left ear lobe. His Valentine's Day gift doesn't quite seem to match hers. He says he's always busy, so the best thing he can give her is some time together. This seems a little unfair because it's Marlene who has the full-time job, and Marlene who spends more time raising their daughter, Chanel. But anyway, last night he took Marlene to the movies. It wasn't a particularly romantic choice. He took her to see *The Replacement Killers,* the new film with the Chinese action hero Chow Yun Fat. He loved it. It's the best film he's seen in a long time. 'Action from the beginning to the end,' he grins.

Valentine's Day is something of a chore for Babyboy, not to mention a delicate balancing act. He's got another girl whom he's seeing on the side right now. Her name is Veronica. She bought him a pair of Nikes for his birthday.

He couldn't be around to take Marlene out tonight. He's 'in the studio'. That means he is at his cousin's house, on Queen Street, near the centre of Inglewood. This is the start of his next project: Babyboy and Budman are going to start recording together again as No Respekt Mob. Sometimes Babyboy just thinks he's the only one interested in pushing onwards. He is becoming frustrated that nothing seems to happen, that no one seems to have faith in him.

Mark Smooth, as his cousin is known, is a musician and DJ with his own bedroom recording studio. He's had his dreams too. On the wall there's a copy of a 12-inch single he recorded as Mark Smooth, 'Play For Me', on Star City Records. Another record that never made it. Mark tolerates Babyboy's presence, and that's about it. He says he can record for three hours: after that, he leaves. But Babyboy lets time slip away once he's recording. 'I like to chill,' he grins.

The big bank of keyboards, drum machines, DAT players and eight-track machines is crammed against one wall. Mark's king-size water-bed takes up most of the space. Stacks of neatly arranged albums and CDs take up the rest. On the shelves that make up the bedstead there's a collection of furry toys: a *Star Wars* Ewok and a pink teddy bear wearing a T-shirt that reads: 'I need your luv.' On the wall opposite is a pine-framed mirror in the shape of the Playboy Bunny symbol.

Babyboy sits down at Mark's Roland JV30 synthesizer and starts recording. He builds an eight-bar foundation of drums, bass and other synthesizer sounds. He's impulsive, trying something, then recording over it, then shouting, in frustration: 'Damn. I liked it the first fucking way.'

His technique is simple: he uses only the black notes on the piano. It works, though. In an hour he's built a solidly funky eight-bar pentatonic loop. 'What do you think, Smooth?' he asks.

Mark shrugs. 'It's different,' he says distantly. He doesn't think much of Babyboy's musical talent.

The trouble is, Babyboy won't stop there. It's so typical of Babyboy: so full of drive, but unable to focus it. He's waiting for Budman to arrive so they can lay down the vocals they've written, and in the yawning hours he goes on piling on sound after sound. He puts in a bird-whistle, and then a sound he likes labelled 'sitar'. He reads the word aloud, pronouncing it 'sigh-tar'. He's never heard an instrument like that before, but he likes the noise it's making.

He starts doodling formlessly, irritatingly, over the track. It is getting so full that the initial funkiness of the beat becomes quickly bogged down. But he doesn't think so. 'That shit is banging,' he insists.

He reaches for the phone for the thirtieth time and calls Budman. 'Where the fuck are you? You're supposed to be here.'

Budman is at home 'in the hood', as he puts it, with his lover, a girl who works for the GTE phone company. He doesn't want to leave. 'OK,' he says reluctantly. 'I'm coming.'

To kill time, Babyboy begs a ride to the liquor store and buys two green dice for 50 cents each. Mark is in the back room, recording a mix tape from his massive record collection for a young friend called Trey and his girlfriend. When we get back, Mark is adding Mase's 'Feel So Good'. This isn't a favour: it's business. He charges for mix tapes. Babyboy has bought them from him in the past to duplicate and sell. It's another form of hustling: there is a huge market for bootleg compilations in school playgrounds, and at the Sunday morning swapmeets that are held throughout South Central.

'You play dice?' Babyboy asks Trey.

'Sure?'

They set the initial bet at a dollar. 'I won 40 bucks yesterday,' Babyboy boasts. The basic rules of craps are simple. It's a two-person game. Both participants place a stake of, say, a dollar. One throws the dice. On his first throw he wins the bet outright if he throws a seven or an 11. If not, he carries on throwing until he repeats the number he's made with that first throw. Then he wins. But if he throws a seven with his second throw, or any after, he loses. If he wins he throws again: if he loses, his opponent takes up the dice.

Everyone plays craps around here. The thrill lies in the fact that the thrower has a slight, but obvious advantage, so that money can flow in one direction fast, until the thrower loses and things start to tip in the other direction. Trey and Babyboy play on the kitchen floor. They plead, swear and whisper at the dice, calling out the numbers they want. It's part of the drama of the game.

Within 20 minutes Babyboy is seriously down. He has lost $20 in singles and has to lay a $20 note on the kitchen floor. Trey keeps on winning and they've raised the stakes to $3 now. 'Three out the dub,' Trey chants, keeping note of the score, 'Three out the dub.' He's won $3 out of the double – the $20 note. Babyboy wins the throw and needs to repeat a throw of eight to win back that three bucks. 'Five three, five three, five three,' he chants.

'Five two,' calls Trey.

Babyboy looks furious. 'Don't put a hex on my dice,' he shouts angrily. But next throw the dice come up with a two and a six and he's won back his three bucks out of the 20 and his luck starts to turn. In ten minutes he also wins back all the singles he's lost. After 40 minutes they are back where they started. Budman arrives, the game ends, and Trey and Babyboy shake hands happily.

As ever, Budman is flat broke. The big, loping boy watches Babyboy pocket his roll of bills and picks his moment to ask for a loan. Babyboy peels off two dollars. He's not feeling rich either. Now the Cougar has died, he's going to need to save to buy a new car.

'Come on, give me a five, nigga,' Budman pleads.

After a brief protest, Babyboy takes the two off him, and gives him five back. Budman tries again, cannily: 'Give me the two as well.' Babyboy tells him to get lost. Budman is so broke he says he couldn't afford to buy his girlfriend anything for Valentine's Day, so instead he wrote her a poem. He says she loved it. When he tells Babyboy about it, Babyboy laughs out loud. 'You know what I bought Veronica?' boasts Babyboy. 'A two–dollar bunch of roses from 48th and Crenshaw.'

'What'd she buy you?'

'A pair of Nikes.'

Bud and he both laugh again, as if they've both pulled the wool over their girls' eyes. What he hasn't mentioned to either Budman or Veronica is that he has a pink application for a marriage certificate in the briefcase that he carries everywhere. Babyboy is always either promising Marlene that he's about to turn over a new leaf or that he's splitting up with her.

Back in Mark's bedroom, Babyboy and Budman start to work on the rhymes for their first song of their new collaboration. Budman listens to the track. Babyboy stands by the computer that they're using as a sequencer, waiting for Budman's approval. 'That shit is bangin',' Budman says, nodding to the track.

'What do you think about "Typical Day" for a name?' asks Babyboy.

'No,' says Budman. 'It's "Everyday Struggle".'

'OK,' concedes Babyboy. The hook has already been worked out, and they've each got a verse ready. It's a simple line about how living in the hood is 'an everyday struggle, an everyday hustle'. But Babyboy wants them to write a third verse together. He pulls out a notebook and tears out two pages. The two friends both start writing furiously.

'I got to think, man,' Budman says, stopping writing. 'I can't think without smoking.' He takes a booklet from Babyboy's briefcase and starts to construct a blunt on it. The photocopied cover reads: 'Music Publishing. By Michael Perlstein Esq.' It's a chapter taken from a dense book on Entertainment Law. Written on the inside cover is: 'This book belongs to Kimeyo Daniels. Property of No Respekt Mob Entertainment.'

Budman kneels at the water-bed, writing. Suddenly he's excited too. Babyboy is scribbling about his everyday struggles:

Had a kid before I learned to control my ding-a-ling.

Kimarre, his eldest daughter, is three now. The eight-bar riff is playing over and over in the background and the two men are excited, shouting lines over to each other.

'No – hold it. I got to get my flow:

Me and my crew we like to stay high, like to stay high,

chants Budman, who's inexorably managed to turn the topic around to weed:

Me and my crew, I don't know about you, we like to stay high,
Me and my crew we from the west side –
South Central Los Angeles,

completes Babyboy.
Budman:

I'm sleepin' through – down the brew, this weed has got me fadin'
Me and my niggas pourin' out this liquor for the niggas who couldn't
make it . . .

Pouring alcohol on to the ground – a South Central ritual made famous in the rash of recent 'hood' movies. An act of remembrance whose roots probably stretch back centuries, but which has become part of gangsta rap's most frequently used images. For a few minutes it has been like it used to be in the old days when Babyboy and Budman first started rhyming together.

Then Mark comes in and tells them they have half an hour left. He wants to go to bed soon. 'Are we going to record this?' Budman asks Babyboy.

'We ain't *going* to record it. We ain't got time,' says Babyboy acidly. It's going to take him half an hour to edit the track down to fit the verses they've written. In his mind Budman let him down by arriving so late. They could have finished the track if he had been here earlier.

'What?' says Budman. 'I came all the way here and we ain't recording?'

They start arguing. 'You should have been here at five. If you'd been here at five we could have finished by now,' shouts Babyboy.

Budman is furious. And if things weren't bad enough, the blunt has gone out and he can't find his disposable lighter. 'Shit. I just bought that.'

He stamps around the bedroom, feeling around the water–bed. Babyboy is counting the bars on his rhythm loop. It's hard to keep tally when he's so stoned. 'One, two, three . . .'

Defeated, Budman lies on his back on the carpet and stares at the ceiling. He hadn't wanted to come out at all tonight. He wanted to stay home. He was hoping that maybe he and his girlfriend were going to have sex. It's Valentine's Day, after all.

'. . . 15, 16, shit.'

'I thought I was only going to be here an hour,' he complains. 'I been here three hours.'

'You've got to do this with me, Budman.' In fact, Budman isn't doing anything much. It's more a plea from Babyboy for some commitment to his grand vision. The fecklessness of everyone around him exasperates him.

The phone rings. Babyboy picks up the mobile handset. It's Marlene asking where on earth he's got to: he was supposed to be home tonight. 'I'm working, baby. I'm working. I'm in the studio,' he says tetchily. 'I'll call you as soon as I finish. Hello? Hello? Hello?' She's hung up angrily. 'Hello!' he shouts into the empty phone.

The red lights of the digital clock by Mark's bed read 12:05. 'Are we done now?' complains Budman.

Babyboy snaps back: 'We could be done if you'd come to work on time.'

Budman looks at him and says defeatedly, 'It's only a game, man.' He's stoned, but the retort has a ring of truth to it.

Babyboy ignores him and carries on counting the bars. He'd meant to complete a whole track, but in the end all they've got is the eight bars he recorded in the first couple of hours.

'Hey,' says Budman suddenly. 'I found my lighter.' It was on the duvet all along.

CAMP ZERO

In Hollywood, a party is going on at the abandoned California Bank building on the corner of Hollywood Boulevard and Argyle. Set Free, a street ministry who take the gospel to the bikers and the gang-bangers, are using it as a club.

New religions seem to like old banks here. A few blocks to the west, the Church of Scientology has commandeered another former bank building and converted it into the L. Ron Hubbard Life Experience.

Hollywood Boulevard is not the fashionable strip it used to be. It wears a decrepit air. On the next block, the white paint peels on Pantages, once the most beautiful of the grand old Hollywood Boulevard theatres. But everything goes in cycles. This year hip-hop breakdancing is back in. Tonight's crowd have brought squares of cardboard to spin on, or skateboard helmets. Boys who look about 13 or 14 are running through the classic breakdance moves that were invented 25 years earlier when the dancing craze appeared on the streets of New York. A boy steps into the circle, 'up-rocks' for a second, to warm himself up, hopping from foot to foot, and then starts whirling around on the floor, supporting his whole body on his flat hands, using the momentum of his legs to twist his body around. The crowd – almost exclusively boys the same age – watch him studiously. The boy flips over and goes into the move known as the continuous backspin, revolving at around 150rpm.

The old bank counter has become a bar. Set Free converts are serving sodas for 75 cents, and bottles of water for $1. A pastor, a white guy, tattooed up to the elbows, with a goatee beard and long black hair tied back in a pony-tail under a black leather baseball cap, steps on to the small stage in front of the old bank vaults and warns: 'I need the breakdancers to be a little more considerable so that everyone can get on the dance floor.'

Around a quarter past 11, the rap group Camp Zero take the stage: nine boys and one girl, Kimmie G. Camp Zero are a group who you can find turning up all over Los Angeles, taking whatever chance to perform they can get. They were at the *Rap Sheet* convention, and they turned up on Lonzo Williams's *Inner City Harvest*. Most rap groups are two or three people. Camp Zero are rare, because they're such a large collective. They live all over the greater Los Angeles area, so these shows are the only chance they ever get to rehearse: they're held together by a slender 40-year-old Jamaican called Duke who's living out his own dream of being a performer through them, and a hyperactive, enthusiastic producer called T-Bob.

Camp Zero make a change from most of the hunch-shouldered rappers who pace the stages of the LA talent shows. They burst with life. The number they're doing is 'Whoop Whoop', featuring Kimmie G, a 19–year-old rapper dressed in blue camouflage fatigues.

Kimmie G is solid, but good-looking in a don't-mess-with-me kind of way. She's not one of the simpering, bare-midriffed girl rappers and singers who survive in this boys' world by playing on their coy femininity. She is loud and assertive. The words of her rap are hardly appropriate to a Christian occasion, but no one seems to mind:

I'm like one of the most beautifulest bitches in the world
My men come to me with money diamonds and pearls,

she announces optimistically.

The show is enthusiastic, but Camp Zero need the practice badly. There are too many people on stage, talking over each other's lines. They still need to learn to work together. They're lucky to have a manager as organized as Duke is. He's put a lot of time into the group and is looking for someone to sign them. It needs to be soon. It's hard holding the group together.

When they started out, they'd rehearse for days in a row, but in the last two years they've only managed to get together to practise maybe five times altogether. These days they all have other commitments. Kimmie has moved out, 65 miles away, to Palmdale: she works there as a hairdresser. But she dreams about being number one in the charts. 'Both *Billboard* and video,' she says.

The crowd of breakers applaud with moderate enthusiasm, then Biggie's 'Goin' Back To Cali' comes on the turntable and they set to dancing again.

C-DOUBLE-E

Herman is finally back from Florida. If he was hoping he would have earned some more money there to save for his MPC 2000 sequencer, he was mistaken. He helped out with the landscaping business, but any money he earned from his father, he spent there just as fast.

He met his younger half-brother and half-sister for the first time: he liked them, but he didn't feel particularly close to them. It felt good getting to know his father, but they don't always get along. All his father's friends in Florida were shocked at the sight of Herman. They couldn't believe how much he looked like his father. A couple of times people actually mistook him for his dad and started conversing with him before the penny dropped.

The strangest thing of all, though, was the way his father reacted to him being there. Half the time, Herman felt that his father was trying to pick a quarrel with him, trying to challenge him to some sort of fight, as if he needed to reassert a father's dominance over a son, or perhaps felt threatened by his son's manhood. When he wasn't acting aggressively, he was trying to persuade Herman to stay, as if he wanted his son to move in with him in order to make up for the years they'd spent apart.

Herman respects his father for making a good life for himself and his new family in Florida. It was good to realize that this man, who had left him and his mother here in Los Angeles, still cared for him. Herman doesn't want to leave LA. Even if life is healthier there, his father lives in what Herman considers the middle of nowhere, outside Jacksonville. LA is a city he understands. He has his corner at Crenshaw and Stocker, he has his dreams of the music business and he has his apartment.

Herman lives alone in the area known as the Jungle, in a small, one-room apartment on Buckingham Road, just off Martin Luther King Boulevard. There are parts in South Central that look blighted: with vacant lots, graffiti-covered walls and tiny old decrepit houses. The Jungle is not one of them. Its sidewalks in front of the two-storey apartment blocks are clean and planted with healthy-looking palm trees. There are swimming pools in some of the backyards of the apartment block.

This used to be a nice area, but it has been going downhill for decades. In the sixties, the elderly Jewish community gradually died off or moved away. The Baldwin Hills Movie Theater is closed now; now the letters that used to advertise movies have been rearranged to read: 'Church of God in Christ'.

The Jungle lies to the east of the junction of La Brea and Coliseum. Over the years it has acquired a reputation for brutal crime. Unofficially some police officers have long regarded it as a no-go area, especially after dark.

The Jungle's proximity to the Crenshaw–Baldwin Hills Mall and the developing Crenshaw Corridor has threatened their ability to attract investment. Officially the LAPD have been forbidden to call it the Jungle: they are supposed to refer to it as 'Lower Baldwin Hills', in an attempt to improve the area's dismal image.

The Baldwin Hills area, to the south-west, was originally the site of the 1932 Olympic Village. It is now a black middle-class area, on the western edge of South Central. In Los Angeles, the moneyed move to higher ground, where the air is cleaner and cooler air circulates. These uplands were originally named after the Irish developer E. J. 'Lucky' Baldwin, founder of Santa Anita Racetrack and one of the region's early boosters, whose thigh-slappingly gung–ho slogan in the 1880s was: 'Hell, we're giving away the land. We're selling the climate.'

The climate below the hills isn't as good as it used to be. This is a Blood stronghold, hemmed in by other hostile gangs.

When I first started driving around South Central, I was oblivious to the coded signs of gang life here. Now, driving down King, through the Jungle, I see notice a 40mph speed-limit sign, crossed out in two red strokes of an aerosol can. Now its message seems to read: Bloods – *the red* – will kill – *cross out* – any member of the Rollin' 40s Crips – *the 40 sign* – who show their faces here.

The Black P Stones have become one of the most notorious Blood gangs in LA because of the viciousness with which they've defended the Jungle against neighbours like the Rollin' 30s and Rollin' 40s Harlem Crips, and against the 18th Street gang. It's this conflict which has given the area such a bad reputation.

The vicious territoriality of LA's black street gangs is famous. Territories are formed around the neighbourhoods the gang members grew up in. They often appear to be based on the catchment areas of the local high schools. The origins of gangs are always hard to fathom: members tend not to keep good paperwork. There is a curious symmetry, though, between the vicious territoriality of the white gangs of the forties, and the black gangs of the following decades.

Throughout the forties, as South Central began to establish its modern geography, the white violence continued. The *California Eagle* diligently noted one incident after another. Whites burned Klan crosses in Slauson, in what is now Babyboy's neighbourhood on Crenshaw and on the University of Southern California campus. Klansmen blew up houses on 30th Street and rioted against the blacks who were trying to move on to East 71st. Schools were attacked too: the *Eagle* reported white gang attacks at several schools in Los Angeles and the San Fernando Valley in 1946–7.

There is an irony about these years. Back in the forties, it was the whites who jealously protected their turf, who torched buildings and daubed graffiti on walls as proof as their rightful ownership. Perhaps it's no surprise if the descendants of the victims mimic their abusers. Some of the aggressively territorial behaviour for which the black South Central gangs later became famous was practised first against the African-American community by white gangs. Some of the younger whites even formed racist gangs, giving themselves names like the Spookhunters. In America, the word 'spook' is less common now but it is equivalent to, and every bit as pejorative as, the word 'nigger'. As the police and the white newspapers mainly turned a blind eye to the violence, white boys were given licence to defend their turf. The prevailing attitude of the years in which the ghetto was formed may have inspired a similar culture among the African-American residents: defend your territory. The line between gangs and vigilante self-defence groups can be a thin one.

From the fifties onwards, territorial black gangs like the Slausons and the Avenues began to appear. For many years before he became famous, Overdose's father-in-law Barry White was a member of a well-known South Central gang who called themselves the Businessmen.

Originally a black political grouping, the Almighty Black P Stone Nation – as they used to be known – were born in the sixties in Chicago. In 1969, a young transplanted Chicagoan called T. Rogers started a cell from his home in Montclair Street, to the east of the Jungle. By the seventies the P Stones had gradually become sucked into competition with other neighbourhood gangs, eventually allying themselves with the new rising force of the Bloods.

A few years ago Herman's fellow rapper Diamond DX was shot not far from Herman's apartment. DX, a one-time gunman himself, was walking down the street near the Crenshaw–Baldwin Hills Mall, when he caught a stray bullet from some feud. It hit him in the hip. 'I wasn't that badly hurt,' he says sanguinely. 'I went to the hospital. I wasn't driven by the paramedics. I went there myself.'

At the time, DX lived upstairs from Herman – he still does. It was while he was stuck at home, recovering from his wound, that the ever-friendly Herman would drop by and suggest that they start writing rhymes together. That was the start of their group.

Herman lives in a brown two-storey apartment block. Apartment 2 is one room, about 20 feet by 15, with a bed in one corner and his stereo and TV on the opposite side.

'I was going to clear up,' says Herman, smiling apologetically. Last night's plates and tomato ketchup sit on the small glass table in the middle of the room. His weights and exercise bench take up valuable space. There are boxes full of the incense he makes himself. His supply of umbrellas waits in a small shopping trolley. The small microwave that he cooks in is perched on the same unit that holds his TV, his stereo, his CDs and his video machine. In the narrow corridor that leads to his bathroom, there is a shelf full of tins of Stagg's chilli con carne.

The walls could do with a fresh coat of paint. The brown carpet on the floor is worn to nothing in some places. There are still cracks from '94's Northridge earthquake – 6.7 on the Richter scale. (Herman woke that night and jumped out of bed just in time to miss one of his large loudspeakers crashing down on top of him.) But the landlord won't redecorate the flat, even though Herman's been living here for six years, paying his $330 a month.

The apartment gets stiflingly hot sometimes. Herman's door is open – with the metal grille locked – to try to get some air into the place. The rains have finished and it's suddenly muggy. 'Earthquake weather,' he smiles.

Southern California is in the middle of an incredible boom. Los Angeles has not had such a period of continued growth in years. The LA Times has just published a short piece announcing the good news that the number of people in LA who earn more than $1 million a year has risen by 66 per cent in the past year.

Herman clearly isn't in that bracket yet. At the other end of the scale, during this apparently heady time of expansion the number of households escaping the bracket of an annual income of $20,000 or less dropped by only 3.2 per cent. Every year the extremes of Los Angeles seem to get greater.

As long as it lasts, though, the boom means that there is more money and more work. The pressure is off. Murder rates are declining, and while there is no evidence to suggest that gang membership or drug consumption are down, the sense of crisis of the late eighties and early nineties has abated.

But there are still plenty of casualties. Some of the people in Herman's block are on drugs. His usually sunny nature wears thin when he says, 'You get these people, and they're crackers [crack addicts] and they pay one month's rent and they don't pay the next two months.' He says it pisses him off that the landlord lets them come here and rip him off, while he has dutifully paid his money each month for years.

It's 11.30 a.m. and Herman lies in bed with a new girlfriend, Shanté: he's taking the morning off. She's 19, pretty, fresh-faced, and has a pierced nose. Shanté doesn't say much; she lies in bed, dressed only in a blue camouflage-pattern T-shirt. Herman pulls on his trousers and winds his way across the room to switch on his new Sony Playstation.

He loads up Tomb Raider. He bought the Playstation a couple of weeks ago. 'I know what you're thinking,' he laughs. 'I should be saving up to buy the MPC 2000.' He starts to guide a pixillated Lara Croft – the large-chested superheroine of the adventure game – into a lion-filled labyrinth. 'But you know, I work so hard I thought I deserved some sort of reward,' he says with a shrug. He sits three feet from his large TV screen, console in his twitching hands. A lion pounces: Lara fires with both pistols.

Shanté picks up a bag of Chips Ahoy Chocolate Chip Cookies for her breakfast and starts to munch away.

Suddenly there's a commotion in the yard outside. A woman wearing a grey and black leopardskin-print blouse is banging on the grill of the adjoining Apartment 3. Herman drops the console and moves to his door. He sees this woman coming around a lot. She's a chickenhead – a crack addict. She begs from the residents there to feed her habit. Herman's neighbour is a nice old man, but he was raised in another era. He doesn't know how to deal with these people. Though Herman told him not to, he once gave this crack addict some money. Herman looks out for some of his more vulnerable neighbours: it's one of the sides of his character that makes him so popular in this block – with everyone but the beggars. 'Don't give them a quarter, don't give them a cent,' he says. 'Don't even give them a quarter of a cent.' But it's too late now; she keeps coming back.

Herman opens his grille, and walks right up to her and orders, 'OK. Go now.'

She flinches. 'What happened? I mean . . .'

She looks in her mid-thirties, but is probably much younger. 'What did I do?'

'Excuse me,' says Herman firmly. 'Hey, you. Get out of here.' The woman whispers, 'I'm sorry'; but she doesn't move.

'No,' says Herman stiffly. 'You need to leave now. 'Cause you keep interrupting him. He done told you he don't want you in here.'

The woman is mumbling now, pathetically. Shanté watches with interest from the bed.

'I'm getting tired of you running in here . . . coming back here all the time. You need to leave. Right now!' Herman shouts.

'I'm sorry,' the woman wails.

'No, don't apologize. Leave.'

She hesitates. In the studio, or on stage, Herman can seem gawky and ill at ease, but in this situation he can remarkably assertive. This is how he gets by here.

'Don't apologize,' he says again, even louder. 'Leave.'

And finally the woman gives way and shambles off, back on to Buckingham Road, to try her luck elsewhere.

'You OK?' he calls in to his neighbour.

'OK,' calls the old man.

Herman calms down straight away. He moves back to his TV screen, where, defenceless in his absence, Lara Croft has been mauled by a tiger. Game over.

BABYBOY

A phone call:

'It's Babyboy. Hey, how you doin', Wes' Side?'

'Fine. How's it with you?'

'It's cool.'

'You finished that track you were working on with Budman?'

'Hell, I ain't fucking with Budman any more. I'm just a solo artist, like I was meant to be all along.'

PART THREE

'Los Angeles is not paradise, much as the sight of its lilies and roses might lead one to believe.'

W. E. B. DuBois, founder of the National Association for the Advancement of Colored People, 1914

12

Blue Moon Things

RAH

It has been the wettest winter on record in Los Angeles. The hills around the city look fresher and greener than anyone remembers them in years.

Most days I drive along the 101. As I pass the Vermont turning, I sometimes think of Josiah Brocks. I find myself timing the distance between the place where the police reports say he was shot, and the off-ramp that the police were called to, a few hundred yards further north. I think of Cash pulling over at the Melrose exit there, with poor Josiah bleeding in his lap.

The murder of Josiah Brocks has not been solved: there is no realistic chance of the murderer being found now. Most murders are like this here: nobody discovers who did them or why.

Detectives Pelt and Curiel of Rampart Division, the area in which the murder took place, are no further along in their investigation than they were the night they questioned Cash about the killing. His is still the only version of events they have. The only other evidence they have to go on is fragments of the bullet that killed Josiah. They're not even sure what type of gun it was: it might have been a 9mm or a .380, because they're basically the same calibre, and they won't know until another bullet that they can match to the same gun turns up in some other case, but they're not holding out much hope.

Pelt and Curiel have appealed for other witnesses, but no one has come forward. They've issued flyers giving the description of the red or maroon two-door Honda, but they've had no response. Pelt blames the emptiness of the normally busy Hollywood freeway that night: 'It was one of those once-in-a-blue-moon things.' There remains no information to suggest there was any kind of traffic dispute before the killing. And it was unlikely to be an attempted carjack. 'It wasn't even a nice car. All I have is a random killing.'

It's an open case, says Pelt, though in Rampart Division there are too many open cases. Rampart Division has one of the highest murder rates in LA: it includes the Echo Park and Koreatown neighbourhoods, and has its share of gang activity, especially from the burgeoning Latino 18th Street gang.

Only a few days earlier, Detective Curiel was standing outside an apartment building at 530 South Catalina Street, asking anyone who knew anything about a triple murder that had taken place there more than a year ago – another in the long list of unsolved cases. Upstairs, three family members had been bound, gagged and then stabbed to death; the murderer had escaped with jewellery and thousands of dollars' worth of rent money. The murderer was in a frenzy – Curiel described it as 'terrible rage': each body had been stabbed about 50 times. Thirteen months after that killing there are still no leads to go on in that case, either.

In these neighbourhoods the clean-up rates are low. Hurts endure, unresolved.

Pelt puts a brave face on the chances of finding Josiah's murderer. 'We work on these things until they're solved,' he told me. 'There's no putting a homicide on the back burner.' It's the right thing to say politically, of course. Not that the detective doesn't mean it, but I can't help thinking that he sounds like he's trying to convince himself as much as anyone else.

★   ★   ★

This is the best time, thinks Rah. A big waxing moon to the west and not a cop car in sight. Three-thirty a.m. Sunday night, and this part of South Central is quiet.

He and Josiah used to work this mile where the road rises up into the Baldwin Hills. As he pulls out his staple gun, a car approaches: he twitches his head round to check it out. He doesn't have to worry, though, because he knows that at this time of night the cops are probably all busy in the Jungle, east of here. 'Right over there on Coliseum – that's one of the worst places. You walk through there and they don't know you? It would be over,' he says.

Last week Rah dreamed he saw the white owl again, floating over the oilfields above here. And in his dream he was with Josiah again, and they were both watching the big white bird float over the city, just as it had the first time they'd seen it together.

As he trudges up La Brea under the moonlight he sees an old orange sticker for the artist A/Z that he and Josiah put up almost a year ago now. They put that sticker everywhere. Tonight he's working on a new account for the Relativity record label: Tupac's former cohort Fatal's new single, 'In The Line Of Duty'. Fatal was one of the Outlawz Immortal. He has fixed the stickers in groups of 12 on to big pieces of cardboard. Rah shins up the first pole and whacks the staple gun on to the cardboard again and again, blat-blat-blat, until it's fixed firmly. Underneath it he has written: 'Josiah Brocks R.I.P.'

Afterwards he steps back and admires his work. Cool sticker, he decides, and walks on up the hill towards where he and Josiah saw the white owl. He is with me right now, he thinks.

BABYBOY

It's almost morning now. Babyboy is cruising around the hood with two guys he doesn't know. On Crenshaw, they drive past a white Chevrolet Suburban van that is covered with posters advertising Fatal's new album. Inside the van is Rah, on the way to do some more sniping late night. Babyboy doesn't know Rah, but he takes note of the van because he's impressed that someone is taking care of their business.

What's worrying him is that the guys he's with are driving like idiots, making illegal turns, driving the wrong way up one-way streets. A little while ago he sold the two of them some weed. When he'd done the deal they asked, 'You want a lift home?' Since the brakes went on his Cougar, he doesn't have a car. He can't afford a new one.

Babyboy needed the ride, but he's always a little anxious about letting people he barely knows find out where he lives. And now, driving with them, he decides that the only people who drive like this around here – with such reckless disregard for road rules – must obviously be policemen.

Now he's really worried: he's just done a dope deal with two undercover cops and then he's told them exactly where he lives. Shit.

Even when they drop him off at the apartment in Culver City, he's still not sure that he hasn't done something stupid. He's going to worry about it all night now. Sometimes Babyboy is a mess of paranoia.

A few weeks earlier, he says, a local dealer asked him if he could supply $4000 worth of cocaine. He doesn't deal in cocaine any more, and certainly not in that quantity. The following day he discovered the dealer had recently been pulled in by the LAPD. He spent the next week convinced the police were trying to set him up. Nothing came of it.

He walks the one flight up to the apartment and lets himself in. Marlene and Chanel are asleep in the bedroom.

He spends so little time in the apartment these days. Marlene puts up with a lot. Sometimes he says he's moving out. Sometimes they fight, and break up, and he really does move out for a few days, though he says he'd whack any man that came near her, because he doesn't want his baby seeing her with other men. But he always seems to end up back here. 'You know how it is,' he says.

On the stereo there are two silver-framed pictures: one of Babyboy, the other of Marlene. On the telephone table in the living room there's a note he wrote to Marlene. Written in his meticulous hand, it reads: 'Thank-you for caring.' He signed it: 'Kimeyo. N Entertainment.'

13

The Most Love

BABYBOY

Breakfast at Babyboy's. He's cooking beef tacos. 'They was the feds, I'm sure of it,' he says. 'But I know people who can find out.'

In all the time I know Babyboy, I am never sure whether these paranoid tales are just an act to impress me, the innocent white visitor, or whether he really believes them himself. Or whether they're not paranoid tales and the FBI really are out there, watching him. All of the above, perhaps.

'I know people,' he says, as he slowly moves the minced meat around the pan. 'I know people who do bad things. I could get some people and they would find where you lived with no trouble at all, and come knocking on your door.'

I sit at the dining table. Marlene has already left for work, taking Chanel with her to drop her off at her parents' house on the way.

'This is a bad place,' Babyboy says, meaning Los Angeles as a whole. 'But I love it. There are people here who would kill you and wake up the next day with nothing on their conscience,' he laughs.

He serves three tacos to me, and three to himself. Before tucking in, he bows his head as he always does, and silently says grace. His faith, he says, comes from his mother. 'She's into religion,' he says. 'That's why I got a conscience. I got a wicked side, but I got a conscience.'

He says, 'I know there are bad people, believe me. I know a guy who will make a man scream for mercy, say, "Please don't kill me, please don't kill me," and still kill him. Who will shoot a man's wife and daughter right before his eyes so he can watch. I know.' He pauses. 'That was my father,' he says. Today he is particularly demon-chased. I wonder what drug he's coming down from. His breakfast conversation is full of psychotic malevolence.

'California is full of badness. And I love it. I love all the corruption and all the evil,' he laughs. 'You know why California has all the prisons? Why it has all the three-strikes-and-you're-out? Because America needs us because we're all the evillest mother-fuckers.'

Then: 'You know what? During the 1992 riot, when they called in the army, they weren't shooting bullets. They were shooting *blanks*. You know why? Because they didn't want to kill us. They want us alive. And why? Because we're the toughest in America, and they know they're going to need us soon. That's why they they've got all these prisons. Because they can keep us there until they need us. You know what the biggest thing in prison is? Pumping iron. And they like that, you know?'

More conspiracy theories, I think. I am struggling to finish my second taco. 'You only want two?' he says, picking up the one I've left on the plate.

RAH

Rah tells me that these days his mother is living at a 'board and care', a sheltered residential home. When I tell him I'd like to talk to her, to hear her version of what life was like for Rah, growing up, he gives me her phone number, then he calls her up and tells her about a journalist who wants to speak to her.

'I had 13 nervous breakdowns,' she tells me on the phone. Her conversation is circular. As Rah has warned me, she forgets what she has said and repeats herself. 'We had a pretty hard time, you know. We had to break up our family, cause we got kicked out of our apartment, so Rah found us another apartment . . .' In fragments, she starts to retell the story Rah has already told me. 'We got kicked out. We didn't pay the rent, and . . . And I was on a freak − and the police picked me up and put me in Metropolitan Hospital − and I was there for a year.'

Several times she asks me how I know Rah, but each time she seems to forget what I tell her and starts asking again. Rah still believes that it was the 'big medicines' that scrambled her brain for good. He blames himself: 'I wish I had been more involved with her medicine and her doctor stuff. Now I think back to them days, I wish I would have went with her to the doctor's appointments and wrote down that, "Yo, she got to be here to do this." '

'I'm in board and care now,' Rah's mother says. 'So I don't see Rah. I call him and talk to him, but he doesn't come by. He came by one time . . . He's busy . . . I have a daughter too,' she tells me, in her defeated, used-up voice. 'I seen her a couple of times. I went down to Jean's house.'

'Who's Jean?' I ask her.

'She's the lady that's taking care of my daughter Christina. She lives down on 54th − but she's having hell out of Christina now, because Christina's 15 and she doesn't want to come home and she got kicked out of school. But I can't help her. I don't have no money. And the lady that's taking care of her, she has custody of her. There's nothing I can do for her now.'

Then, proudly and a little sadly: 'I used to be a model myself . . . I used to be a professional model.'

'I know. Rah told me,' I say. 'You've had a tough life.'

'Yes, I have. A really tough life. He has as well.'

I ask her about Rah's older brother, the one who was a member of the Crips, but she says she doesn't know what he is into now. She tells me she didn't know anything about him being involved with the Crips. She says she's going to hang up now: she doesn't want to talk about the past any more. 'That's enough,' she says tiredly, 'that's enough.'

STRANDED

Nerv is a graffiti artist who shares an apartment in Downey with Sleep, the street promoter who runs Mad Pro. He's showing me his work.

Standing up at one end of the kitchen there's a larger-than-life portrait of Tupac, copied in aerosol paint from the famous photo portrait of him looking at his most thuggish, with a blood-red bandanna around his head. Sleep is also showing me some of the work he is commissioned to do these days, including the logo he has designed for a band named Stranded. I haven't heard of them.

The logo is a highly stylized piece of calligraphy, the sort you see sprayed on railway carriages all over America: the letters explode into new shapes that become so intricate it's almost impossible to read the word itself.

'They're the band on Rodney King's new label,' Nerv explains.

'Rodney King is setting up a label?'

'Yeah. Stranded have a launch party this Monday – I can get you in if you want.'

In Los Angeles so many people are trying to become celebrities – like Philly, Herman's friend from Crenshaw and Stocker. Rodney King's fame is of a more accidental kind. He never set out to become a household name, but between 1991 and 1992 there can have been few corners of the world that didn't know who he was.

Sleep calls me the next day and says, 'You're on the guest list.'

TIBU

Belltown's finest, Mr Tibu, moves out of Cavi's place. His girl-friend, Keyna, is doing a course in Business Studies at California

State University's Dominguez Hills campus. She is sharing a student apartment there.

Tibu moves in with her. Life is good now. The only drawback is that it's a long trek from there to USC Hospital, where Josiah Brocks was finally pronounced dead. Some days Tibu doesn't even make it to work.

One day he visits the Wherehouse record store in the Lakewood mall, because the rapper WC is there, signing copies of his solo album *The Shadiest One*. WC used to run a group called the Maad Circle, who included the apprentice rapper Coolio. More recently he has served as a member of Westside Connection.

When Tibu arrives at the store he discovers that WC's security have closed off the area where the rap star is sitting. You can only meet him if you're wearing a wristband, and you can only have a wristband if you've bought a copy of *The Shadiest One*.

'That's bullshit,' says Tibu. 'When I'm famous, I ain't going to act like that.'

STRANDED

Monday, I'm dressing to go out and watch Stranded. The TV is on. KTLA news anchor Hal Fishman is reading out a bland item about the LA riot; about how much things have improved since those days. 'Fifty-five people were killed after rioting started at the junction of Florence and Normandie . . .'

My ears catch half of another sentence: '. . . say that 80 per cent of the 1100 buildings damaged in the riots have now been rebuilt . . .'

Hal is a lugubrious-looking man, with a frizz of grey hair and a big pair of glasses perched on his lined face. He's been reading news for 30 years now. Despite his demeanour, he's doing his best to make the item sound upbeat, with all the drama that such a considerable achievement deserves, though of course a ride through some of the parts of South Central that I've been visiting would account for the other 20 per cent that hasn't been repaired or rebuilt.

Belatedly, I figure it out. Wednesday is the anniversary of the day the grand rumpus of burning, looting and rampaging started. By arranging the launch of the first album on his new label this week, Rodney King is marking the event in his own special way. A little extra publicity for a start-up label is no bad thing.

An Armenian plumber called George Holliday had bought a new video recorder. It was fresh out of the Styrofoam, and as boys are when they've bought some new hardware, he was eager to find subjects to try it out on.

Arnold Schwarzenegger was making a movie just down the street in Sylmar in the San Fernando Valley, where George lived with his wife, so George took the camera out and managed to catch a smidgen of Arnie on tape.

A few nights later, on 3 March 1991, at around half past midnight, his wife found she couldn't sleep because of the noise of police helicopters overhead. So she got up and looked out of the window at all the flashing lights, to see what the fuss was all about. Several others from their sprawling housing complex were already there, gawping at the ugly scene.

'George,' she said. 'Maybe you should get the new camera . . .'

Next morning she rang the Foothill Division station and asked what had been going on last night, beyond the protecting fence of their gated community of condominiums. The cop who answered the phone was dismissive and gave her the brush-off.

There have been plenty of beatings of non-whites by policemen in and around Los Angeles. In itself, it was not a particularly remarkable event. As LAPD detective Mark Fuhrman once put it so choicely when he thought the world in general wasn't listening: 'See, if you did the things that they teach you at the academy, you'd never get a fucking thing done.' The only remarkable thing was that first Mr Holliday captured it on video, and second Mrs Holliday, peeved at her dismissive treatment by Foothill Division police, suggested: 'Maybe we should call up KTLA news?'

KTLA don't appear to have thought at first that there was much remarkable about the video tape. When the Hollidays talked to the assignment desk at the station, they were just asked to drop the tape off with the security officers at the main gate. Only when the station actually ran the video tape did the news staff at KTLA begin to realize the potential of what they were dealing with.

So KTLA dispatched one of Hal Fishman's most famous colleagues – Stan Chambers – to interview George. KTLA has a reputation for showing breaking news, and Stan is a minor legend in the business: he's been with KTLA over 50 years. Stan was there when they effectively invented the whole TV genre of 'breaking news', back in 1949, when a three-year-old called Kathy Fiscus fell 100 feet down an abandoned well in San Marino. KTLA reported from the scene, making it the first major live news event to reach viewers all over America. For two and a half days Stan and the news pack reported the desperate attempts of the rescuers to reach the girl. Billy Wilder fictionalized the story for his dark 1951 movie *The Big Carnival* (released in Britain as *Ace In The Hole*). Fiscus was long dead, of course, by the time the rescuers managed to reach her, but during that 54-hour rescue, Los Angeles had yet again helped create a new media model for the twentieth century. The best breaking news gives you a front seat to someone else's personal disaster. Rodney King's personal disaster made irresistible TV.

King, who was just approaching his twenty-ninth birthday, was on parole after serving a year's sentence in the California Correctional Center in Susanville for robbery of a store in Monterey Park. He was therefore anxious not to be caught offending by police. So when a police car tried to pull him over late one night on the Foothill freeway for speeding, and probably because he had been drinking, he stupidly tried to outrun the car in his white Hyundai. King was driving with two friends, Junior and Poo. Police cars and the pursuit helicopter finally trapped him in the Valley.

The tape shows a black man on his knees. He is being truncheoned, while about a dozen officers stand around watching. The man, who is obviously large, starts to stand, then falls on to his front as the blows rain down. He rolls on to his back and is beaten again on his stomach. When the man tries to get up again, he is hit several times on his back. Another cop kicks him to the ground, and another colleague steps in to stomp on his neck. Finally, as he starts to rise again, the officers standing around crowd in to handcuff him. At no point in the tape does King offer any serious resistance to the beating. You can count about 40 blows on Holliday's tape.

Later the cops who beat King, or who stood and watched others doing so, would successfully claim that their violence was inspired by events that had happened before the camera started rolling, that the video had distorted the truth of what had happened. It hadn't shown, they said, the threatening gestures King had made when he had emerged from his car, before the beating started. 'We thought he was high on PCP,' they protested to the Simi Valley jury. Which he wasn't.

There was an awful lot the tape didn't show. One witness later said the beating had already been going on for three minutes by the time Holliday figured out how his new camera worked. Sergeant Stacey Koons had twice already fired barbs from his Taser at King, burning his flesh. Other witnesses from the same block as Holliday's say they didn't see any attempt to resist arrest.

The tape doesn't show what happened afterwards, either, after the badly pummelled King had been taken to Pacifica Hospital. Standing by King's bed, Officer Laurence Powell told the victim, 'We played a little ball today, didn't we, Rodney?' The nurse later recalled him saying, 'We played a little hardball. We hit quite a few home runs. We played a little ball and you lost and we won.'

Later Powell's attorney insisted this was just 'banter'.

Rodney King calls his label Straight Alta-Pazz, in recognition of the neighbourhoods he grew up in – Altadena and Pasadena. He, like everyone else in the game, is giving his neighbourhoods their due.

He runs Straight Alta-Pazz with his cousin Ontresicia Averette. They've written a mission statement, full of desperately high-minded optimism:

'Through life's trials and triumphs, Mr King and Ontresicia, understanding the importance of bringing family together and creating cohesion between men and women within the home and work place, decided to set a positive example by showing that African American family members, both, man and woman can work together and make a positive contribution to benefit the community at large. He and his cousin have decided to take an aggressive approach in fulfilling President Clinton's quest to unite and create harmony in our society, and economic stability simultaneously . . .'

I arrive, foolishly early, at 9.30 p.m. at the ugly seventies niterie that King has booked, on Hollywood and La Brea. According to their record company biog: 'STRANDED IS AN INCREDIBLY TALENTED NEW "RAP GROUP", THE MONUMENTAL FIND OF RODNEY G. KING.' Their single, 'Do It How You Wanna', is 'AN UNFORGETTABLE SOUND GUARANTEE-ING "STRANDED" PLATINUM IN '98 (WAAACHOUUT!).'

Stranded are a two-piece comprising Papoose and Buzz, and their forte is mildly bawdy party rhymes. Papoose (his mother called him that) was born in Compton. He was raised on hip-hop mix tapes bought at the Compton swapmeet. The people he knew hung around with Suge Knight. Papoose made a demo and was signed to Death Row, but he never managed to release a record before Suge was imprisoned. Instead he met Buzz (named for his fondness for weed) and then Rodney King, and they pressed a demo on him.

It's a break of a kind. King has a little money paid to him as a result of his beating and, more importantly, he has notoriety too.

Papoose and Buzz hover in the large guest room, just off the main dance hall. Sandwiches are being served. Papoose is a dark-skinned man who sports a goatee. He is heavy set and looks like he works out hard. Tonight he's on top of the world. After years of waiting for his chance, then seeing it slip through his fingers when Suge Knight went to jail, he finally has a record out. He tells me they're thinking of making a video too. Buzz, the younger of the two, says, 'Me and Papoose want to re-enact a police chase. With Rodney driving . . .'

Buzz and Papoose intend to act the part of Rodney's two friends Junior and Poo, who were in the car with him during the famous police chase. I ask, 'How's Rodney going to react?'

Papoose is laughing. 'We already told him. He'll do it. He says, "Whatever it takes to get this thing moving."'

With his height of six foot three, you can't miss Rodney King. Close up, though, the 32-year-old seems less than powerful. He is a shy man.

This label has been a dream of his, he says. 'Music is, like, real touching.' He talks slowly, hesitantly. Even before the beating he was a reticent man. The attack, however, has affected his behaviour; he claims he suffered from brain damage as a result of it.

'I feel like I'm a touching person myself. And so, you know, it's a nice way to express yourself. Through music,' he explains.

I ask him what his favourite track on the album is. 'I like them all,' he laughs abruptly. Then, as if he's been caught out, he says, 'Number four. That's mine.' He doesn't seem to know the songs by their title. We make more small talk before he stops the conversation equally abruptly to contradict himself: 'Number five is the one that sticks in my mind. I'm sorry,' and then laughs some more.

Track five is called 'Another Brotha Gone' – yet another elegy to the universal ghetto victim, on which Buzz rhymes, perhaps a little insensitively:

I must admit I was a sucker for the drink
Until I saw what they did to my man Rodney King . . .

Much of LA now acknowledges that the trial of the four officers accused of beating Rodney King was condcuted in a way that loaded the dice in the defendants' favour. Because it was held in Simi Valley, a white neighbourhood and a popular retirement area for LAPD members, a verdict declaring the policemen not guilty was always likely.

After the verdict was read out, King had something approaching a mental breakdown. The prosecution had declined to call him to the witness stand, believing that the video testimony would be enough, and that it would be stronger without his ineloquent contribution. King, who had been hospitalized by a brutal beating, had not even had his chance to give his own version of events to the court.

That afternoon, King fell apart, locking himself in his Altadena bedroom as he watched the TV replaying shots of the four officers smiling and throwing their arms around each other. Friends and relatives say he was groaning, 'Why, why, why? Why are they beating me again?'

At 3.43 p.m. on Wednesday 29 April police received the first reports of a disturbance at West 67th Street and 11th Avenue in the wealthy Hyde Park district. A young man had thrown a brick at a passing truck. Fighting broke out. A white pedestrian was chased, beaten and thrown into a skip.

At 4.17 reports started coming in of a serious disturbance at the junction of Normandie and Florence. People who looked white were being dragged from their cars, beaten and robbed.

At 6.30 the most famous moment of the whole riot came when trucker Reginald Denny's 18-wheeler blundered into the junction and was stopped by the rioters, who dragged him from the cab and beat him until he was saved from being killed by a group of African-Americans. The attack was recorded by TV news cameras in the helicopters overhead.

By ten that night King still hadn't emerged from his bedroom. His attorney of the time, Steve Lerman, announced: 'Right now, the guy's completely unglued. I got a client who's on the edge of his seat. He's trying desperately to hold on to his sanity.'

All over Los Angeles, demonstrators were chanting King's name. Since the beating, he had refused all requests for interviews. Now, shaken by the way his city was going up in flames, he finally agreed to meet the press on the Friday. In the TV interview, King appeared perplexed and bewildered about what was going on, about having become a household name all around the world. Last night, on his own TV, he had watched President George Bush talking about him. 'People, I just want to say . . . can we all get along? Can we get along?' King pleaded. 'Can we stop making it horrible for the older people and the kids? We've got enough smog here in Los Angeles, let alone to deal with the setting of these fires and things. It's just not right.' It was a pained, rambling statement. 'It's not right, and it's not going to change anything. I'm neutral. I love everybody. I love people of colour . . . I'm not like they're . . . making me out to be.' He spoke slowly and quietly, rubbing his fingers. Newscasters had been talking about the dozens of dead, some killed trying to defend homes and stores. News channels had showed shots of armed Koreans, waiting to defend their businesses.

'We've got to quit. We've got to quit,' King went on. 'I can understand the first upset for the first two hours after the verdict, but to go on, to keep going on like this, it's just not right. It's just not right because those people will never go home to their families again. And I mean, please, we can get along here. We all can get along. We've just got to, just got to . . .'

Six years on I tell King I'm surprised to see him doing this, revisiting that time again to promote his hip-hop band. 'It's hard,' he says. 'I won't lie. It's a part of the business. I realized that when . . . when I got caught up, March 3, with them police officers' – he pronounces it 'po-leese' – 'I knew that life was not going to be easy.'

I suggest, lamely, that maybe there is something healing in remembering the anniversary of the time when things were so out of control for him. I'm not really sure what I'm saying, but King seems to agree, whatever it is: 'Yeah. It is, it definitely is. It's a part of history, you know. And like any part of history, we have parades, we have celebrations of Christmas . . . so it should be in memory. Because people died on that day, to cut a long story short.' He dries.

In the liner note to Stranded's brand-new CD, I notice a phrase in quotation marks near the bottom of the page, and realize it's taken from that sad, shaky, desperate statement, made six years ago: 'Can we all just get along?'

In fact, though Rodney King's name was the rallying cry that inspired the hurling of the first bricks and stones, the riot had been waiting to happen for some time. Like the Watts uprising 27 years before, it was just waiting for the spark.

For some, it was just a sense of release. Kokane told me how much fun it was to be there, tearing up the place. 'Oh shoot,' he laughed, like it was the funniest time of his life. 'I was doing a *gang* of looting. All of it got lost, but I got a gang of shit.'

'I loved everything that was going on,' Ice Cube said. 'It was bad that some people got hurt, but it was definitely a statement, and it seems like the only thing that America hears is violence and destruction. If black folks would have just marched, that would have just been on the news for 30 seconds.'

'It wasn't just the black people that was looting. There was more Mexicans than black people,' says Kokane, the happy rioter. His impression is right: 51 per cent of those arrested for rioting over those six days classified themselves as Hispanic. The Watts riot had been contained in a relatively small area; this time the sense of rage was far more widespread, both geographically and ethnically.

Ice Cube was 22 at the time. From the house where he was living in the middle-class Baldwin Hills district, he watched the smoke rising around him. It made him feel proud. His group NWA had put South Central Los Angeles on the map when he was a teenager, and now the rioters were putting it on TV all around the world. The rampage resulted in 53 deaths and 2382 injuries, and nearly all those killed or hurt were 'civilians'. Only 66 police officers were injured in the rioting. A total of 1700 businesses were damaged, and the insurance claims totalled over $750 million.

'Everybody with eyes knew what it was about,' Cube said. 'Putting it on the Rodney King incident – that's small. There's day-to-day things that go on in the black community that are unseen by a camcorder. It's just a heartache, man. You know, they give the black community so many pacifiers, and a pacifier doesn't do no good, and if we don't have a bottle, we're ready to explode.'

At the time, Cube had had his own production company, Street Knowledge, based in an office on Crenshaw. When the first bout of fighting died down, he took his 9mm Glock and rode down from Baldwin Hills to check out the premises. When he arrived there he saw that someone had sprayed the words 'BLACK OWNED' on the building. It had escaped the fury.

'I felt a sense of unity, a sense of pride, a sense of control. We felt satisfied. They say two wrongs don't make a right, but it damn sure makes it even.'

Riot, rebellion, uprising – call it what you will, everyone has their own stories of it. Papoose and Buzz remember it well. Being on

King's record label, they know full well why the media would be interested in them. They've written a track called '4-29-92' about the riot:

> *I remember that day so clear*
> *4-29-92 was the day people lived in fear*
> *Burn baby baby burn, when you gonna learn*
> *That if you keep the people down*
> *They'll be crawling out the underground?*

Papoose's rap echoes the slogan that some of the radicals had shouted during the Watts uprising a generation earlier: 'Burn, baby, burn.'

He remembers the '92 riot as a fine time. He too was raised in an aggressive Blood neighbourhood in Compton, the same Mob Piru neighbourhood that Suge Knight came from: that meant there were many parts of the city where he didn't feel safe. He puts his finger on one crucial reason why so many African-American young men have such a rosy memory of the riot, saying emphatically, 'It felt good because the tension was gone against the blacks. It had gone in another direction. I walked in neighbourhoods I have never walked in my life, so it felt good to me.' For a brief second, ghetto youths stopped regarding their neighbours as their principal enemy.

For five days the normal rules of engagement were suspended, and a strange thing happened. Remarkably, many of the gang territorialities which had existed for decades broke down. There was another enemy, whether it be the LAPD, whites or the Korean storekeeper defending his livelihood.

White Angelenos are so paranoid about South Central that many never go there. Yet, paradoxically, it's often safer for them than it is for many of the African-Americans who live there. It's difficult for them to understand the sense of release that the riot gave to so many young men.

For the first time there was a semblance of the unity that had been dreamed about for so long. For many, it was the first chance they had to explore parts of Los Angeles they'd never been to before, for fear of being challenged by gangs from other neighbourhoods. There is something very sad about the way that Papoose says, 'It is the most love I ever got from other brothers, you know?'

Nothing happens until after midnight, when the celebrities from the guest room suddenly start to fill the hall. Rodney King takes his place to the left of the stage. Tonight he's feeling good. A couple of TV crews have turned up to record the event.

When given the chance, King complains to people who want to hear about the fact that everyone thinks he's rich now. In fact, following his action against his attackers, he was not awarded punitive damages. He was awarded $3.8 million, to compensate for pain and suffering and to cover medical bills. Of that, he has so far seen only a fraction. He tells me that nearly all the money he was awarded in the settlement went to his attorneys. He took them to court too, but the judge died halfway through the case, and a new trial date has not yet been set. 'Once I got slaughtered by the police. Now I'm getting killed by the system,' he says. 'Nothing has come easy, all the way from the beating, the brain damage, the heart attacks. I'm fighting so I can kick back and enjoy all these millions that they say I've got. Quote unquote,' he says, with sad belligerence.

I look around and I wonder if King is going to have another disaster to add to his list of woes.

Power 106's Big Boy has been hired to do Stranded's warm-up. The massive Big Boy is a regular fixture on the LA gig scene. He has his shtick down. It's the same every time. He and a sidekick divide the crowd up into two, making them run through familiar chants like 'Make money-money, make money-money' and shouting, 'I can't hear you,' until they're loud enough. But it's Monday, the crowd is thin, and no amount of shouting 'I can't hear you' is going to make the crowd bring the house down.

The party vibe is not helped by the fact that Stranded don't come on, until way after midnight. When they do, it's a performance remarkable only for their lack of rehearsal. The moment they appear the stage is crammed with their friends, who are either too drunk or too inexperienced to know that they're not really helping out much up there. Not that they care. They are proud to be on stage with Buzz and Papoose. No rappers of any note from West Covina have ever made it. Their homeboys are fiercely proud of Stranded and have come to show their support. Unidentifiable hangers snatch the mike and shout, 'West Covina's in the house!'

It's not an auspicious launch. Looking at Rodney King standing to the left of the stage among the cocktail tables, I wonder how much he paid for all this. I hope he hasn't invested everything in the label. This was supposed to be a big Hollywood launch, but it looks like a small party at a club anywhere in LA County.

Poor King isn't enjoying himself either. He doesn't like the way everyone has come up on stage. You can't see my artists, he's thinking sadly.

14

Spittin' Game

BABYBOY

Around the same time as Stranded's inauspicious album launch, Babyboy finally gets a break, just when he's really starting to despair of getting anywhere.

His hustling appears to have paid off. He met a girl who said she was a singer, told her about N Entertainment and said that maybe they should do some business together. I have witnessed Babyboy give this same spiel to other performers he has met: Babyboy never lets on that N Entertainment exists only in his head, and that the company has yet to make a buck. The singer doesn't know what to make of his advances so she speaks to a black Hollywood actor she knows called Glen Plummer: 'I have this guy called Babyboy Delatorres who's interested in working with me. What should I do?'

Glen Plummer is a successful movie star: he was in the hip-hop flick *Menace II Society* with Ice-T and he starred with Ice Cube in *Trespass*. He was also in two movies that did so much to fix images of LA gang life in the minds of viewers around the world: Dennis Hopper's *Colors*, a wildly fictionalized version of Bloods versus Crips warfare, and *South Central*. But Plummer doesn't know much about the music business, so he in turn contacts a friend.

At the time Plummer is working on an independent black movie called *Love Beats The Hell Out Of Me*. The movie's producer is a middle-class African-American called Paul Goldsby who used to be in the music business himself. Compared to his other pictures, this is a low-budget movie for Plummer. He is doing it for love. It's about black men and their relationships, an attempt at a male *Waiting To Exhale* or *Soul Food*. Plummer is Goldsby's ace card: the biggest star on the project, and his biggest chance to win bona fide distribution for the movie.

So when Plummer mentions to Goldsby that he has this friend who needs some advice about the music industry, Goldsby readily agrees to meet Babyboy for lunch. He calls Babyboy and they meet at Johnny Rocket, a fifties retro burger restaurant on La Cienega in West LA. Of course, the moment that Babyboy discovers that he's meeting a card-carrying film producer, he changes tack fast.

'Are you havin' a *soundtrack* with this movie?' he asks. It's a reasonable question. Movie soundtrack cross-promotion has already proved a massively successful device for black American filmmakers. It turns out that, yes, Goldsby is doing a soundtrack; he doesn't have a label for it yet, but he's looking around. Babyboy asks him a little about the movie. After the meal, Babyboy buys a Johnny Rocket souvenir pin and goes home.

When Goldsby arrives back in his office, there is already a message on his answerphone. He plays it and hears Babyboy rapping the lyrics to a song he's written that he says, somewhat audaciously, will be just right for his movie. 'Fallin' In Love' is an old rap of his. It's about falling in love ('though I don't say who I'm fallin' in love with,' he laughs) and making a woman pregnant, so it could be Marlene. He lets her think so, anyway. Babyboy is a philanderer, unable to commit himself to just one woman, but he is also a romantic. In the song at least, he commits himself to her: he implores the woman to take his mind, his heart and all his money. It's torrid, purple-phrased, lovers' rap:

Come over to my place like I was Teddy P
And let me put my tree
Up inside the garden, so we can start breedin' . . .

Teddy P as in Prendergast, the soup love-balladeer.

Goldsby had intended to include only r'n'b songs in the movie, but he is won over by Babyboy's pitch. He has pulled this movie together with his credit card and his own enthusiasm, so he respects hunger when he sees it in someone else. 'If you can get that song recorded,' he says, 'I'll put it on the soundtrack.'

Babyboy is ecstatic. When he drives up to Hollywood to meet Goldsby again, it makes him want this even more.

Goldsby is using a white friend's house as his production office. The friend is a musician too. He's earned a substantial amount of money working for groups like Guns 'N Roses and is living in a luxurious house high above the city on the steep slopes of the Hollywood Hills. The whole house is painted white. The living room is a huge, wide, open space with a double-height ceiling.

Babyboy goes there to watch some of the movie's rushes on the TV in the basement, where an editing suite has been set up. 'The shit is hot, man,' he says. 'This motherfucking shit is dope.' The more he sees, the more he wants to take charge of the whole soundtrack to the movie. Suddenly he is in another world. This is the way things should be. There is only one fly in the ointment. He is flat broke. All Goldsby has heard is the rap on his answerphone. Babyboy needs to get a professional recording of his track.

BIG AL

In early summer 1998 MTV starts using street teams to promote a new national talent show it's organizing. *The Cut* is to be a showcase for urban music. Big Al, the 300lb king of the talent-show scene, first heard about it back in April. He turns up with his two backing tapes to S.I.R. studios in Hollywood along with about 200 other people, takes a numbered ticket, fills out the waiver forms and waits. It's a long evening.

When it's his turn, he goes into the audition room and belts out 'Freez Up' and 'Lyrical High'. The MTV people cut each track off after about 30 seconds.

Afterwards he goes to a third room, where they train a video camera on him and ask a few questions. 'Where are you from? What's "Lyrical High" about?' He tells them the song is not about drugs: it's about how he gets high on lyrics. It's a brutally brief audition but he's confident he made an impact. Besides, he recognizes a woman who has helped organize the Los Angeles heats: she was the woman who had organized the *Rap Sheet* convention last year. He knows he impressed her back then too.

They tell him they'll be in touch.

BABYBOY

It's three in the morning and Babyboy is angry with himself. In his mind he has decided that if he can get 'Fallin' In Love' recorded, everything is going to work out for him. Hip-hop film soundtracks are increasingly successful these days. Babyboy wants to record the track with the producer Overdose, who's offered to give him some music in the hope that Babyboy will finally make it.

The chance seems to be slipping away, though. Babyboy can't lay his hands on enough cash to buy studio time. He's trying to raise it by selling weed, but dealing drugs is no easy way out, whatever the stories. It's a time-consuming business. Babyboy was supposed to be having another meeting with Goldsby today, but he missed it because he had an appointment to fulfil.

He has driven here in Marlene's car – because he hasn't his own any more – along Sunset and up through Beverly Hills looking at all the 'big ass houses'. He feels that he should be living in one: that soon he will be if he doesn't mess up.

This right here is my motivation, he thinks, looking at the size of the houses, and the massive wealth they represent. 'Damn. Somebody could be living on your property for a year and you wouldn't know they exist.'

He picks up the mobile phone.

'Did I wake you?' someone is asking me.

It is three in the morning: I am standing naked by my bed, having been scrambling for the phone in the darkness. I recognize Babyboy's voice. 'Yes,' I say.

'I'm just thinking, man.'

I switch on the light. Babyboy is saying, 'I'm thinking. I got to make a decision. Which path am I got to take? Right now I got two careers. I got to choose one of them.'

'Why?' I ask, confused.

'Because I can't do both.' He sounds tired, stoned, depressed.

'Are you telling me you're trying to give up hustling?' I say.

He laughs and says, 'Man, we're born hustling in California. This whole state is born hustling. It's in us.'

'So what happened?'

I can hear him breathing heavily. 'Well, today, I was supposed to do something with this film soundtrack guy. But I had this other business,' he says euphemistically. 'I spent all the day doing the other business . . .'

'So you missed your meeting?'

'Yeah.' He sounds wrecked and wretched. He's worried that by missing his meeting with Goldsby he's blown the one big chance he has been offered so far. 'Sorry I woke you, OK?' he says. There is a long pause. 'Later, Mr Shaw,' he says, and rings off.

A couple of days later Babyboy calls me again, this time ecstatic. 'Bipolar' is how some of the friends I've made in Hollywood would describe him. He and Overdose have recorded a studio-quality version of 'Fallin' In Love'.

Later he tells me what was going through his head that night he woke me at three a.m. He was starting to think that the only way he would find enough money to make the tape would be to start dealing in cocaine again. 'I was about to become Nino Brown,' he boasts grandly, 'and infect the whole of LA.'

Luckily Marlene finally stepped in. Whether she realized that Babyboy was about to jump back into dealing serious drugs or not, she decided to raise the money for the track herself.

'As a matter of fact,' says Babyboy, 'my fiancée Marlene paid for . . .' He stops himself and choses words that are more business-like. 'Marlene *executive-produced* the song.'

Now Babyboy's mood shoots skywards again. Goldsby hears the finished track and OKs it for the movie. Babyboy is telling people he's about to make $60,000 from putting Goldsby's compilation album together, even though he hasn't seen a cent from the track yet and, in reality, Goldsby hasn't agreed to any such deal.

Babyboy's confidence, though, is infectious. Now he finally appears to have some momentum, it's easier to get things done. He books another block of studio time at the Edge and starts to record a track for his next project, Babyboy Delatorres's debut CD.

After 'Fallin' In Love' he goes on to record a number he has written called 'Spittin' Game'. Playa Hamm, the rapper who sometimes hangs around Wilton, has agreed to appear on the track. This is a coup for Babyboy. Hamm has a little weight locally: not only was he half of the Ruthless Records duo Tweed Cadillac, but he also raps for DJ Quik, one of the best-known producers in LA. Babyboy has been chasing Hamm for weeks for a favour. This is part of hip hop's system of patronage. New artists can gain attention by persuading more famous figures to make guest appearances.

Something else is new in Babyboy's life. The other day he met

Kimmie G from Camp Zero at a show. He asked her, in the grand way that he has, if she wanted to guest on a track on his album too.

They ended up in bed together. 'I didn't mean to,' he grins sheepishly.

TIBU

Tibu has lost his job. The hospital lost patience with his time-keeping. Now he's back to relying on selling weed to raise the money for studio sessions.

He gave up on Dave's studio in Cerritos. Dave took too long to get anything done and was always losing pieces of music in his computer. Now Tibu calls me up most weeks, asking if I'll drive him all the way from Bellflower, or from the Cal State campus, to a new studio in Studio City. This one is run by a white guy too, an r'n'b songwriter called Todd.

'Can you pick me up from the house on Eucalyptus?'

I pick up Tibu and Boldface. Boldface is the youngest member of the Vietnom click. He's just 16. 'But that don't mean shit,' Boldface says belligerently.

Boldface says he's Italian. On his shoulder he has a tattoo of a rearing horse, with a caption that reads: '100% Italian Stallion'. The '100%' is dubious: his mother is from the Far East, and he's part Latino too, but he clings to his Italian heritage. He wants to use Boldface The Italian Stallion as his rap name, but Tibu tells him he should just stick to Boldface.

Boldface isn't so sure. He says to me: 'Caucasians aren't accepted in this business but I thought if I let them know I'm Italian . . . Italians are more accepted, maybe. What do you think?'

I drive them down Eucalyptus, pausing at the corner with Alondra. The 706s are all there. One flashes a $10 bill at the car.

Today Tibu wants me to pick up another singer too. Patrice is 17 years old and wild. Her parents found her too much to handle, so now she lives with her grandmother in an upscale, mostly white cul-de-sac east of Eucalyptus.

While we're waiting for her to emerge from her grandmother's house, Tibu says casually, 'I fucked Patrice once. She still wants to fuck me, but I don't want to mess with her any more.' He says that Keyna, his girlfriend, wanted to come to the studio today too, but he didn't think it that it was a good idea to have Keyna and Patrice in the same room together.

Patrice comes out of the house wearing a pair of sweat pants and a sports top. She has a slim, muscular body. An intricate henna tattoo is drawn around her belly button. 'I have to sit in the back?' she says, horrified.

'Just get in,' orders Tibu. She pouts and gets in next to Boldface. Around Tibu and Boldface, she is both shy and flirtatious at the same time. As we drive off she complains, 'I'm not ready for this.' Patrice is a drama queen: she hates not to be the centre of attention.

'Shit,' says Tibu. 'I know when you're ready. Stop stressin'.'

'I never sung in a studio before,' she whimpers.

As we drive off, up the 110, Tibu orders her to stop acting like a prima donna. All she has to do is sing. He knows she can do it, so she can do it. She sits in sulky silence for the next 45 minutes as we drive to Studio City. Patrice has sung in church choirs and at karaoke contests, but she's never done anything like this. She doesn't even like rap music much.

Studio City is a section of the San Fernando Valley, just north of the Hollywood Hills. It changed its name from Maxwell in 1928 in an attempt to stake a claim to part of the burgeoning film industry. Todd's small recording studio probably isn't what the city fathers meant. It's a tiny bedroom, 10 by 12 feet, overlooking the dismal concrete culvert that is all that's left of the Los Angeles River. When he's recording, Todd has to close the window and the door to reduce the noise. In the hot LA weather, the room quickly becomes stifling.

In the studio, Patrice announces dramatically, 'I don't know if I can do this.'

Tibu is curt. 'Just sing,' he says. He's paying for this session. 'Come on,' he orders.

'What?' she protests. '*What* do you want me to sing?'

'Make something up,' Tibu instructs. 'It's about money. Sing something like, "Everybody's chasing paper."' He sings the line in falsetto.

Patrice laughs and picks up a copy of *Vibe* magazine and starts staring at the models. 'I'm just looking at these swimsuits,' she announces airily.

Tibu is losing patience. 'Sing!' he tells her.

'Mmm. This is interesting,' she says, peering at the magazine.

'Sing!'

'I got some panties like that.'

Boldface, wearing an embroidered 'Vietnam' baseball hat, the sort you can have made up at malls, perks up. 'You got them on right now?' he asks, smiling at her lewdly. She scowls at him.

Eventually, when she's assured herself that she's the centre of attention, Patrice tries a take. Standing apprehensively in front of the mike, she improvises:

You know you want it? Why don't you have it?

Her voice is beautiful. She sings quietly, without frills, but her voice has a strong, very pure tone. 'Does that sound all right?' she asks innocently, knowing just how good her voice sounded.

'Just do it. Stop bullshitting,' says Tibu gruffly.

She sings again and again. Each take sounds better. 'How was that?'

215

Even Tibu is smiling now. 'Stop asking questions and just do it again. Come on, 'Trice.'

The next time her take is perfect. 'That's it!' shouts Boldface, who jumps right on to Patrice, pushes her down on to the sofa and starts dry humping her right there.

'Get off,' she giggles, embarrassed.

Grinning, Tibu turns to me and explains: 'Boldface has this thing about women with beautiful singing voices. He wants to have sex with them.'

Now Todd makes her repeat the phrase four times, panning each vocal on to different channels. 'That's what Babyface does,' Todd explains. Then Todd makes her sing the same phrase an octave higher, again four times. The r'n'b producer Babyface is one of Todd's heroes.

On the way home, Tibu is pleased. The track worked out well. Todd is so impressed by Patrice's voice that he's asked Tibu if she can do some demos with him. Tibu is daydreaming that maybe Todd will give him some free studio time for hooking them up. Maybe Todd will make her a star, and then he can be Patrice's manager.

'Look at that,' Patrice shouts from the back of the car as a new 4WD accelerates past us. 'I want one of those.'

'Nah, I want a Navigator,' Tibu quashes her. 'But I'm going to buy a house first. When I blow up, the first thing I'm going to buy is, like, Tibu Mansions.' Tibu has been pretty much homeless for the past two years, moving round to friends' and relatives' houses. 'A big house with, like, four bedrooms. That's what I'm going to get right there.'

All the way home Boldface asks Patrice questions, flirting with her.

'Where do you work?'

'I go to school still, but I work in McDonald's in Long Beach. I got another job too, but I ain't talking about that one.'

'What is it?'

'I ain't talking about it,' she says flirtatiously. 'All I'm saying is *The Players Club* – that's all.'

A look of comprehension dawns on the Italian Stallion's face. 'I do that too.'

Boldface and Patrice have something in common: they're both strippers. Though Patrice is just 17, she says she's been doing it for some time. Boldface is even younger, but he's only recently started performing at strip clubs. Once Patrice learns that he's a stripper too, she stops talking so coyly. 'The women – they're the wildest,' she says.

'Oh yeah,' Boldface agrees knowledgeably. 'Which do you like the most? Stripping for males or females?'

'Females. I'm bisexual, you see,' Patrice says precociously.

Boldface is ecstatic. A teenage fantasy come true. He whoops. 'See? That's what I like about females. They're so honest. They're so upfront.'

We drop Patrice off outside her house in Bellflower. As she gets out, Boldface begs her phone number and says, 'Can you hook me up with the people you strip for?'

'Sure,' Patrice tells him.

BABYBOY

Kimmie G and Duke – Camp Zero's manager – have come to the studio to listen to the backing track Babyboy wants her to appear on. It's called 'Janine'. She listens to Overdose's backing track, sitting cross-legged on the floor, scribbling lines in a writing pad, then goes home to work on her verses.

Babyboy is recording another track right now. He's in the room below, which serves as a vocal booth. He stands there excited in the darkness, waiting for Overdose to give him his cue. He waits the eight bars before bursting in with another of his paeans to life on the dub:

I don't gang-bang homie
Forget flossing like Pooh
Red is a dope colour but I prefer to wear blue
It's just this thing I do, hanging out in the street
Leanin' on a post conversatin' with the O.G.s
While they drinkin' O.E.
Me I'm sippin' Hennessy . . .

'Flossin" is pretending to be something that you aren't. Archetypally, hip-hoppers are accused of flossin' when they pretend to be affiliated to gangs, when in fact very few are – something he's accusing the LA producer DJ Pooh of being.

It may not be the greatest lyric, but it's one that is true to Babyboy's life. It's what he does. As the song says, Babyboy has never gang-banged, despite his father's underworld connections. Despite his admiration for the Crip O.G.s who live in his neighbourhood, and the fact that he wears blue, like many of the people around Wilton and King do, he's never been affiliated to the Harlem Rollin' 30s Crips who run that area. Some of his relatives are Bloods, and some are Mexicans, so he never felt like it was a family thing for him, as it is with some of the younger gang-bangers today.

'I don't gang-bang' is a timely thing to be saying too. After what happened to Tupac and Biggie, no white-run label is looking to sign anyone who boasts too loudly of their affiliation.

When his verse is finished he leaves eight bars for the chorus.

Playa Hamm comes upstairs to listen to it, and to work out where he's going to drop his own verse. 'That's tight,' he says. He's impressed by Overdose's work too, but not by the chorus. At the moment, all Babyboy has is a phrase: 'I'm spittin' game . . .', repeated eight times. 'Spittin' game' just means talking, but talking about the sort of things that hood boys talk about with other hood boys.

'You want to say something more than that,' says Hamm. 'Just sayin' "Spittin' game" is a waste . . .'

Babyboy, usually the one with the mouth and the opinions, respectfully says, 'OK.'

'You want to say something like, "I'm spittin' game . . ." Then I say, "You spittin game, my nigga?" And then you come back with something like . . . I don't know . . . "Yeah, I'm spittin' game . . . and my name is gettin' bigger." '

'Right,' says Babyboy, eager to learn from the older hand. 'I'm feelin' that.'

Together they sit down and write out a chorus.

Hamm goes downstairs and lays down his verse. His delivery is much more confident than Babyboy's. He's been doing this for years and it shows. 'Hell,' asks Babyboy in a rare moment of humility, 'you think I'm going to sound weak after that shit?'

'Don't worry, it's tight,' Overdose tells him.

Reassured, Babyboy bounds around the room, saying, 'This is the shit.' Finally things are moving for him. He's not just hanging around someone else's recording session. This is his turn.

He takes out a blue biro from his ever-present briefcase and starts to scrawl on the clean white studio wall. He draws a large letter 'N' and a circle round it, and then slowly and methodically starts colouring it in. N Entertainment.

15

Motherfuckers Come to Take Their Lives

C-DOUBLE-E

The summer is starting. On the big old jacaranda trees that rise up occasionally on the sidewalks, the last of the shocking purple blooms are dropping.

On a Saturday at the end of May, I catch a snippet of news. Orlando Anderson, the suspected South Side Compton Crip widely believed to have been responsible for killing Tupac Shakur in 1996, has been shot dead during a gunfight at a Compton car wash.

The Compton police are quick to quash reports that he was murdered in revenge for Tupac's murder; this, they say, was just the result of an argument over some money. Tupac's death ignited an outburst of violence between the Mob Piru Bloods and the South Side Compton Crips. Fortunately for the police in this case, the two others killed in the fire-fight were not Bloods, but Corner Pocket Crips.

The first time I met Tupac was at the overripe, pink, palm-treed fantasy that is the Beverly Hills Hotel. The property on Sunset Boulevard is owned by the Sultan of Brunei, sometimes described as the richest man in the world. Originally built on the site of some bean fields in 1911, it was remodelled extensively in the fifties by Paul R. Williams, a black architect who was born in 1894 in

Downtown LA on 8th and Santee. Williams was a rarity, someone who sidestepped the prejudice of the times, becoming one of the most fashionable architects of the city. He designed homes in places where local ordinances forbade him to spend the night. His granddaughter recalled how he learned to write upside down when dealing with his customers, because it was thought to be inappropriate for a black man to lean over alongside a white person.

Tupac had recently signed up to the Death Row label when I met him. Suge Knight had for a long time been trying to include the controversial young rapper in his stable. His opportunity came when Tupac was sentenced to two and a half years in prison for the first-degree sexual abuse of a fan. Tupac contested the judgement and denied any part in the assault, but by then legal fees had left him broke, and mainstream record companies nervous of associating too closely with him. This gave Suge the opportunity he needed to step in. On condition that Tupac became a Death Row artist, Suge raised the bail of $1.4 million and Tupac walked out of Clinton Correctional Center in Dannemora, New York, pending an appeal.

Now we sat at a table in the posh Beverly Hills Restaurant. 'I hate to point to the obvious irony of it, but after 11 months inside, it must be something of a relief to come to a place like this,' I said.

'Exactly,' said Tupac. 'When I sat there, this is what I thought about, coming to places like this.' And he ordered a double helping of soft-shell crab and some hot tea with lemon.

The Tupac I'd read about was violent and moody and had been arrested several times, on weapons charges, assault charges and once for shooting at two off-duty policemen (though it later turned out that the cops were drunk, using illegal guns and had started the fight).

This Tupac appeared urbane, witty and erudite. He quoted poetry, talked about his movie roles and pointed out other celebrities who were dining near us, like Anthony Hopkins and

Emma Thompson, silently mouthing their names across the table. He was happy to be out of jail, hoping that his time as the media bad boy was over.

But during the rest of the day I spent with him, his optimistic mood quietly evaporated. We were driving to Tarzana, in his open-top Jaguar, when a nearby car backfired. He flinched at the wheel.

Later he told me he did that all the time when he heard loud bangs. He was still suffering from post-traumatic stress from the shooting in New York. If he saw people running he'd tense up, ready to duck. He said he got nervous if people stood behind him.

We went into Can-Am studios, where all the greatest Death Row artists, like Tupac, Snoop and Dr Dre, recorded their material. You entered through an armoured front door that was locked behind you. The industrial unit had been turned into a well-armoured fortress. In the first room there were armed guards. Beyond that, another door locked behind you.

Tupac started smoking weed heavily the moment he was inside the studio, surrounded by cousins and friends he'd recruited as part of his new click, the Outlawz. Most of them were dressed in military fatigues, waiting for whenever he might need them to lay down some vocals. This was Tupac's chance to spread his patronage among his family and friends. He introduced them to me proudly, as he slicked apart some Dutch Masters cigars. His cousin Kadaffi teased a pit-bull puppy called Scandalous, trying to teach it to fight.

As he smoked, the sunny side of Tupac disappeared. He became sombre, telling me what it was like when he was shot that first time. 'It was like something grabs me, and it's black.' He added, 'I knew I was going to get shot. Right now I know I'm not going to live for ever. Nobody is. But I know about it. I know I'm going to die in violence.'

'You know that?' I said.

'I know.'

'Does that make you afraid?'

'No. I'm afraid that I won't finish the things that I set out to do. I'm not afraid of the niggas coming for me, or what they might do. Because it's going to happen. All good niggas. All the niggas who change the world die in violence. They don't get to die in regular ways. Motherfuckers come to take their lives.'

I think, at the time, I found the words pompous. A little ridiculous, even.

According to witnesses, the events that led up to Tupac's death started with a question: 'You from the South?'

In the MGM Grand Hotel in Las Vegas Mike Tyson had just KOed Bruce Seldon in a mere 109 seconds. Tupac was on top of the world. *All Eyez On Me* – rap's first double album – was on the way to going multi-platinum and he must have felt invincible – like Tyson.

A TV crew caught him emerging from the ringside. 'Did you see Tyson do it 'im?' he told the cameras. 'We bad like that. Come out of prison and now we running shit,' he said, comparing Tyson's career to his own.

Then one of the entourage, Travon 'Tray' Lane, spotted a young man with a Kobe Bryant haircut and a small moustache in the throng in the lobby. His name was Orlando Anderson. Tray pointed him out to Tupac. An informant later told Compton police that Tray had been part of a group of three Piru Bloods, affiliated to Death Row, who had been assaulted by several South Side Compton Crips at a Foot Locker outlet in Lakewood Mall, just to the south-east of Compton. During the scuffle, Tray had had his gold Death Row pendant snatched – a pendant that had been given to him personally by Suge Knight. In the MGM Grand lobby, Tray apparently thought that the young man was one of the South Side Crips who'd assaulted him.

Tupac, jolt-full of testosterone and ever keen to prove his

manhood, confronted the smooth-faced boy. 'You from the South?' he asked. The classic gangsta confrontation. Geography mapped as a challenge. Manhood envisioned as territory.

Tupac's fist smashed into the side of Orlando Anderson's head, and the young man fell to the ground. The rest of Tupac's entourage crowded around, many – including Suge Knight – joining in kicking Anderson on the hotel carpet among the mechanical blips and ker-chings of the gambling machines around them.

It was over quickly. Suge and his bullyboy entourage swept out through the lobby. Hotel security invited Anderson to file a complaint with local police, but the young man, who had turned 22 just a few weeks earlier, refused, as people from his neighbourhoods have become so used to doing, and he too disappeared.

Less than three hours later Tupac was travelling in Suge Knight's BMW when he was fatally shot by an unidentified man in a white Cadillac with California plates.

In his apartment on Buckingham, Herman keeps a big collection of videos, taped off BET and MTV, and he has a collection of rap CDs too. He has a lot of Tupac. Los Angeles rappers are almost universally respectful of Tupac. After all, he was a New York-born rapper who adopted their city, and who shouted out for it. And he embraced, perhaps a little too wholeheartedly, the whole local lifestyle. Tibu adores his work. Herman is a huge fan.

Herman tells me that he was in Las Vegas on 7 September 1996, the night the 25-year-old Tupac was murdered there. He and a friend, who works in real estate and who had some money, travelled there and booked into the Flamingo Hotel just to hang out on the night of the Tyson–Seldon fight, to party, to try to meet some girls and do a little gambling. Hotels in Las Vegas are cheap: it's the gambling that's expensive.

It was Herman's first time in Vegas. His friend with the money rented a car for the night, but with so many people in town for the fight, the police were on edge. It was a mad night. Everywhere they went there were members of the r'n'b aristocracy, just hanging out, like they were. They spotted K-Ci, a singer from the band Jodeci, and rappers like Foxy Brown, Mase and Vinnie from Naughty By Nature. It was a trip.

They tried also to get into Death Row owner Suge Knight's new club on Flamingo Road, the 662, but it was full. Tupac and Suge had been heading there too, when their car was attacked, but Herman knew nothing of that at the time. The police moved them on from the parking lot at the 662 because it was so busy, so they tried to get into the Shark Club, and on the way there they noticed that Las Vegas Boulevard was barricaded and blocked. They just assumed it was the police acting up again. They had no idea that Tupac had just been shot three times. 'There was a lot of crazy things going on that night in Vegas,' Herman says.

The next morning they had to return their car and return to the normal world. When they were in the car lot, a girl standing near them suddenly collapsed on to the tarmac. 'We thought: What happened? Did somebody *hit* her?'

It turned out that someone had just told her that Tupac had been shot; she had fainted, right there in front of them. And that's the first Herman heard of the attack on the rap star.

Tupac lay in the hospital for six days. Like a lot of people, Herman didn't really expect him to die. Tupac had been shot before in New York in 1994 during an assault that he himself believed was an assassination attempt, taking five bullets, including one to the head, but had survived. 'We all thought he was going to pull through,' says Herman.

Six days later Herman was standing in the Crenshaw–Baldwin Hills Mall when he heard Theo, the smooth-voiced DJ from 92.3 The Beat announcing that Tupac was dead. He felt his face go numb.

Back in his apartment, he taped all the news shows and tributes he could find about Tupac. He picks out a video and switches on the TV to show me it.

BABYBOY

The deal with Paul Goldsby isn't working out as well as Babyboy hoped.

Babyboy wanted to help compile the movie soundtrack. He dreamed of earning a fat fee from it, but Goldsby has turned him down flat. Now all Babyboy thinks he stands to earn is about $6000 if and when 'Fallin' In Love' is included on the soundtrack.

But at least the ball is rolling now. Babyboy has made a little money hustling and invested it in some more tracks he made at the Edge. Havoc Da Mouthpiece, whose father was a member of the Chi-Lites, guests on one number. Havoc was a member of the group Southcentral Cartel, who had gangsta hits back in the early nineties and were signed briefly to Def Jam. The track is intended as an intro to Babyboy's putative CD. He has a concept for the album, which is going to be called *The Lesson*. 'It's everything that I learned from birth to 24,' he says.

This one's for the Babyboy . . .
Get ready to learn your lesson . . .

Havoc intones.

But the most poignant track by far is one that Babyboy calls 'Dear Dad'. It's about the father he met only six times in his life:

Dear Dad
How you doin' up in heaven?
Remember July 7, 1992, when you left me here alone?

No need to worry, your son is full grown . . .
You should have seen the mountain your son had to climb
I hope I'm in your heart, you know you're in mine,

It may be mawkish, but the love for the father he never really knew is painfully real. Then, as the rhyme progresses, it becomes angrier. This is as naked as Babyboy gets:

Damn dad, I need your help
Why d'you leave me here stranded all by my self?
Damn dad, why did you have to leave?
What happened to the cards you kept hidden up your sleeve?

The final chorus changes to:

Damn dad, I'm still tryin' to understand
When did I change from a boy to a man?

And it ends with his voice continuing, after Overdose's beat has finished, with one last 'Damn dad'.

16

On Chrome

BIG AL

On Thursday nights as the summer gets underway, I take to visiting Leimert Park, just off Crenshaw Boulevard. Leimert Park used to be a posh, whites-only district. Now it's the heart of African-American middle-class bohemia, with its restaurants and jazz clubs. Project Blowed, held there in a small corner room next to the Vision Theater, is a small, earnest affair, but it's a different scene from Khop's or Babyboy's. It's not a nightclub, its devotees insist: it's a 'hip-hop seminar'. There is no drinking. A few flyers for other events are routinely scattered around the place. Hip hop has already reached its high classical age. The boys who cram in here every night treat MC-ing as a high art and stand, nodding at each other's rhymes, until their turn comes. It's a different crowd in here: a few are black college kids. A couple of women are usually dressed in kente cloth.

A couple of the nights I visit, I recognize a rapper from the Camp Zero click, standing at the back, carefully taking in the high-speed rhyming of those on stage. He calls himself Don Heroin; not that he takes the drug: 'The only thing that's high about me is the music,' he insists.

I tell him, 'Everyone here looks so serious.'

'Project Blowed is serious. Everyone here is trying to be a rapper,' he says. 'It's not about having fun.'

A rapper on stage is rhyming so fast I can barely make out the words. Somebody shouts, 'Wack!' from the crowd, throwing the performer. The DJ suddenly stops the turntables and the woman who acts as stage manager takes the mike and upbraids the heckler. 'Who said that about wackness?' The crowd goes quiet. 'You got to get up here on stage if you're gonna talk about wackness.' The protester stays just where he is.

'That's the way it is here,' says Don Heroin, with a grin.

Before Project Blowed there were the open-mike sessions held in the Good Life wholefood café on the corner of Crenshaw and Exposition. These ended after eight continuous years. Old Good-Lifers – 20-somethings like Big Al and Babyboy's neighbour Volume 10 – sound like nostalgic old men when they mourn the club. As members of an older generation always do, they insist that Project Blowed doesn't have the same spirit.

The Good Life's open-mike sessions were run by a woman known as B. Hall, who laid down the event's strict rules. There were three of them: no 'dissing'; no leaning on the paintings; and, most importantly, no 'cussing'.

Big Al used to love performing there. The Good Life café was a haven for hip hop – as opposed to just rap. Subtle demarcation lines have been drawn between rap and hip hop. For the most part, the terms rap and hip hop are interchangeable. But purists insist that hip hop refers to the whole culture, not just the MC-ing. To those purists, plain rap has taken the attention from the true skills of mike controlling, MC-ing, with its obsession with violence and money, its dreams of Lexuses and Glocks. Hip-hoppers look down on mere rappers. It's a broad generalization, but those African-Americans who call themselves hip-hoppers – as opposed to rappers – are more likely to be middle-class and educated. In LA, hip hop, in the stricter meaning of the term, tends to thrive north of Wilshire, in bohemian areas like Vermont, in fashionable hip-hop clubs like Pedros and vinyl-only record stores like Phat Beats, all of which attract a mixed crowd. Hard-core rappers from the poorer working-class neigh-bourhoods like Watts, Long Beach, Lynwood and Compton, in return regard the metropolitan hip-hoppers with suspicion.

Al first went to the Good Life café in '92. If you wanted to perform, you added your name to the list. Back then he called himself 'Alski Rock', but when he came to write his name it suddenly seemed old to him; a cheesy, mid-eighties sort of name. He wrote down 'Big Al', and it stuck.

From then on he went religiously every Thursday to the Good Life. He became one of the 'Lifers', the community of rhymers who honed their skills at the mike. The venue provided a spring-board for a few moderately successful careers. Freestyle Fellowship, Volume 10, Pharcyde and Jurassic 5 all cut their teeth there, groups who generally value wordplay over gangsta narratives. When the chance came around, Al helped compile a Good Life compilation tape; it was called *Please Pass The Mic* – a homage to the venue's policy of enforced civility.

Everyone who went to the Good Life seems to remember it fondly. Diamond DX, Herman's fellow rapper, used to act as security on open-mike nights. He remembered Big Al, Volume 10 and others performing there. It reminded him of the good days at Radiotron. 'We need to go back to those days,' he says nostalgi-cally. 'Back in those days, we just used to come out and do everything for free. It was all about giving respect to the nation of hip hop.'

For ten years a small scene that has nothing to do with gangsta rap has thrived below Wilshire Boulevard, on Crenshaw. A few white faces turn up in the crowd, but rarely more than a handful. The major record companies from Hollywood and Beverly Hills don't often show up. That might be because they think the music here is too earnest and too uncommercial for them to sign, or it might also be that they prefer to wait for the acts to appear in the Hollywood clubs, north of Wilshire.

Peter Cohen, the man from the dance label 550 that Al met at the *Rap Sheet* convention, goes to Project Blowed sometimes. He notices how few A&R men ever make it past that borderline of Wilshire and into the South Central clubs. 'It's kind of shocking,' is how he puts it.

KHOP

Khop and Kidub roll up to Roscoe's Chicken And Waffles, on Pico, in Khop's brand-new, shiny maroon, two-door Lexus, and park out back. Roscoe's is a black music industry haunt. It's not so upmarket as the Shark Bar, on La Cienega, which has become the new in place for the hip-hop élite to dine, but the plates are always fuller at Roscoe's. 'What's up?' Khop greets me.

He looks every inch a star. He has had his hair straightened, and it's falling in neat symmetry on each side of his face. His goatee is carefully trimmed and he's wearing a new orange Pelle Pell sports shirt, topped off with a neat silver necklace. Khop is the cat who has got the cream.

I say, 'So you're not in the '84 Caddy any more?'

Khop laughs. 'Changed from a 'Lac to a Lex,' he declares proudly. The Cadillac has been sitting outside his parents' house for months now. It doesn't run any more. Somebody tried to steal it a little while ago, not realizing there was no battery in it.

'A number five with waffles,' he orders, and also asks for a Sunrise. This is a Roscoe's speciality – lemonade poured over orange juice, so the colours merge halfway up the glass.

Over lunch, Khop tells stories of his new life. The other day he filmed a second video for 'We Be Clubbin'' – the remix version featuring the rapper DMX. There is a fashion for making 'R'-rated videos now: they're shown only on the adult channels, and their value as promotional tools is limited, but they project an appropriate 'playa' image. This video follows the movie's theme of the strip joint: the set was packed with strippers, performing for Cube, Khop and DMX. It was Khop's idea of fun.

'Yeee-ah, yeee-ah. Off the *hook*. Afterwards I had nightmares of titties in my face!'

Fame changes people in the end, but Khop has only just started to discover what it's like. The other day he appeared with Cube on *Vibe*, the new TV show based on the magazine the same name. The next day, he went to the mall, basking in the recognition. 'Weren't you on TV last night?' 'Off the *hook*,' says Khop.

In the lyrics he's been writing for Ice Cube, Khop has been representing, shouting out for Inglewood – 'the City of Champions' he calls it. Inglewood is mostly a middle-class suburb, though it has its share of gang life, poverty and crime.

'Where we live is cool,' says Kidub. 'There ain't too much going on and the scenery is right. But the streets are the streets . . .'

'Yes,' says Khop.

'And it's always going to be the streets. That's why we don't try to be there all the time. Keep it rollin'. Keep it safe.'

'Would you move somewhere else?' I ask.

'*Hell* yeee-ah,' says Khop, looking at me like my brain is soft.

'It's not because of *us*,' says Kidub. 'I got two girls, so I would have to be gone.'

'Man,' agrees Khop. 'I'm gone.'

'I'm outta here.'

Khop says, 'Man, I love Inglewood. I grew up in Inglewood. But you can't stay. Niggas is jealous of you.'

C-DOUBLE-E

Herman calls me up one day and invites me to a gig that A Nu Creation are playing: 'At Magic Johnson Park. This Saturday.' It's a Juneteenth celebration – the start of the hot season. Herman is excited about something else, too. 'Did I tell you? I got the MPC

2000. I haven't messed with the Playstation for three weeks. It's in the box,' he giggles.

Herman loves to talk. He will chatter for hours on the phone if you let him. He starts telling me all about the wonderful machine he's bought, how it's going to make his career. How he's figured out how to use it in three weeks. 'Some people spend a year just finding their way around it,' he says.

The MPC 2000 cost him $2100. He spent weeks browbeating the store owner and managed to beat the shop down $400. All the same, the sequencer represents six months' rent.

'Aren't you worried, having such an expensive piece of equipment in your apartment?' I ask him.

'I don't tell many people about it,' he says. 'You know, I was wondering if I should get the MPC or if I should get the car. Now I know I was right not to get the car. Soon I can get myself a whole lot of cars.' He laughs.

BABYBOY

Because Babyboy is usually out on a bud run or some other business, his time-keeping is erratic. We have a meeting place at the dub, the corner of Wilton and King. I park and wait for him there. Sometimes I can wait two hours before he finally appears. It's high summer now and hot. Today he is late. He usually is.

In midsummer the temperature in the low-lying land of South Central soon climbs above 100 degrees. The concrete soaks up the heat. In the middle of the afternoon, the air is solid and still.

Ice-cream vans buzz lazily back and forth from east to west and back again, across the intersection of 38th and 39th, gradually meandering closer. In South Central they sometimes look like low-budget armoured cars. I remember Babyboy laughing and telling me once how, when he was a kid, he and his friends used to snipe at the vans with BB guns.

One that's yellow and orange gradually winds its way closer. All the windows, including the windscreens, have wire mesh over them, as if they were army vehicles from Belfast. A recorded tinkling noise plays over and over. Far away, it's hard to make out what the tune is. When it finally gets to Leighton I can make out the tune. With beautiful incongruity, the van is playing the old English music-hall song 'A Bicycle Made For Two'. 'Daisy, Daisy, give me your answer do . . .' Passers-by crane their necks at me as I sing. Babyboy, with his typical love of the dramatic, has said: 'If they didn't know that you were with me there, they would've fucked you up.' I suppose he's exaggerating, like he so often does, but I'm never too sure. There is always fresh Rollin' 30s Crip graffiti on the road signs and tree trunks: gangs are like dogs, forever marking their territory.

A boy of about ten, dressed in a black T-shirt, holds two plastic toy guns and runs around pretending to shoot at the girls: 'Bam-bam-bam.' A guy with slicked-back hair walks his Rottweiler.

An old Toyota comes up alongside me and a guy in a Wilson golfing T-shirt leans over and asks, 'You waiting for Kimeyo.'

'Yes.'

The boy holds up his cellphone and says: 'Kimeyo says he's on his way,' then drives away again.

A black and white LAPD squad car rolls up behind me. It slows as it comes past my car, then cruises away again.

Two minutes later it is back, repeating the same manoeuvre. And then a third time it returns and parks on the opposite side of the road from me. And waits.

The two black officers must be wondering what a white guy is doing in a beat-up car parked here. Presumably they think I'm up to no good in such well-known gang territory. Do they think I'm here to buy drugs?

The boys from Wilton Place wander slowly up the sidewalk and position themselves on the far corner from the squad car. It is obviously an irritation to them to have a white intruder drawing the attention of the police, but it's the police that they focus their attention on, not me. The boys fold their arms and just stare at the car, waiting for something to happen.

For the next ten minutes the police car waits to see what will happen. And nothing does. So eventually it drives away again.

Later that night, as I'm driving Babyboy down Leighton, a voice calls in the darkness. 'Hey, Kimeyo, what the fuck are you doin' riding around the hood with a white boy?'

Babyboy laughs, but I have no idea whether the comment is a joke or not, or whether it's someone who was annoyed by the attention the cops gave them earlier.

This incident sticks in my mind, because in the whole time I have been hanging out in South Central, this is one of only two incidents of anti-white racism that I ever encounter – if it was even that.

When I first began visiting South Central, I admit, I was very aware of my own colour, even in relatively mixed places like the Crenshaw–Baldwin Hills Mall. Some didn't want to answer my questions, but no one made me feel unwelcome. Friends in Hollywood who asked me where I spent my days were sometimes surprised at this. They say they expected hostility.

There was another occasion when I was made abruptly aware of my race while in South Central. It happened when I listening to three boys freestyle for me on the tarmac of some empty school playground. One of them, the most obviously talented of the trio, launched into a violent verse:

I'm here to shoot ya
With a Luger
And many weapons that will do ya
My hollow points will go through ya . . .

This was all familiar territory, but from there it suddenly lurched into an anti-white polemic:

Soon to be the massacre in white America
That's a true solution
Get ready for the new world order, revolution
Retaliation, a must
Devils will be crushed by the NOI . . .

In the NOI – Nation of Islam – cosmology, the white race are 'devils'.

The sentiments are fairly common on rap records, but I had never had them expressed to my face before. The curious thing was that the boy delivered this aggressive, anti-white couplet solely for my approval of its skills. Maybe I missed something, but it seemed to me that none of the animosity was directed personally at me. Maybe, I wondered at the time, I was not being counted as part of 'white America' anyway. So far I have found that my English accent is an asset. It marks me out, at least, as a curiosity.

No one I meet in South Central questions my right to be writing about them. I have met no one who objects to me hanging around, though I'm under few illusions why people let me, even encourage me. All of the people I meet want to further their career: they're not simply waiting for fame to strike. They live in neighbourhoods dislocated from the entertainment industry's power base north of Wilshire. I represent a connection, a contact. Every time I visit a talent show or a convention, I return home with a wallet bulging with business cards.

The only person who does object to what I'm doing is Harry. Harry drinks at the same Hollywood bars as I do. I bump into him on several occasions. He's about 60, I'd guess, a short five foot four, always elegantly dressed, and he loves to drink. Each time I meet him he is usually drunk, or on the way, and has totally forgotten who I am. So he repeats the same stories of his life. He is a musician who has travelled the world.

'You're English?' he says each time he sees me. 'I've been to England. Brighton. A lovely town. Beautiful girls in England,' he says, without fail.

In the bars he's something of a mascot. The bar habitués are ambitious, mostly white 20 to 30-year-olds who more than tolerate the way the older African–American interrupts their conversations to retell the same tales: they clap him on the back and share their cigarettes with him.

'You're writing a book?' Harry exclaims one night. 'That's a terrific thing. Truly a terrific thing. Tell me: what is this book about? Is it an adventure story or a love story?'

So I tell him that it's about the young men who grow up in South Central who are trying to get into the music business, about their lives and about the place they grow up in.

Harry's brow darkens. 'I grew up in South Central,' he says. 'Just on Crenshaw.' He mentions a junction somewhere around 50th.

'Really?' I say. 'All the times I've met you, I never knew that.'

'I don't know how you think you can do that,' he says.

'What?'

'I grew up there. What the *fuck* do you know about South Central?'

'Not much, I suppose,' I'm saying. I realize that the usually smiling, grinning, affable Harry has gone. He's furious at me.

'What the fuck do you know about it? I don't know how the fuck you think you can do that? It's impossible,' he says. 'You don't know a damned thing about the place.'

'Tell me what you mean,' I keep trying to say.

'You don't know one fucking thing about it. How can you write a book when you don't know anything about it? That is fucking arrogant.'

The barman, in his mid-twenties, is surprised at the outburst, but he comes up and says to me, 'Don't mind Harry. He likes a drink, that's all.'

'You can't write a book about it,' insists Harry. 'You don't know a single thing about it.'

'Calm down, Harry,' the barman orders. 'Calm down.'

C-DOUBLE-E

Herman enjoys taking a white boy around.

'You feel kind of out of place here?' says Herman, grinning. Earvin Magic Johnson Recreation Ground is on Avalon, north of El Segundo, in the heart of South Central. It's the Juneteenth weekend – an African–American holiday. It's a sort of black Independence Day: 19 June 1865 was the date Texas, the last state to declare emancipation, finally freed its slaves.

'Not many white people here,' Herman jokes again. None immediately visible, in fact. Dennis, the big DJ, rolls his eyes skywards, exasperated by the way Herman just babbles all the time. I guess he is embarrassed by the comment. Even if Herman obviously meant the comment lightly, the implication is that whites feel threatened when they're so far away from their own.

Herman is always hyperconscious of the fact that he's inviting me to places where there aren't many white people. One day, outside his apartment off King, he watched as a woman pulled out into the middle of the road, not even seeing a Cadillac driving north on Buckingham. 'Stop! Stop! Stop!' he shouted. The woman braked just in time to avoid a smash. Herman recalls: 'She wasn't looking at the traffic. She was just looking at you wondering what the hell a white person is doing around here.'

Despite the fact that it's the Juneteenth weekend, there aren't many people of any colour here in the park. A few Hispanic families sit under umbrellas. A line of elderly African–Americans sit patiently holding fishing rods over an artificial lake. Near a modest fun fair, a small stage has been set up in the sun. The event is sponsored by the County Recreation Department.

The show itself is a lame affair, but the small crowd of about 50 middle-aged women and listless children applaud each act politely. A Hispanic woman with more gusto than sense of pitch sings 'You Picked A Fine Time To Leave Me Lucille' to a karaoke tape. A dance group of African-American children called Tiny Toons come on next. Their choreographer chides them loudly from in front of the stage as they dance along to a couple of hip-hop tracks by Missy 'Misdemeanour' Elliot. By the side of the stage, a bored mariachi band, dressed to the nines in black leather and white cotton, chain-smoke as they await their turn.

And then the MC announces, with no shame at all: 'Everybody, I want you to please give a warm welcome to one of the biggest rap bands in the Southland. A Nu Creation!'

Afterwards Herman is buoyed up, as ever. The band played 'Nine Times Out Of Ten' and a new track I'd never heard before. Herman had written the backing track on his MPC 2000. 'What did it sound like?' he bubbles. 'Did it sound good?'

As they make their way back to Dennis's car a man from a family who have been picnicking about 50 yards from the stage shouts, 'You were good. You got a CD out?'

Herman smirks happily. 'Not yet. In a month we'll have one,' he promises, ever optimistic.

A decrepit-looking middle-aged guy comes up on a bicycle that's too small for him and asks them the same question. 'You got a record out?'

He tells them he has a record shop on 115th Street. 'When you get a record out, come and bring it to my store.'

'You got a card?' asks Herman.

'I think I got one left,' says the man. He ferrets around inside his jacket, pulls out a grubby wallet and hands over a battered business card.

Herman peers at it and says, 'This is for a bail-bond office.'

'It's a record shop on one side, a bail-bond office on the other,' says the man, as if that arrangement is perfectly normal. 'An' if you know anyone who needs a bail bond . . .'

Herman cracks up. 'No! I don't know anyone . . .'

BIG AL

'You have reached the 24-hour hotline of Hollywood Connections. We are currently conducting a nationwide search for the most exceptional spokesmodels and musical acts of all ages to perform for television film professionals, casting companies, record label A&R, producers, managers and potential investors . . .'

Another talent show. The preliminary heats are being held at the Roxy on Sunset Boulevard in Hollywood – one of the string of anodyne venues on the Strip usually used by labels to showcase rock bands. It's 10.30 p.m. and Camp Zero are on the stage, performing a new song, 'We're On A Mission'. As always they crowd the stage, all dressed in the blue fatigues which are so fashionable this summer. There are 65 acts on the bill tonight. There have been nervy, self-conscious girls, all attitude and make-up; and underconfident, chip-on-shoulder boys, caught like rabbits in the spotlight as they wait for their DAT tracks to start. Most betray their lack of experience. Some acts have the track shut off after just a few seconds and are hustled off stage for swearing.

'If there's any profanity,' insists the organizer, Ray Jarreau, 'don't let that fool you it's going to get you into the finals. On the last round we had about a dozen acts that were disqualified for using profanity.'

The profanity rule is a way of keeping the gangsta element from competing, or at least hobbling it so badly that it's unlikely to win. After 20 or so of the dour, hunched-shouldered performances that have filled the bill so far, Camp Zero are a breath of fresh air. As a touch of showmanship, they have brought electric torches on stage with them and are shining them at the crowd as they chant:

It's all going down at the Camp Ground . . .

Their performances improve every time. They lift the grim mood of the talent show briefly. And then a fight breaks out to the left of the stage.

The speed with which the crowd disperses at hip-hop shows when this happens is a sign of how bad things have been. The floor empties in a second to leave two boys, one belting the other in the side of the head, the other trying to protect himself. Women rush for the exit. Security is on top of the situation fast, and one of the fighters is being dragged out on to the sidewalk, punching the air and struggling, but out-muscled.

Already Camp Zero's T-Bob is calming things: 'Come on. Increase the peace. It's all good.'

Ray Jarreau joins him: 'Everything is going to be all right,' he says soothingly.

The DAT restarts, but the moment has passed. Kimmie G gets her turn on the mike, urging:

Take a trip on me in my cool Camp Z,

but their three minutes are up. 'Camp Zero. Camp Zero. Camp Zero,' the band chant into empty space, trying in vain to recapture the energy they had before the fight.

It takes Big Al, three acts later, to reignite the atmosphere. Dressed in a huge pair of beige trousers and a woollen hat, the big man launches into a manic version of 'Freez Up'. He runs around the stage like a madman, determined to be noticed, the DAT cranked up. Suddenly the evening is alight again. It's Al's high-speed ebullience that is so infectious:

Lyrical weed, you use speed of confidence
I'm in this game to maintain
I be flippin' flows like omelettes . . .

The Camp Zero click surge down to the front of the stage to cheer him on, grateful for the opportunity to dance and let their hair down. Few of the other performers on the bill have any idea of stagecraft: with so few clubs in Los Angeles putting on live hip hop, there aren't that many places to learn it outside of the talent shows. Halfway through his brief three minutes, with a well-practised theatrical gesture, Al whips off his woollen cap and shakes out his short dreadlocks, and a cheer goes up from the room.

Outside in the Hollywood night air, Camp Zero's affable manager, Duke, is not worried by their interrupted performance. He thinks he's found a backer for his group. The owner of an Inglewood limousine company, 'EJ' Jackson, has seen the band and likes them. He's told Duke he wants to set up a record label and put out Camp Zero's album.

'It's a done deal,' Duke says.

BABYBOY

I'm back in the hood, thinks Babyboy.

There are boxes, still unpacked, in the living room of the bungalow. Last night Marlene, Babyboy and the two kids moved from the apartment in Culver City into the guest house at the back of Marlene's mother's house.

The upside of the move is that Babyboy is living rent-free back in his beloved dub at Wilton and King. But the downside is that now he's relying on Marlene's family for charity. The house is small – one bedroom, a petite living room and dining area, and a workable kitchen. Guest houses, crammed into the backyards of family houses, are a common feature in Los Angeles. This one looks like it was built sometime in the fifties. You reach it by a small metal gate to the left of the main house.

Babyboy hasn't slept properly in three or four days now. His capacity for staying awake is remarkable. The last few nights he's been driving around, getting stoned, going to parties in Hollywood, visiting the house up in the hills where Paul Goldsby has been trying to conclude the final deals to find distribution for his movie. That lifestyle seems so close right now.

After a few days awake, Babyboy's brain seems to work overtime. He says aloud, 'I'm in this bitch. Whoop whoop whoop. I'm maxing.' Everything appears more intense to him. He sits in the small living room of his new home listening to a new backing track he has written. One of the first things they set up was the big stereo, putting it up on the shelves that now seem to fill an entire wall of this small living room.

Babyboy loves this track. It's something different. Through friends, he's met some new producers who are interested in working with him. They're a couple of Iranians who live in the Valley, called Bruce and Benny Ferat. Like so many others, they are interested in breaking into the hip-hop scene. They've written this track for Babyboy and he's just starting to add lyrics to it. The music has a sort of smooth, wide-open feeling, as if it was culled from a seventies movie soundtrack. Babyboy thinks he'll call it 'Fast Lane'. He has some words going round his head that he might use that seem to fit: 'Dippin' out of traffic, tryin' to survive in the fast lane . . .' Something like that. 'If you can't handle the speed then you shouldn't try and survive in the fast lane.'

He wants it to have a sort of *Miami Vice* flavour. He thinks that maybe it should be about a drug dealer trying to make cash, flippin' ten bucks to make a thousand. He tries a verse out loud:

Started off with just two ounces of llello [cocaine],
Sitting on the corner trying to make it flip
So you got a dollar, I can make you holler.

He's not really got the words down yet. My shit is going to be hot, he thinks. I know my shit is going to be hot.

'Wassup?' he says, looking at the door. Budman stands outside: the big man has managed to scrounge a ride from the apartment where he lives in the Jungle and has come to hang out.

'This yours?' he asks, stepping inside as 'Fast Lane' plays.

'Fo' sheezy,' says Babyboy proudly. 'It's, like, some new twist I got going on. You like it?'

It's a hot, lazy Sunday in June. On afternoons like this, there is time to waste. 'Hey,' says Babyboy. 'You got a blunt on you?'

Budman never seems to have anything on him, least of all money, so they take Marlene's car, ride over to a nearby gas station and buy a couple of dollar Garcia Y Vega English Coronas. Babyboy rummages in the coat closet where he keeps his weed and emerges with a small polythene bag, dropping it in front of Budman, who sets to work slicing the cigar from one end to the other, and then pulling out all the tobacco leaves, to replace them with grass.

A young woman, smartly dressed in a sensible kind of way, knocks for Marlene: it's one of her girlfriends. 'She's in the bedroom,' says Babyboy. 'Marlene?' he shouts. 'Betty's here.'

'I'll be out right now,' comes Marlene's voice.

The young woman stands, waiting for her friend. Deciding he should listen to the whole tape one more time, Babyboy goes over to the stereo to rewind it. 'Uh, Betty, this is Rahiem,' he says as he moves across the room.

Budman looks up from the small glass table where he's carefully building his joint and nods at her. From his reddened eyes, it looks as if he's already been smoking today. 'Hi,' says Betty politely.

Marlene bustles out of the bedroom with Chanel under one arm and a bag of diapers under the other. 'I'm going out now,' she says.

'You takin' the car?' asks Babyboy.

'Yes,' answers Marlene, gazing with what looks like resignation at Budman and her dining table covered in weed.

'OK,' says Babyboy, with a deliberately sickly smile. 'Goodbye, *sweetheart*,' he adds, in as treacly voice as he can manage. When her back's turned, he sticks his tongue out.

He's found the track he wanted. 'Janine', the one he recorded with Kimmie G, comes on:

Met this bitch named Janine
Age 19
Had her own green
Sniffed her on the team . . .

'I fucked Kimmie G again,' announces Babyboy, with a little, only-slightly-ashamed grin on his face. 'I wasn't going to, just like the first time, but you know . . .' He giggles. She's a fine woman, he thinks.

Kimmie G's chance may be finally coming around too. Camp Zero's deal with the Scooter label has finally gone through. The summer is full of promise.

As Babyboy sees it, 'Janine' is about how you meet a beautiful woman – even though you've already got a woman of your own – and she starts flirting with you and one thing leads to another. And then you realize that you don't want to go through with it, and you try to leave it alone, but that thing just keeps on happening because she doesn't let you go and so you fight with her, and she fights with your baby momma . . . He insists the song's not based on real life.

It's all because of you why I did what I did
I found through your people about your baby momma and your kid
That you never told me about,

raps Kimmie G, her icy syllables shining with girl-gangsta contempt

And now I'm feelin' kinda bad about knockin' the bitch out.

Her delivery is vicious. She enjoyed her verse too. She always imagined she was going to be a solo performer. Sometimes it's hard, taking her turn along with the rest of them in Camp Zero. The track gave her a chance to let her hair down.

Budman finishes making the blunt, and is about to put it to his lips to light it.

'Hey,' protests Babyboy. It's his grass, after all. Budman passes it over, and Babyboy takes it and lights it himself, and they listen to the music, passing the blunt back and forth. Babyboy's small black cat jumps up on to the window ledge and stares at the two of them. The tape plays through until it reaches 'Fast Lane' again.

Budman nods his head discerningly. 'That's tight, nigga.' He inhales, coughs and splutters. His veiny eyes water up. Suddenly his wheezes turn to giggles. It's the weed. Seeing the boxes of Marlene and Babyboy's possessions on the floor has reminded him of something funny. When he stops laughing, he asks Babyboy out of nowhere, 'What was your first sexual experience . . . How old were you?'

'I was . . .' Babyboy stops and thinks. 'I was 17.'

Budman says. 'Hell, *I* was 13, or 14.' He pauses and tries to suck something from the last centimetre of the blunt, then laughs again and starts to tell his tale: 'This big woman – shit, really big woman – she was 350lb – said, "I'll give you $20 if you come back to my house and move some shit for me."'

Babyboy leans back in his chair. All this weed is making him hungry. He has to find something to eat soon. Maybe some red snapper from Stevie's On The Strip.

'Twenty bucks was a lot of money for me back then . . .' Budman is saying. Babyboy has heard this story plenty of times before, about how a woman picked up the young Budman in her car and drove him to her apartment, and when he got there there was just one box in the middle of a room. The big fat woman told him to move it into another room. Is that all? thought Budman happily, and asked for his $20. 'No,' she said. 'You still ain't earned it. You got to do something more.'

'What?' he wondered.

'You gonna have sex with me.'

Budman is giggling again, remembering the story. He would have run out of the apartment right then, only he was all dressed in blue, because Wilton was a Crip neighbourhood, and this woman lived in a district that was run by Blood gangs. He was convinced that if he went out on the streets dressed like that, someone would kill him, for sure.

He had only one option. To fuck her. So he did it, and then she drove him home.

'Oh, did she smell. She stank. I couldn't get the fuckin' smell off me for a week. I got home and I washed my dick with Ajax. Still couldn't get the smell of her off.'

Babyboy, too, is laughing now.

The phone goes. Babyboy stops laughing and picks it up. It's this guy he knows who used to be a musician. Now he's working for one of the major labels. He lives out in the Valley and he wants to buy some chronic. Can Babyboy get him some? For Babyboy, it's all about what he calls transactions. When he's making transactions in the music industry, he's happy. He stands there with the phone, wishing he still had his old Mercury Cougar and wondering how he can get over to the Valley now Marlene's driven off somewhere in her car. Maybe he'll wait till she comes back.

Two days later he's looking for that fucking tape. He can't find it anywhere. Budman must have stolen it. He probably copied it and is selling the bootlegs right now.

'Hey, Wes' Side. What's going on?'

'Nothing much.'

'You want to go down Crenshaw this Sunday?'

'I'd love to.'

'Hell, yeah. I know. You want to go the 'Shaw and find some pussy?' he taunts. 'Hey, wait, I want to ask you something. You got my tape?'

'Which tape?'

'My tape, you know. The tracks for *The Lesson*. My tracks.'

'No. Last I saw of it was in your tape player at home.'

'Hell. Somebody stolen it then. Shit. By now somebody will be making copies and they'll be all over the hood.'

Bootleg tapes are part of the currency in South Central. Tapes of unreleased Tupac bootlegs sell for $15 or $20 each. But I can't see anyone paying money to hear Babyboy's music yet.

'Budman stole it.'

'No,' I say. 'Budman wouldn't do that.'

'Hell he wouldn't.'

TIBU

Boldface, the Italian Stallion, isn't going to get much of a chance to be a stripper this summer. His family have decided to send him away to live with relatives out of town. They're worried about him getting into trouble in Bellflower.

A few days before he goes away, Boldface decides to visit Keyna's apartment on Cal State campus, where Tibu is staying full time now.

Tibu likes living on the campus. Cal State is an oasis at the southern end of Central Avenue, a wide green space in the middle of the inner city. Tibu doesn't have much money since he was sacked from his job at USC Hospital, but he doesn't have to pay any rent here. With the small amount of cash he makes from hustling, he can still afford to visit Todd's studio every week or so.

Keyna's parents were OK about Tibu moving in with her at first, but relations soured when he and Keyna borrowed her stepfather's car 'for a few hours' and ended up keeping it for the whole weekend. After that, her stepfather said he wanted to meet Tibu and have a talk with him. It never happened, but Tibu says he would have 'fucked his ass up' if he'd had to.

Keyna and Tibu first met when Tibu was 16. He first saw Keyna with another girlfriend at the bus terminal. He approached her friend first, but she said she had 'something like a boyfriend', so he talked to Keyna instead. It wasn't until one year and four months ago that they started going out properly.

These days Tibu likes to boast in front of his friends about how Keyna sucks his dick. 'Anything good happened to you recently?' 'Yeah, my girlfriend gave me head.'

He sounds oddly proud, too, when he tells his friends about all the arguments they always have. 'She just *bullshits*. Her whinin' that shit is the worst.'

Sometimes he plays her the tracks he's recorded. She'll say in a deadpan, unimpressed sort of voice, 'That's cool.'

Tibu snaps back, 'Shut your lyin' ass up. You lyin' motherfucker. It's better than cool.'

Until she got her place studying at Cal State, he never really considered going to university. Now he thinks he'd like to go. It's not the quality of education that interests him, just the fact that the campus has a free recording studio. He'd have to go back to school, though. He never graduated from school when he was younger.

Keyna's apartment in block M is small. It has two bedrooms, and they share with another female student. Keyna and Tibu argue a lot.

'Damn!' Tibu is shouting. 'Shut up. Shut the fuck up. That's fucked up. You're just trippin'.'

Keyna has accused Tibu of looking a little too interested in her room-mate. 'I was *not* looking at her!' he protests.

She puts up with a lot from Tibu. Today she just buttons her mouth and refuses to speak to him. Tibu hates that. 'Talk to me,' he orders her. 'Talk to me!'

She purses her mouth still more. Tibu has a temper. His anger rises up. 'If you don't start talkin' to me,' he says, enraged, 'I'm going to throw you off the balcony.'

He could easily pick her up and toss her over. It's not that she's particularly small – it's just that Tibu is big. When he still doesn't hear her saying anything, he grabs Keyna and hauls her right over the apartment's first-floor balcony and holds her there. It's only about 15 or 20 feet to the ground, but it would still hurt her badly.

Keyna screams. Tibu notices people staring at him, shocked, from the block opposite. He pulls her back over the balcony.

Later they make up. Tibu rolls a blunt, because he's expecting Boldface to arrive any minute. And when there is a knock at the door, he goes to open it, expecting it to be him. Instead it's the police. Ah shit, Tibu thinks, wishing he'd asked who it was first. Someone from the campus must have seen him holding Keyna over the balcony. He claims he would never have dropped her, that he was only joking, but he knows they're going to arrest him, so he just walks out of the room, arms behind his back, ready to be handcuffed.

BABYBOY

On Saturday, Babyboy rides over to Jayo Felony's house in Beverly Wood, south of Beverly Hills. He's working on keeping his connections alive.

Jayo Felony is a star. He had a hit back in '95 with the single 'Sherm Stick' and now the hip-hop label Def Jam is renting a $1000-a-month apartment for him and his producer T-Phunk while he completes his second album. T-Phunk is a New Jersey producer whom Babyboy is eager to enlist to help him complete his demos for *The Lesson*. 'T-Phunk has been around some of the best on the East Coast, and he told me my shit is tight,' says Babyboy. 'That motivated me.'

Jayo sits on the couch in his living room, a slight yet strong-looking man, his hair braided tightly. He took the name 'Felony' after being sent to jail for dealing in crack: Jayo used to run with the Crips in San Diego, where he grew up in the housing projects. He saw the word carved on a desk in prison and decided to appropriate it. 'I'm not ashamed of my past,' he says. 'But I'm not happy I went to jail. I don't feel that's something to brag on.'

He has all but finished work on his second album: now he's waiting for it to be released. The album could be his big break from the underground of 'Sherm Stick' into the mainstream. It's been hard for all the gangsta rappers like him since Tupac and Biggie were killed. People have been reluctant to put out product from the harder edge of rap.

'It's got calmer,' Jayo says. 'Everybody's getting back, getting focused on telling your great grandchildren, yeah, I was doing that. This is how we got this. That's what it's all about. You got to break that cycle of not passing 25, you know what I mean.'

Babyboy listens respectfully. Jayo says he's going to call the album *Justice Against Y'All Oppressors*, an acronym of his name, and also the title of a track he's recorded with Ice Cube and the Bay Area rapper E-40.

Jayo's beefs with the police these days are less serious than they were in San Diego, but he still has his problems. Last Sunday he had planned to perform a show with the group AllFrumTha I at the Vision Theater, in Leimert Park. AllFrumTha I's added novelty value is based on the fact that one of their members is an ex-Crip, while another is a former Blood.

Every summer on Sunday nights, the 'Crenshaw Cruise' starts. And every summer, the LAPD tries to close it down. The day of the show, the police erected barricades to close off Crenshaw Boulevard. The show had to be called off.

'They're not only shutting it down, they're harassing,' Jayo complains. 'Within ten blocks from the freeway to where the

251

show was at, all you see is cars getting towed. I saw, like, eight or nine people's cars getting towed at one time. I guess they're having fun,' he says bitterly.

TIBU

'Hey.'

'Tibu?'

'Yeah.'

'What's up?' I have not heard from him from a few days.

A sigh floats down the phone line. 'I been in a heap of trouble. The police locked me up.'

'How long for?'

'Just a night.'

'What did you do?'

'Drugs . . . I had some weed.'

Slowly at first, Tibu explains his version of what happened on Cal State campus; how another student snitched on him for holding Keyna over the balcony, and how the police came in and found him smoking a blunt. 'I wasn't going to hurt her,' he insists. 'I was just messin'. She knew that.'

The police found his grass; now he has to go to court. When they released him the next morning after the arrest he headed straight back to Cal State. A couple of days later a letter arrived from the campus police. Because he was seen acting violently towards a student, he was banned from going anywhere near Keyna's apartment; if he contravened this order, he would be arrested again.

He discovered they really meant it when the police came to block M shortly afterwards and found him there. They arrested him again. Now he's going to have to pay another fine.

BABYBOY

Every form of pop music has a sacred geography. New Orleans jazz has Bourbon Street, the mods have Carnaby Street, psychedelia has Haight-Ashbury. For fans of West Coast hip hop, there is Crenshaw Boulevard.

Central Avenue, the great wild street of the first half of the century, was already losing its shine in the late forties. Rich African-Americans had already been pushing westwards, to the more fashionable west side. As Chester Himes wrote: 'Past Western, this was the West Side. When you asked a Negro where he lived, and he said on the West Side, that was supposed to mean that he was better than the Negroes who lived on the South Side: it was like white folks giving a Beverly Hills address.'

As soon as the deed restrictions were ruled illegal at the end of the forties, the epicentre of South Central moved westwards. Soon Crenshaw Boulevard began to replace Central Avenue as the South Central meeting place.

On an ordinary weekday Crenshaw will disappoint. For the most of its length it's just another unremarkable South Central thoroughfare. It runs from Long Beach in the south up to Wilshire Boulevard, where it ends. The fact that Crenshaw stops dead at the northern edge of South Central – at the point where the racial mix starts to change rapidly – gives the street its own significance. Since the fifties, Crenshaw has been a street which African-Americans can think of as pretty much their own.

Other than that, the only other notable peculiarity of Crenshaw's geography comes around the junction with Slauson: at this point it becomes the widest street in Los Angeles, divided by a central reservation, laid out long ago with a grand ambition that somehow it hasn't yet lived up to, except once a week, on Sundays, when the street really comes alive.

During a Sunday's daylight hours, Crenshaw's sidewalks are full of respectable churchgoers. Huge crowds, immaculate in their Sunday best, pour out of the Church of God in Christ, or throng outside the smaller storefronts that have been transformed into places of worship. On the corners, a few crisp-suited followers of Louis Farrakhan hold up copies of *The Final Call*, hoping to win some converts, jostling for space with Christian evangelists who clutch picket signs that proclaim the gospel.

As the day winds on to the afternoon, the atmosphere changes dramatically. The shiny cars start to appear: the Sunday-night cruise is about to begin. From Adams, past the Crenshaw–Baldwin Hills Mall, through Leimert Park and down to Imperial, the youth come out in their shiniest clothes and cars to see and be seen.

Babyboy found the tape after all. Budman hadn't stolen it: it was in the player in Marlene's car.

On Sunday I drive up to Wilton to pick up Babyboy. I wait at our usual meeting place. In blue, someone's sprayed 'HARLEM CR1P' – with the figure '1' replacing the 'I' – on the back of the 'Stop' sign at the junction with Leighton.

It's dark by the time Babyboy arrives with a stocky, smiling friend I don't recognize. 'You mind if this guy comes along too? He's a friend of Jayo Felony's, visiting from Jersey.' The young man shakes hands and gets in the back of the ancient VW Rabbit convertible I'm driving; Babyboy introduces me, but I don't catch the guy's name.

'He wants to come along and see what Crenshaw's all about, where all the beautiful west side girls is at,' Babyboy explains. The New Jersey boy giggles, and steps into the back of my car; Babyboy gets in the front.

'Where you going, Kimeyo?' calls one of the guys standing on the corner of Wilton and Leighton.

'Where we goin'? We goin' to cruise the 'Shaw,' Babyboy shouts loudly, happily.

'The cops have got Crenshaw locked up, man.'

'They'll let us through. We got the white guy with us,' Babyboy laughs.

I put the car into drive. 'How long are you here?' I ask the stranger in the back.

''Bout a week.' He explains that he's a concert promoter; he's here trying to do some business with Jayo.

'You like it here?' I ask.

'It's different. We don't have palm trees back in Jersey,' he laughs. He says that sometimes he feels like he's in a movie, driving around South Central.

'Would you move here?'

He looks at me like I'm an innocent. 'I don't think this is a good place to live. You know all the colours and shit? It's a little too crazy for me.' He sits back. I drive off down Wilton, turning on to King. 'You know what? It's real cold back here,' New Jersey complains. 'And I've only got a T-shirt on.'

It's June, but the night air feels cold because the top is down. In the front with the heater on it's warm, but the guy is starting to shiver. I turn left on to Crenshaw, heading south, and pull over next to a liquor store so Babyboy and I can put the top up.

When Babyboy gets back in the passenger seat, he says to me, 'You turned off the engine?' I look at him blankly. Babyboy never switches off the engine when he's in a neighbourhood he doesn't trust. He admonishes me: 'You don't do that. Got to leave the motor running, case you have to move off in a hurry.'

'Oh,' I say. 'Right.'

The LAPD are low-key tonight. The barricades that had stopped Jayo from performing his show at the Vision Theater a few weeks earlier are nowhere to be seen.

In 1994 the City Council passed an ordinance which allowed police to shut down a three-and-a-half-mile stretch of Crenshaw.

The police have been trying to crack down on the Sunday-night cruise every summer for years now, starting the season off by erecting roadblocks, issuing parking tickets and towing away illegally parked cars, and searching the cruisers for drugs and weapons.

Residents resent the noise of the cranked-up stereos, the jammed-up traffic and the occasional groups of gangsters, flicking hand signs to announce their presence. The business community, trying to promote the Crenshaw corridor as a newly thriving, high-growth district, resent the image that comes with the whole jamboree. Local stores complain that they have to shut down or face their parking lots being filled with loud boys in cars who scare away the regulars.

But for the youth of South Central, Crenshaw on a Sunday night is like watching a play and being on stage simultaneously. It's the time when African-American and Latino youth gets to rule three miles of tarmac. The Crenshaw Cruise is a carnival that anyone can join, and it's free, at least as long as you're not one of the many who rent a flashy car just for the day in the hope of impressing girls as they drive down the street.

These days the fashion is mostly for new models: Mercedes, Acuras and Lexuses. There are fewer low-riders than there used to be in the cruise's seventies and eighties heyday, though you'll still see old Chevrolet Impalas bouncing proudly down the street. These cars have been carefully customized. Hidden in the trunk are rows and rows of car batteries to power the hydraulic pumps that make the cars jump like carriages on a funfair ride. LA was the world's first true car town; it's still the place in which having the most impressive wheels is crucial.

The origins of the Crenshaw Cruise go back to the fifties, when African-American boys who lived in what was the wealthier west side of South Central were putting their own spin on the white fashion for 'car clubs' by forming their own associations.

Those who remained on the east side, and in the southern end of South Central, in Watts and Compton, were now regarded as the poorer relations of the showy, well-heeled people from the west side. It was the west-siders who had enough money for cars. This was in the days before Bloods and Crips, when gangs like the Low Riders, the Road Devils, the Avenues and the Watts Farmers scuffled for territory. The car clubs formed one of the prototypes for the gangs that emerged in the sixties. One of the car-club era's gangs was the legendary west-side grouping the Slausons – forerunners to the original Crips – who took their name from the Slauson Boulevard area. Earlier, Slauson – like so many LA streets – had taken its name from one of the city's founding oligarchs, J. S. Slauson, a late-nineteenth-century land developer and director of the Los Angeles Bank. In this way, the names of millionaires and upright citizens are purloined and given new meaning by those at the opposite end of the social spectrum.

Today the car clubs are largely gone but boys in new clothes still stand proudly beside their 4WDs, pumping out music from their tapes. If the police let them park for long enough, they'll dance around the cars as it gets towards midnight.

'I bet there isn't anywhere in the whole world like Crenshaw,' Babyboy whoops. 'Look at those females,' he hoots joyfully at a group of girls.

Some cars are parked by the side of the road, with their stereos turned up as loud as they can. Boys in baggy pants slouch around them, trying to impress the 'Crenshaw cuties' – as the local rap group called the Pharcyde once called the girls who come here on a Sunday night. The girls stand around and collect phone numbers of boys who want to hook up with them. Later they complete the ritual by comparing lists with their girlfriends and boasting about who has gathered the most numbers.

Babyboy points out various groups: one packed Jeep contains members of the Crip Rollin' 30s, from Babyboy's neighbourhood.

Huddled around another car are 18th Street members; since the truce of '92 this gang has emerged as one of the most powerful in Los Angeles. Like Babyboy says, there is nowhere in the world quite like Crenshaw when it's like this:

Any nigga that claim they bossin'
Why don't you bring your ass on over to Crenshaw and Slauson
Take a ride through the hood . . .

rhymed Kurupt on Dr Dre's album *The Chronic*.

'I want to shoot my first video, right here on a Sunday night . . .' says Babyboy, still bubbling. Then: 'Know what? They're trying to change the name of Crenshaw.'

'To what?' I ask.

'To Malcolm X Boulevard,' he says disgustedly. 'Malcolm X Boulevard. Shit. What they want to mess with that for? That's tradition.'

This is his special street. He's irate at the idea that the uniqueness of Crenshaw could be subsumed into what is to him a vaguer notion: the idea of creating a national African-American history

'It's always been the 'Shaw,' Babyboy complains. Always since 1904, at least, when it was named after yet another oligarch, the wealthy entrepreneur George L. Crenshaw, popularly known as the Banana King because part of his fortune was based on importing the fruit.

'Shit. "I'm gonna meet you on X?" What does that mean?' he fumes. 'Like King. It was better when it was Santa Barbara Boulevard.'

All over America, streets have had their name changed to honour the memory of the civil-rights leader Martin Luther King. Inevitably they are always in black areas. The young comedian Chris Rock, who's filled Richard Pryor's shoes in recent years, tells a dark joke about it: 'When he was alive, Martin Luther King stood for non-violence. Now he's dead, he's a street. And I don't care where you are in America, but if you stand on Martin Luther King, there's going to be some violence going down.'

For Babyboy, the change has made his neighbourhood sound just like any other part of black America. 'They changed that King around '83,' he fumes. 'They even changed Santa Barbara High to Martin Luther King High. Santa Barbara is better, don't you think? It's much more . . . real.'

Santa Barbara Boulevard he could claim for his own; but King Boulevard is such a common name now, it means nothing to him. It's still all about geography and identity: who you are and who you want to be.

'Make a U-turn here,' Babyboy orders, and we head back north-wards.

At the lights we pull up next to three young girls driving a silver import. Babyboy leans across me towards them and shouts, 'Hey, girls. What you doin'?'

The girls turn, check us out, then pointedly stare straight forward until the lights change. They accelerate away up the road.

Ahead, a car has been pulled up by the police. Babyboy laughs and says, 'They'll probably think we're two black guys who kidnapped a white guy.'

'And that's what I'll tell them,' I laugh.

Babyboy looks horrified. 'Hey, don't joke, man. Don't joke. I mean it. That's fuckin' serious.'

We pass the police car. 'Shit. If they stop you, you're going to spend 15 minutes up against the wire, even if you got your licence, your insurance and your registration with you.'

At which moment I realize that I've left my car rental documents at home, so I don't have my registration with me. Being white and foreign, I don't bother much about these bureaucratic details.

Getting into trouble with the police isn't a major worry for me, normally. Now I wish I'd put them in the car.

On 92.3 The Beat the DJ is playing Militia's 'Burn':

Ride, until the sun burns your eyes
Keep drivin' till it sets on the west side
Ride, just ride all night
Just ride, just ride all night . . .

At Adams, Babyboy tells me to turn at a gas station forecourt. The gas stations and their parking lots become meeting spots on the cruise. 'We're not stopping here. This is Blood territory right here,' says Babyboy.

We head back south. This is what the night is: driving up and down the 'Shaw, looking at the boys and the girls, seeing old friends, hoping to gather a few phone numbers, or find out where a party is going to be. There are so few places where young men can hang out together in South Central, can meet new friends and pick up girls. There is little public space, and local parks routinely become the territories of individual gangs. The bigger streets, like Crenshaw, which often form the borderlands between gang turfs, are neutral ground, as long as you stick to the street itself. This lack of safe space for people to meet feeds back into the gang animosities: as one gang counsellor once told me, if there were more situations in which members of different gangs could socialize together, there would be less mutual fear.

'Hey, take a left here. Pull up on this forecourt.' Babyboy has recognized someone at another gas station at the corner of Brynhurst. He gets out and walks over towards a parked car, leaving me and New Jersey. This time I leave the engine running.

A black 600 series Mercedes moves slowly away from the pumps: the driver, a man in his thirties, is eyeing the girls. His car has ultrathin tyres on 20-inch bright-chrome rims. Lines from one of the tracks Khop recently recorded with Ice Cube come to mind:

> *I see you, over there, looking like something's wrong*
> *'Cause I'm over here, sittin' on some chrome . . .*

'Sittin' on chrome' has become one of the catchphrases of the past couple of years. This year, the most important thing to customize on your car is your wheels. Brooklyn-born rapper Masta Ace not only put out an album called *Sittin' On Chrome*, but he's opened his own wheel shop. He declares: 'Whether you're pushing a '98 S600 Benz or something a little more modest, you want to make sure your whip is buttery. And one thing that will make your car stand out from the rest is the rims you tuck under your ride . . .'

It is all about – to use Masta Ace's magnificent phrase – making sure your whip is the butteriest. Standard car rims are between 16 and 17 inches. Older low-riders might replace these with 14- or 15-inch rims and fatter tyres. The fashion among the 'ballers' now is to push up the rim diameter as far as they can, leaving space for only a few inches of rubber. It's an expensive fashion. As with everything, it's important that you sport the right brand. A set of four 18-inch Brabus rims will cost you $2500. Or you can pay an extra $200 for a set of coveted 20-inch Syncros.

Mechanically, there is a drawback to this automotive peacockery. Performance cars are hobbled by the thin tyres these massive rims need. Understandably, the fashion for big chrome wheels doesn't cut as much ice back east in New York, where the roads are so much less welcoming. I'm the duller sort who sees a car merely as a means of transport. To me, the Benz's large chrome wheels and thin black tyres make the vehicle look like a game of consequences in which someone's drawn in a set of wheels without seeing the car.

All the same, the butteriness of his whip is working for the man who drives the Merc. He calls over to a young woman who's with some of her friends in another car. She gets out and wanders over to him, deliberately slowly, like she's impressed but trying not to look it. She's beautiful, dressed in a one-piece black nylon bodysuit, with long, straightened hair. When she finally reaches the car she leans slowly into the driver-side window, facing away from us.

New Jersey and I have been watching the whole performance. 'Hey,' he says excitedly, looking at the girl as she bends over, ass towards us. 'Look at that. She's not wearing any drawers!'

He's right. As the nylon on her backside stretches, it becomes transparent, revealing the round skin of each buttock as she leans into the Benz's pale leather interior.

'I don't believe it,' he shouts happily. 'She's not wearing any fuckin' drawers.'

Babyboy brings over two of the boys he recognized earlier. One of them, a short, angular-looking guy with long braids that poke out from under his woollen cap, holds out his hand. He wears neatly pressed trousers, with the fly fully unzipped and no belt. It's a style thing. The trousers are continually slipping down to the bottom of his striped boxer shorts, before he yanks them back up again.

'This is Badazz,' says Babyboy.

Badazz is an up-and-coming LA rapper. His career has recently been given a huge boost by Snoop Dogg, who's guested on a new track, 'We Be Puttin' It Down', which has become a much-bootlegged pre-release cassette around South Central. Babyboy is moving again, keeping his connections warm.

The 600 pulls off the forecourt, leaving the girl alone. New Jersey saunters over to her as casually as he can and starts chatting.

Badazz and Babyboy are in earnest conversation. Babyboy drops Jayo's name and Badazz looks interested. The rumours are out that Jayo's album is going to be a big one. Badazz is interested in meeting him, maybe doing something together.

'Oh yeah. I'll hook you up,' says Babyboy. 'Sure.' He says they can ride over to Jayo's apartment later tonight. Babyboy is always working, keeping the hook-ups going. Maybe one day he'll get the payback.

'You in the entertainment industry?' Badazz's lieutenant asks him.

'That's right,' says Babyboy. 'I got a production company.'

'What's the name of your company?'

'N Entertainment.'

'M Entertainment?'

'No,' says Babyboy. 'N. Like this.' He turns and lowers the neck of his shirt to show the big five-inch circle with the letter 'N' in it that he had tattooed there two years ago.

'Oh, I see. That's serious.'

'Serious,' says Babyboy sombrely. 'Yes, it is.'

'Hey,' says New Jersey, returning excitedly with a scrap of paper. 'I got her phone number. I got her fucking phone number.'

17

Flesh and Blood

TIBU

Now Tibu is homeless. He is facing two court appearances and his only possessions are a few clothes, some tapes, a notebook full of lyrics and his pager.

Yesterday he decided to go on General Relief. He went to the GR office and queued up from nine in the morning. It wasn't until three that they finally processed his claim. Eventually they gave him some vouchers to stay at a hotel – the Magnolia in Long Beach. But that's too far away, so Keyna is now paying for him to stay for a couple of nights at the Willow Tree Hotel at the southern end of Central Avenue, just on the other side of the 91 freeway from Cal State campus.

At the GR office, Tibu had looked around at all the other claimants and had thought: This is something else. All of the people who were there had looked like losers to him. Everyone had the same refrain: 'The moment I get my money, I'm going to flip it.' Flipping it: the entrepreneurial dream of the perfect hustle in which a buck makes ten, a gram of cocaine makes a kilo.

BABYBOY

In summer, when it's hot like this, Babyboy takes off his T-shirt and shoes the moment he gets inside the small house. It's stifling in the living room, and his torso is still in good shape from his days in the Marines. They have put a fan on the ledge of one of the small open windows, to try to make the air circulate through the small windows.

Babyboy and Marlene are fighting a lot. Maybe it's the weather; or maybe it's because Babyboy resents the fact that he's living off the charity of her parents now. This morning he found her wearing a pair of his track pants. He's furious. 'I just don't like her going through my stuff.'

When he goes to lay his breakfast out on the small, round, glass dining table, he finds there are still dishes in the sink. 'Marlene,' he calls. 'You haven't done the dishes.'

'I haven't had time to do the dishes yet,' she complains.

'Whatever,' replies Babyboy furiously.

Now Marlene has had enough. She raises her voice, starts shouting at him. 'You say I don't do anything but you don't do anything around this place. All you do is complain. Why don't you do something around here?'

Babyboy shakes his head and looks darkly at her.

'The next time you ask why something didn't get done, I'll give the same answer you always give: "I didn't get around to it," ' she says, mocking Babyboy's drawl. Then she screams at him: 'I still haven't got around to washing the motherfuckin' dishes.'

'Thank you, Marlene,' says Babyboy through thinned lips.

But there's no stopping her now. She stamps out of the house.

Babyboy raises a middle finger at her back as she crosses the tiny yard to her family's house.

Her parting line is the most vicious: 'You're always talking about the things you're doing. The things you're gonna do . . .'

RAH

Rah just made the 'dub one' – he is 21 years old. 'Betcha thought I'd never make it,' says the message on his answerphone. Sometimes he wasn't too sure he would either. 'Leave me a message or hit me on my hip.'

'Hit me on my hip' means 'Page me', pagers being traditionally designed to be worn on the belt. Rah still talks to Silas on the phone. He still likes to think that they're part of a team. In reality he works alone now. He is used to doing things himself: he has been doing it most of his life.

Rah still talks about Josiah a lot. It's as if after all these months he's still obsessed with trying to put everything right. He still writes Josiah's name everywhere, on the back of the flyers he hands out, on the side of his cap, on the elaborate promotion displays he sets up at King Records on Crenshaw: 'In memory of Josiah.' On his answerphone now, he ends his message: 'We'll never forget you. We're always keeping your spirit alive. We're gonna innovate in '98. We're not gonna hate, we're gonna create.'

He talks to Josiah all the time in his head. 'Yo, man. I wish you was here right now, man. I wish you could see how I'm doing right now.' It's still back-breaking work, but Transit Promotions, as he calls it now, is picking up.

BIG AL

An MC called Blind Method is struggling through a rap, 'Why Do I Sometimes Break Down And Cry?':

For my little brother, R.I.P., who got hit in a drive-by . . .

The audience is ignoring his rap to his dead brother. It has been a long day.

At the Roosevelt Hotel in Hollywood, the finals of Ray Jarreau's Hollywood Connections hip-hop competition are ending. In its heyday, the Roosevelt was once one of the finest hotels on Hollywood Boulevard, and it still has a grandeur about it. Entrants have sold tickets at $25 each to their relatives and friends to fund tonight's show. Duke, Camp Zero's spindly, businesslike and besuited Jamaican manager, thinks that it's between his group and Big Al. On the Sunday afternoon, the hip-hop performers have a last chance to perform upstairs in an unatmospheric, brightly lit, formal hotel room.

Blind Method stomps off stage, furious that the small crowd talked through his act. However sincere the sentiment, it was a lacklustre performance. 'Niggas ain't got no attention span,' the stand-up comedian who is hosting the show commiserates with the rapper. 'Two minutes and niggas are ready to go to Roscoe's,' he giggles.

It's Camp Zero's turn. In contrast to Blind Method's sombre rap, Kimmie G and the boys perform a wild, if unruly version of 'Whoop Whoop':

You work all day and the shit don't stop,
But the party ain't over till six o'clock,
Whoop whoop!

T-Bob strides around the stage, waving an unfurled umbrella. A group of fans dressed in blue Camp Zero T-shirts crowd the stage to dance with them. On the back of the shirts is the logo of Scooter Records – 'EJ' Jackson's new label. Camp Zero's single is going to be Scooter's first release.

T-Bob takes the mike and booms, 'Do my ladies run this motherfucker?'

'Hell yeah!'

'Do my niggas run this motherfucker?'

'Hell yeah!'

They have abandoned Jarreau's 'no cussing' rule. Camp Zero don't seem to care whether they win or lose. They're just here to have fun.

When they finish, the DJ puts on Busta Rhymes's 'Notorious' while he waits for the next act to appear. But Camp Zero, hyped up, refuse to stop. Off stage, they push aside the chairs and start dancing on the carpet. Others join them. An ebullient Kimmie G reverses the usual hip-hop gender roles, bending boys over on the dance floor and pretending to spank them, thrusting her groin at them.

On stage, the stand-up comedian who's acting as MC tries to restore order. 'This is fun, isn't it? Hey, you in the suit,' he calls to Duke. 'What you wearing that for? Y'all still from *Compton*,' he mocks.

'But seriously,' he continues, 'there's some dope shit here today. Look, even the white guy has been nodding his head.' Eyes turn to look at me. 'No wonder he's smiling. He owns the building.' Everyone laughs. 'Only messing with you, friend . . . OK, I want you to put your hands together for another very talented young man. His name,' he checks the list, 'is Big Al . . .'

And while Al performs 'Freez Up' one more time, Camp Zero move to crowd the front of the stage, shouting encouragement, pumping their fists in the air.

In the end, neither Camp Zero nor Big Al wins. A young woman called Treasure, who dresses from head to toe in Tommy Hilfiger, wins the contest. Neither Al nor Camp Zero seem to mind much. 'That's Hollywood,' says Camp Zero's Don Heroin with a shrug.

TIBU

Tibu pleads guilty to the marijuana charge, and says he's out of work and broke. The court fines him $247.

His only income now is dealing weed and the GR cheque, when it arrives. The Los Angeles County's General Relief roll covers 48,000 unemployed, as well as some of the mentally ill and others with substance-abuse problems.

This summer the County has been slashing the GR budget. Monthly payouts have been cut from $287 to $221, and long-term claimants are having their eligibility withdrawn. An estimated 8000 people who have been claiming for over five months will have their payments stopped on 1 July 1998. The Board of Supervisors is of the opinion that the buoyant US economy means that there are jobs out there for them if only they'd learn to start looking for them.

Poverty activists like the Los Angeles Coalition to End Hunger and Homelessness predict a rise in homelessness, substance abuse, crime and other poverty-related social problems. Eighty-eight per cent of those on GR use the money to pay the rent or other housing costs.

Somewhat politically incorrectly, given the battle that is being fought to try to restore the GR budget, Tibu is hoping to use some of the money they're going to pay him to cover time at Todd's studio.

In the meantime he can't afford to record any new material. He hates it when he's not making new music. But luckily Sneak calls him up and asks him to produce some tracks with him. Sneak wants the tracks because he's decided to leave Bellflower and move to Las Vegas, and he wants to take some of the Vietnam click music with him so he can play it to any rappers he might meet up with there. He is sick of being broke all his life. It's becoming tougher to make a living selling weed and cocaine on street corners. He's 19 now and he's decided to try to find a real job. But he can't get work easily because he doesn't have a driver's licence. Without a licence, he can't do any jobs that require any driving, and employers are suspicious of job-seekers who can't produce one as ID.

The trouble is, Sneak has been a bad boy for too long. He has so many outstanding fines in Los Angeles from previous police convictions that even if he were to pass the Department of Motor Vehicles test, they wouldn't issue a licence until he'd pay them all off. 'Too many thousands of fines,' he says wryly. 'Can't pay them.'

So he's going to have to look for work outside the state, where he has a clean record. Las Vegas is a boom town: these days it is one big building site. He's not sure what work he'll find there, but he's sure there'll be something he can do. 'A bit of hustling. Whatever. Same as here.' He has cousins who live there who can set him up: there's a chance of a job in a pet store. He'd rather stay in Bellflower, but he doesn't feel he has any choice.

He's saved up a little money to record one final demo tape so he can show off his rhyming skills in his new home. Tibu's happy to help out. It gives him another chance to record tracks at Todd's studios.

In front of the mike, he starts to read the verse he's written on a piece of lined paper:

It's seven-oh-six in the morning
I'm on the corner of Alondra and Euccy and I just started yawning . . .

Sneak has spent half his life hanging out there, with bags of weed ready to sell in his pockets. Most mornings for the past five years he's been there from early in the morning, not always as early as 7.06, perhaps, but that licence allows him to represent for his click, the 706s:

. . . standing on the corner selling llello and dodo.

Cocaine and weed. It's about the everyday grind. In the verse Sneak turns up to find someone else already hogging his pitch. He ends it by saying loudly into Todd's mike: '*Motherfuck!*' After he's cussed, he smiles sweetly and giggles. Tibu had suggested that last touch.

Back in the days when the corner of Euccy and Alondra was at its peak, Sneak claims, he could take home $300 on a good day. These days it's not so easy. The police have tightened up. Sometimes

Sneak sees the plainclothes men sitting in the KFC, or in one of the restaurants across the street, just watching. It's a big day now if he can bring home a couple of hundred bucks. Selling drugs on the corner used to be fun. It used to be daring. Now it's just boring, standing for hour after hour on a street corner watching the cars go by. That's another reason why it's time to leave.

After the session Sneak and Tibu head back to Bellflower. Terence, Sir T of the Vietnam click, is standing there at Eucalyptus and Alondra.

'Wassup, 'ler?' Tibu shouts at him.

Sir T, a dark-skinned, handsome boy with a dry, sharp-witted way of talking, is from Jackson, Mississippi, and grew up there. His cousin used to visit relatives in Los Angeles and bring back stories about how wild it was out there in the West. One time the cousin brought back all these crazy tapes by a band called NWA. Sir T and all his friends didn't know anything about rap music; they'd never heard any gangsta rap before, but they loved what they were hearing. 'This shit is tight,' they told each other. 'It's bumpin'.'

Soon the only thing they were listening to was West Coast acts like NWA, Eazy and the DOC. 'That was the shit.'

Sir T came to LA thinking Jackson was a kind of mellow backwater, a decent place compared to this immoral city. But the atmosphere in the Southern cities has become so much darker over the past ten years. Now when he goes back, Sir T is astonished at how much his hometown has changed. Last Christmas he went to a club in Jackson and wound up in an argument with a member of a local gang called the Vicelords. They decided to take it outside, but the moment he got outside they knocked him down, before he was ready. It all happened so fast, he thought he'd been shot. All he saw was a guy whipping the gun out. Boom. Luckily the gang-banger had only pistol-whipped him. Sir T now has a neat scar on his forehead, where the gun tore the flesh.

Somebody has obviously thumped Sir T again today. As he comes over to lean into the car, there is a bright trickle of blood running down the left side of his head. 'Just had a fight with Melvin.' He wipes the blood from his ear. Normally Sir T wears an earring in the top of his ear; the skin there has been torn, but it's only a small wound. Melvin is a great big jock of a basketball player who used to live around here; he moved away to Florida, but returned at the weekend, on a visit to catch up with his girlfriend Rebecca.

'Why were you fighting?' asks Tibu.

''Cause he found out I was fucking Rebecca,' Sir T explains.

Melvin thinks Rebecca is his girlfriend, but when Melvin's away in Florida she doesn't always remember this. Sir T dabs gingerly at his bleeding ear.

Later Tibu says, 'Melvin's stupid, man. He goes to Florida, that Rebecca is going to fuck. She's a hoodrat. She's just a ho.'

Hoodrats, that's what Tibu calls the girls around here.

Sunday afternoon, Big Al is appearing at a summer talent show at Cal State Dominguez Hills. Tibu tries to persuade the people running the show to let him on stage too, but he hasn't signed up in advance, so he has to just watch. Tibu has never performed live. He knows it's something he has to do, sooner or later. He watches Big Al instead. Al's upbeat hip-hop delivery isn't really Tibu's style of rapping, but he seems to get a good response from the crowd.

A young man is wandering around, passing out flyers. Tibu takes one. The small mauve piece of paper reads: 'The Unlimited Break Talent Show – Are you good enough?' Underneath that taunt are two boxes, one marked 'Yes', the other 'No'. Next to the 'Yes' box it says, 'Give us a call'; the 'No' box says, 'Leave it alone'.

As he does so often, Al wins the second prize. When the show's over, Tibu looks around for Keyna. She promised to meet him here: they were going to ride back together to Long Beach, where he's staying now. But she hasn't showed up on time. He has only a few cents in his pocket and can't afford the bus. He's hoping she'll lend him the money.

From a phone booth he calls up Keyna's apartment. It's only a few hundred yards away, but he daren't go there because he knows he'd only be arrested again and receive another fine.

The phone rings and rings. She's not home. 'Stupid bitch,' he says.

With nowhere else to go, Tibu has moved into his grandmother's apartment in Long Beach, just north of Pacific Coast Highway. It's an ugly, cheaply built four-plex. The building is a simple rectangle, two homes on each floor. There are no frills or decorations. It's just a box.

He's getting $221 a month plus about $120 in food stamps from GR, but his grandmother makes him pay her for housekeeping. This drives Tibu crazy.

Keyna is usually there for him, lending him money, putting him up when she can afford to, but his own family? He thinks bitterly: I got a fake-ass family. They're as fake as fuck. If he blows up big in the rap game, well, maybe he won't even give them a cent. I'll be the shiestiest motherfucker to my family, he says to himself.

Tibu's dad is in jail: he has been for years now. Tibu doesn't visit him much. He's been inside a lot of Tibu's life. He was sent down the last time for supposedly dealing cocaine. Tibu says, with contempt in his voice, that in fact the cocaine wasn't even his. He'd just been asked to carry it in his car for some friends. The police pulled him over, caught him with it and that was that.

His father converted to Islam recently, as a lot of convicts do. Tibu doesn't think much of that, either. They don't really have a great deal in common, these days, his dad and him.

Fatherlessness is a theme that runs through so much modern hip hop. There are plenty of boys that I meet who come from conventional, stable households. Big Al still lives with his parents. Khop wouldn't be where he was now if it wasn't for the support not only of his two parents, but also of his extended family, who have encouraged him and helped hook him up with both his record company and with Ice Cube.

Herman, Babyboy, Tibu and Rah all grew up fatherless. In Herman's case, his father's desertion is a simple fact. He has no great desire to know his father better, nor does fatherlessness seem to have left any particular scar. He is entirely self-reliant. In fact, others seem to rely on him. Tibu doesn't talk about his father much, but it's clear that his mother found her son hard to cope with on her own: that's why he's been more or less looking after himself from the age of 16. But for Rah, and still more for Babyboy, the absence of a father is a raw wound. Both talk about their fathers a lot, even though they hardly knew them.

Tupac Shakur was someone who wore his fatherlessness in public. The inferiority he felt about growing up not knowing his father ran through many of his rhymes:

Growin' up as an inner city brother
Where every other had a pops and a mother
I was the product of a heated lover,

he rhymed on his song 'The Streets R Deathrow':

Nobody knew how deep it screwed me
And since my pops never knew me
My family didn't know what to do with me
Was I somebody they despise?
Curious look in their eyes
As if they wonder whether I'm dead or alive . . .

I asked him about this once. A few days after I had talked to him at Can-Am studios I visited him again, in an upscale, white-carpeted apartment on Wilshire Boulevard that he was just moving into.

'When did you first start looking for a father-figure?'

'When I started seeing other people, and how they handled it,' the young rapper answered. 'I was like, "Damn! I got a cowardly deficit. Why am I acting that way? Why do I have to drink? Why can't I sleep? Why do I grind my teeth when I sleep? Why is it so mandatory that I get respect?" I know other people who are just as successful as me, you can call them bitch and . . . I know some people, hard just like me . . . somebody call them shit and they just smile. If you call me bitch, I don't care if we're in court, we're going to fight. That's mandatory. And it's still the same. That's what I have constantly to work with. It was reinforced that they was a man. It wasn't reinforced that I was a man. So I can't let nobody shake it because I might die that second they called me bitch, and that can't be the last thing they called me.'

Tupac's mother, Afeni Shakur, was a former Black Panther who had married the activist Lumumba Shakur but had affairs, one with a drug dealer called Legs, another with a Panther called Billy Garland. When she told Lumumba that the child she was carrying was not his, he dumped her.

Tupac grew up believing Legs was his father. 'Even though he wasn't there, he represented himself to be my father,' said Tupac. Afeni raised Tupac alone in Harlem and the Bronx. It was a struggle. They were sometimes homeless, forced to stay in shelters. When he was a teenager, she hooked up with Legs again, and he introduced her to crack. She became an addict. Legs died of a heart attack when Tupac was around 15, probably brought on by smoking crack. Tupac was distraught.

Then, nine years later, Tupac was shot in Times Square in the attack he believed was an attempt on his life. One of the visitors at his bedside was Billy Garland, who told him that he, not Legs, was his father. The attack coincided with the rapper starting his two-and-a-half-year sentence for first-degree sexual abuse of a fan.

'I had to be there,' Garland told me. 'He's my son. I've never asked him for anything – not money or nothing. I just wanted to let him know that I cared. How could I feel like that? He's my flesh and blood. Look at me. He looks just like me. People who I had never seen before immediately knew I was his father.'

The visit churned up the 24-year-old Tupac. Now, looking at Garland, who looked so much like him, he no longer knew what to think.

Afeni, too, visited her son, after he was sent to the Correctional Center at Dannemora.

'It was bad,' Tupac told me. 'I can remember me and my mother talking about, like, "Who's my father?" Deep shit. Right there in front of the guards. Her crying and calling me names.'

Even when I talked to him about a year after he had met Garland he was still not absolutely sure who his real father was. He had considered taking a blood test, but had so far decided against it. 'The man who claimed to be my father, who represented himself to be my father even though he wasn't there, is deceased. The man who is supposed to be my father, who looks just like me, he's alive.' He was still also struggling with his memories of Legs. 'I've got my memories of somebody who claimed to be my father, and on the other hand I've got another man who didn't want to be my father until just now.' To admit that Billy was his father would be to betray the memory of Legs. 'It's a difficult position,' he said. He was still working it out.

He said that, in the meantime, he was keeping in touch with Garland. 'We friends,' he said. 'We homies.'

It wasn't just Watts that exploded in the summer of 1965. There was unrest throughout black America. That was the year the

Democrat Assistant Secretary of Labor, Daniel Patrick Moynihan, produced a report commissioned by President Lyndon Johnson to investigate what was going wrong in what was then called the 'Negro' population.

Moynihan's conclusion came in his report 'The Negro Family: The Case For National Action'. He wrote: 'At the heart of the deterioration of the fabric of Negro society is the deterioration of the Negro family. It is the fundamental source of the weakness of the Negro community at the present time. There is probably no single fact of Negro American life so little understood by whites . . . There is one truly great discontinuity in family structure in the United States at the present time: that between the white world in general and that of the Negro American. The white family has achieved a high degree of stability and is maintaining that stability. By contrast, the family structure of lower-class Negroes is highly unstable, and in many urban centers is approaching complete breakdown.'

Since the report, the debate over the state of the African-American family has become a battlefield. Years of welfare paid to single parents appeared to have done little to change the situation; more recently a new centre-right consensus has decided that welfare is actually one of the root causes of family breakdown. Attempts to reverse the welfare cycle have begun. Obtusely, though, fatherlessness has yet to show any sign of declining. The divorce rate among African-Americans is now over double that of the rest of the population.

To Moynihan, the pattern of fatherlessness was evidence of a 'pathology' at work in the African-American family. Echoes of Moynihan resurface in the nineties 'shock jock' polemics of neo-conservatives like Rush Limbaugh, who blithely declare, 'There are no role models for the blacks' and tut-tut sententiously about the breakdown of the African-American family.

The stories of those who have the roughest ride – the Rahs, the

Babyboys, the eloquent Tupacs – bolster this idea. They are narratives of extreme pain. Yet it's among the mass underclass that 'the fabric of society', as Moynihan put it, is really coming unstitched. As long as it has been in Los Angeles, working-class black culture has been under such extraordinary pressure, and the pressure is not getting any less. The disproportionate incarceration and murder rates for young African-American men mean that there are, quite simply, fewer of them out there. The extremes of wealth and poverty and of geographical isolation are greater than ever. This situation plays itself out in personal disasters.

Much of black society is working just fine, of course. There are other hunky-dory narratives of people like Big Al, living at home with his parents, keeping a steady relationship going, but they don't make headlines. And African-American society has the advantage at least of a stronger extended family structure: witness Khop and the way he, his parents and his baby momma look after his child.

The peculiarity of black society in America is that more than any other minority, it is characterized by its failures. In no other minority does the underclass come so totally to represent the whole. Nowhere has this been more starkly obvious than in 'reality rap', or 'gangsta rap', a genre which is taken to be a more authentic, grittier representation of African-American culture than any other.

Meanwhile the carrot-and-stick attempts to put the nuclear family back together do little to change the basic mechanism of disadvantage. No amount of government cajoling is going to bring back Babyboy's or Tibu's father. Both of their dads were in prison for most of their sons' juvenile lives. Babyboy's murdered father is no longer in any position to offer parental advice and financial support.

In the Long Beach apartment, Tibu's grandmother is always after him to keep the house clean. 'She screams like a motherfucker.' Today she wakes him at 5.30 a.m. and tells him he has to tidy up the place. He is supposed to go down to the GR building for an appointment, but after being woken so early he decides he is too tired to go.

Instead he calls up the number on the flyer for the Unlimited Break Talent Show. As he waits for the phone to be answered he picks up a pen. 'Are you good enough?' asks the flyer. Tibu scrawls a big 'X' on the box marked 'Yes'.

'First,' says the voice, 'you have to audition. Can you make Tuesday at 3 p.m.?'

18

A Braggadocious Thing

BIG AL

Al doesn't give up easily. After investing so many years, it must be hard for him to contemplate failing.

The Urban Focus Music Conference held at a music college just off Hollywood Boulevard costs $50. Al has recorded a new track produced by Click Tha Superlatin, a local Peruvian immigrant who has become a Latino rap celebrity. Al pays his money and turns up, demo tapes in his backpack.

Outside, on the Hollywood sidewalk, Al plays the track on a boom box. A crowd of boys quickly surround him, nodding their heads. 'Man, that's tight, you do that?'

'Mm-hm,' nods Al.

'That's the shit.'

The Urban Focus Music Conference is a higher-power event than last autumn's *Rap Sheet* convention; but with that come disadvantages. Within a few hours it's obvious that there are simply too many people like Al, clutching their demos, eager to be listened to, and not enough time in the weekend to listen to them all.

'I was promised one-on-one listening sessions,' complains Al. Within hours of the usual opening speeches, the event has descended into a first-come-first-served scramble for attention.

Upstairs, in one of the crowded classrooms, a white A&R man from Universal Records has been listening to tapes for over an hour. A cool young producer called G-Wiz has passed him a tape. G-Wiz dresses in sixties chic, looking like a young Black Panther. Next to him is a beautiful woman in sunglasses, leather waistcoat and Afro who looks the spit of a young Angela Davis. G-Wiz's song is called 'Get Your Guns'. The A&R man stops it the moment it hits the first chorus.

'Look. I'll say this straight out,' he says. 'I'm looking for something I can promote. Radio is not going to tell America, "Get your guns."'

'What about underground?' asks G-Wiz.

'Underground is a whole other thing,' the Universal Records man says. The underground: a place in which everyone can be cool, where crass commercial imperatives cease to operate, and in which struggling young artists finally get the respect they deserve; also a place that no one seems to know the way to. 'I'm not looking for underground,' the A&R guy declares. 'I'm looking for something your grandmomma can sing in the kitchen. This is not it.'

G-Wiz stares back, as coolly and contemptuously as he can.

'I'm looking for things which don't say times is hard,' the A&R man continues baldly. 'Because nobody in the industry wants that. They're looking for a positive, commercial record. If it don't make dollars . . .'

'It don't make sense . . .' the room murmurs back.

'Exactly.'

'Is that *all* we should be doing?' says G-Wiz archly. But his time is up. The next song is already being cued. It's a funky, synth-based r'n'b song. Mr Universal Records is tiring. He cuts the song short again.

'I don't know,' he sighs. His head is in his hands. 'That's some different kind of shit. Next.'

A tall, dark woman standing in the throng by the door interrupts. 'Can you do just a *little* better than that?' she says acidly.

The room murmurs angrily. The unfortunate A&R man looks

up. She has paid her $50 and she expects better treatment. 'Oh, I'm sorry. Is that your song?'

'Mm,' she answers, her lips pursed tightly. Her gaze is furious: he buckles under it.

'Uh. I just didn't feel it. That's all.' He pauses uncomfortably. 'Like, I missed a lot of things,' he excuses himself, trying to make her feel better. 'Some things I just don't *get* the first time around. I mean, I missed Montel Jordan as a matter of fact,' he says by way of encouragement.

'I used to sing with Montel Jordan,' the woman fires back. 'He said a lot of people passed on him.'

'Well,' the guy smiles, as disarmingly as he can. 'I was one of them. I'm sorry. I didn't mean to disrespect you.'

The tension dissipates.

After the first few hours, when it became obvious that it would be impossible to attract the attention of all the record-company representatives at the conference, Al carefully chose to direct all his efforts at an A&R man called Alex Meija, from the Virgin subsidiary label Noo Trybe. Meija, a young, enthusiastic Hispanic guy, has announced he's looking for hip-hop acts.

Al goes up to the room and his heart sinks. The room is already full. Every chair is taken: people are sitting on the carpet. The janitors are complaining that they're breaking fire regulations, but no one moves.

Meija has been conscientiously listening to his immense pile of tapes, trying to comment thoughtfully on each one, for all of the allotted hour. But the pile is too big. There's no way he can get through it all. Al stands in a corner, waiting for his turn to come. Meija runs over time. The session was supposed to be an hour long, but after two hours there are still about 20 tapes to go. He still hasn't played Al's tape. People are starting to complain that Meija still hasn't played their demos. A voice pipes up: 'Hey, how come you ain't listened to a single tape by a woman yet?'

'OK, the next one is going to be a woman.'

'And how come you ain't played any reggae?' asks a West Indian voice.

'Sure, I'll listen to some reggae,' says Meija.

Suddenly the running order that Al had patiently queued up to add his name to is torn to shreds. Everyone is crowding down to the desk at the front of the seminar room, trying to get their tape played.

Al meekly stands against the wall. It's not his style to shout, to push himself forward like that. He does all his shouting on stage. But he realizes that no one is going to listen to his tape today, and he's furious. He registered for this conference weeks ago, because the advertising appeared to promise that anyone who registered early would be first in line when it came to having their demos heard. Out in the corridor, shaking with rage, he fumes: 'What's that guy saying? "How come you ain't played any reggae?" Where did they say they were going to be playing reggae anyhow?' The large man takes his tape and heads back home to Inglewood in a thunderous mood.

TIBU

Western Avenue is one of the longest streets in Los Angeles; originally it was just a dirt track that connected Hollywood to the docks miles to the south in San Pedro. Rowe Entertainment's offices are at 700 Western Avenue, in one of Western's most run-down sections, just north of Figueroa. It's a large, old, decrepit hall in a deserted part of town. 'Color Lab Photo' says a sign at the front. The front door is open, but a locked security door blocks the way in. Tibu walks around the building looking for another entrance. It looks abandoned. He goes back to the front door and shouts, 'Hello?'

Eventually a young guy in a plaid shirt, jeans and a pair of black suede shoes appears.

'What do you want?'

'I've an appointment for a, uh, audition,' says Tibu.

'Oh,' says the boy. 'OK. Come in.' Tibu follows him into the building. The building smells of old dust and fresh paint. Rowe Entertainment has done its best to spruce up the building. It has covered the walls in purple paint to try to disguise the fact that the place used to be a colour-film processing laboratory. The boy walks in a noisy shuffle because he is wearing shoes that are several sizes too big for him. They look like they'd fall off if he raised his legs too keenly.

'I'm Leonard,' he says, and leads Tibu into a large, windowless room that is panelled in dark imitation wood. Inside, James Rowe of Rowe Entertainment sits behind a large desk, wearing a blue sweatshirt. He is watching *Bonanza* on TV. 'Turn that off,' he orders Leonard, as if he's suddenly shocked to find that it is on at all, and Leonard shuffles obediently over to turn off the huge old set. Sitting on top of the TV is a recent Father's Day gift: a white baseball cap embroidered with the word 'Superdad'.

Apart from the TV, a filing cabinet, a stereo and Rowe's huge desk, the room is empty. 'Fetch some chairs,' Rowe orders Leonard. Leonard scuffs his way back, carrying two chairs.

'OK,' says Rowe. 'Sit down.' He motions Tibu to an old chair. 'What's your name?'

'Ah, my real name or my stage name?'

'Both.'

'Caleb Candler is my name. My stage name is Mr Tibu.'

'T-Bone?' Rowe says.

'T-I-B-U,' Tibu spells it out.

Leonard, who's pulled up a chair next to his boss's desk, writes down this information carefully. 'Thought you said T-Bone,' says Rowe jovially. 'That one's already taken. You know T-Bone from Da Lench Mob?'

'Of course,' says Tibu.

'They were discovered at one of my showcases,' says Rowe warmly. Actually, Da Lench Mob were a group discovered by Ice Cube back in the early nineties, but Tibu keeps his scepticism about Rowe's claim to himself.

'We've been running these talent shows for 17 years,' says Rowe. 'We started at the steak house down the road. These are our new premises. We just got them,' he says grandly. 'Where you from?'

'Compton . . . That's where I was born. I'm living in Bellflower now.'

'Well,' says Rowe. 'You're lucky because I got one space left for the show on the 22nd. First the ground rules.' He lifts up a stapled sheet from the table. 'This is why we're the number-one talent show in the Los Angeles area: we got ground rules,' he boasts, not entirely accurately.

Rowe hands Tibu the five-page contract. Page one deals with ticket sales. As is usual for these talent shows, Tibu has to sell ten tickets at $10 a head in order to qualify. 'That's the entry fee.' Rowe reads the page out loud to Tibu, then asks: 'OK? You understand everything?' Some of the contestants he deals with probably don't read that well; if he reads it out, there can be no misunderstanding.

'How many contestants are you going to have?' asks Tibu.

'Fourteen.'

Tibu does a quick bit of maths. That means he could be performing in front of 140 people. 'If you want a video of your performance, that will be an extra $25,' says Rowe. 'Next: language. No profanities may be used.'

'What you mean by that exactly?' asks Tibu, shifting in his chair.

Rowe picks up a small California State flag on his desk, and fiddles with it, twisting it around on its pole. 'Your subject matter can be as hard as you like, but the moment you use a cuss word, we're gonna turn your music off. You can use words like "damn" and "hell", but,' he extemporizes, ' "Fuck that bitch and cut her neck off" – no way.'

Tibu laughs. 'I'll save that for the record.'

'Well, that's professional,' chuckles Rowe. 'No one's interested in gangsta rap anyway. Reality rap. That's what they want.'

Tibu's hackles rise. This man is acting like he knows more about rap than he does. He doesn't know how fuckin' much I know, thinks Tibu. He hates it when people try and tell him what is what about rap music. He feels like getting up and slapping Rowe. He's full of bullshit. Gangsta rap and reality rap are the same thing anyway.

Rowe continues blithely: 'And this is the part which you should be really happy about, because what it means is I'm gonna work really hard to make sure that the record companies are gonna come and watch you.' Page three is an agreement that says that should Tibu be signed by one of the talent scouts as a result of them seeing his act at the show, the record company will pay 10 per cent of the advance to Rowe Entertainment. He continues to read the contract aloud, then looks up. 'So, if you get a $50,000 advance, the record company pays you $45,000, and $5000 comes to me,' he says optimistically.

On the back of Rowe's flyer is a list of record companies that supposedly support Rowe Entertainment's talent shows: 'Deff Jam [sic], Epic Records, Motown, Loud Records, Bad Boy Records, Tommy Boy, A.M. [sic] Records, MCA, Capital [sic], RCA, EMI, Scotti Bro [sic], Warners Bro [sic] . . . . and more.'

Like all talent shows, it's a business based on a promise of better things.

Next is the audition. Maybe it's a face-saving ritual for both parties – the pretence that the artistry is the important part, not the ability to sell ten tickets at $10 apiece.

Leonard leads Tibu into the hall; *fsssht, fsssht, fsssht*, the scrape of his shoes is amplified by the emptiness of the room. He and Rowe have done their best to turn the space into a nightclub. When the processing lab's equipment was torn out, it left an uneven concrete floor. They have painted it grey. A bar has been hastily built at one end, jutting out into the hall. The walls are painted the same dark purple as the entrance hall.

They have arranged about 20 metal tables around the room, covering them with purple tablecloths, each with a candle on. Two collapsible metal chairs are placed beside each table.

On the small stage, Tibu performs a rhyme called 'Hustle Man', to a backing track recorded at Todd's studio. On an ancient boom box the track sounds tinny. Tibu doesn't have a mike, but he pretends to be holding one as he performs. Leonard stands holding a clipboard, as if he's judging some gymnastic event. Tibu falters a couple of times over his lines, usually where an obscenity used to be. Leaving out the 'fucks' wrecks the rhythm.

Rowe doesn't listen; he stays in his office. When the track is finished, Leonard holds out the clipboard so Tibu can sign the contract.

Tibu has never performed in front of a real audience, and he knows he has to get some live experience behind him. He thinks the place is a dump. It's fucked up, but he knows he should do it, if only to start getting his name around.

Rowe emerges from his office when Tibu is done, and says, 'One more thing. You must tell anyone who sponsors you by buying a ticket that they can't bring any alcohol, or food. And we got a dress code. No jeans, no caps, no tennis shoes. We want this to be a nice occasion for you. Nobody wears anything that makes them look like a gang-banger. Not that I'm saying you're affiliated, but you never know, your friend may have a friend . . . you know what I mean?'

'Uh-huh,' says Tibu.

'OK, be here at 7 p.m. – 7.30 at the latest,' says Rowe. Leonard carefully counts out ten tickets and passes them to Tibu.

'Will you buy a ticket?' Tibu asks me.

'Of course.' One down, nine to go. He'll have to persuade some members of the Vietnam click to buy some. He wonders if his mother will buy one. They haven't always got along so well, but maybe she'll come up with ten bucks.

BIG AL

Al is keyed up. Alex Meija, the A&R man from Noo Trybe who didn't have time to listen to his demo last week, has agreed to meet him, briefly, to listen to his demo. Alex is new in A&R at Virgin. He doesn't carry much weight yet, but he's always on the lookout. These days every A&R man seems to be looking for a new upbeat act: no one is looking for anyone who is too obviously affiliated, or too violent. It's time for the music to have some *fun*, is what Alex thinks. In theory, at least, Al should be perfect.

The Noo Trybe office in Beverly Hills is a slick, cool-looking building. A classic fifties space-age design TV has been rebuilt with a colour tube; it's blaring out the BET – Black Entertainment Television – channel. This is the lobby where nine months before Rah had shown Sleep the photo of Josiah. Al waits patiently, clutching his backpack, in the reception area until he's called.

Alex shakes hands in a businesslike manner, and leads him into a conference room with a huge wooden table surrounded by chairs, and a video and stereo. At the Urban Focus Music Conference, Alex was affable and eager. There he was on show, representing his company. Here things are different. This is Alex's workplace.

'You don't have representation?' he asks. The fact that Al doesn't have an attorney or a manager present is a minus point, even before he's sat down. 'I don't usually see people unless they have representation with them.'

Al is uncomfortable in this environment. 'Are you connected? Is there anyone you've worked with?' Alex is asking him.

Al could talk to friends from the Good Life about the compilation he put out, about his deal with the Warlock label, but now it's as if his head has gone blank. He mentions he's worked with Click The Superlatin, but Alex looks blank.

'I've not heard of him,' he says. Though Al and Alex are the same age, Al is acting like a candidate at a job interview.

'What have you got for me?'

Al hands him a tape of 'Freez Up'.

Alex looks at it. It's not properly labelled. Another minus point. 'What sort of category would you put this in?'

'Well, it's kind of like a braggadocious thing,' Al suggests, meaning it's in the battle-rap tradition: a rapper boasting of his chops, demonstrating his superior wordplay.

'Braggadocious?' puzzles Alex. 'What is that?'

He puts the track on. It's quiet, so he turns it up louder. 'I can't hear it. Your voice is too low in the mix. What are you saying?' The chorus finally arrives. Alex switches the tape off. ' "Freez Up": what does that mean?'

'It's like, other DJs will freeze up when I get on the microphone.'

'Well, I didn't get that. It's not a great chorus. You have to make that clearer. It needs to be more professional.'

In the last minute, Al gradually starts to sell himself. 'I have a reputation as a live artist,' he volunteers. 'If I put on a showcase, would you come down?'

'Of course,' says Alex, handing him a card. 'Fax me the details.' Then he hands the copy of 'Freez Up' back to Al. 'You're not ready yet,' he says.

Afterwards Al looks pale.

'I can respect that,' he says.

He is silent for a while. Then he says, 'I'm just going to have to get some money together to do another demo.'

This has been a big knock-back for his confidence. He has been struggling at this business for so long, it is painful to be treated as if he is a newcomer. Alex's harsh words – that he's not ready yet – still ring around his head. If he's not ready after ten years, he'll never be ready. 'It hurts,' he says quietly. 'Right inside here,' and he lays his hand on his big chest.

TIBU

Tibu has a dream. It's the second time he's had it. Master P is performing at some little stupid-ass local show. Tibu thinks his shit is corny, even when he's awake. So when Master P comes to the mike and says, 'Uuungh,' the grunt that is his vocal trademark, Tibu just walks right up to him and snatches his chain off.

The day before the Unlimited Break Talent Show, Tibu calls me. He is fuming.

'What's happened?' I ask.

'I'm going to have to cancel tomorrow night's fuckin' show,' he says.

'What?' I say. So far, Tibu has never actually performed live. I wonder if he's having first-night nerves.

He says the backing tape of 'Paper Game' that Todd had mixed down for him has disappeared. He's convinced that his aunt, in whose apartment he's now living, has stolen it. I ask him why on earth his aunt would steal a tape, but he doesn't know. He has no idea at all why she might have it. He's just convinced it's her. 'I'm going to kill her,' he says.

'Can't you use anything else?'

'I'm going to see if Montrie [Sneak] has a copy. I just paged him.' Tibu sounds despondent. He hasn't got the money to get another copy off Todd. He says, 'I'll refund your money for the ticket, don't worry.'

Tibu rages on for the rest of the day. His temper is fearsome, when it breaks out. Whenever he sees his aunt he screams at her to give him back the tape, but she says she doesn't have it. So he goes to the kitchen and finds a knife. He's not sure whether he's going to stab her with it or just threaten her. Luckily he pauses long enough to think: Do I want to go to prison? I'd be there if I stab my aunt. So instead he gathers together a pile of her clothes and starts shouting at her that if she didn't give the tape back, he'll set light to them.

Afterwards, when we talk about this, there is no sign of any remorse at what he has done to his aunt. Or any belief that he could have been mistaken. Inside Tibu there is a fearsome rage that can burst out suddenly, from time to time, just like when he dangled Keyna over the balcony. He laughs when he says that all the time his aunt was just screaming at him: 'I didn't do it. I didn't do it.'

19

Ciscoed Up

TIBU

Sir T has been cajoled into appearing on stage as Tibu's hypeman. I give both of them a ride from Bellflower.

Tibu never found the backing tape he'd lost. He's having to make do with another track. About three blocks north of the venue we pull into a mini-mart so Tibu can buy a packet of Hall's Mentholyptus pastilles to keep his throat loosened up. Sir T and I wait in the car park of the Cameo Liquor Mart. The sign that says 'Groceries – Meat' outside the shop has been defaced by gang graffiti. The name 'KW7' has been written up several times and then crossed out each time with big 'X's. Whoever KW7 is, somebody doesn't like him much.

'Damn, it's like *Boyz In Tha Hood* in there,' says Tibu when he returns, clutching his pastilles. The movie featured a scene in a grocery store run by paranoid Asians. 'They got, like, eight cameras.'

The shop looks like it's under siege. Opposite the counter there is a bank of old TVs, stacked up. Each is connected to a surveillance camera. Every corner of the store is covered. An elderly Asian woman sits behind two-inch thick layers of bulletproof perspex; each has a hole in it, so you can pass her the money and she can pass you change, but the holes are staggered so it would be impossible to get a clear shot at her, should you want to rob the till.

Los Angeles invented the supermarket, just as it has dreamed up so much of the mechanics of the modern city. An enterprising European Jew called Isadore M. Hattem opened Hattem's on Western and 43rd, a little way north of this desolate store, on the day after Boxing Day in 1927. For the first time shoppers could park their automobiles in the lot and load them up with the goods they themselves selected, all bought under one roof.

The principle is similar in the Cameo Liquor Mart, but nowadays assistants watch the groceries much more jealously. The irony is that though this is the area that gave the world the first supermarkets, the larger supermarkets have generally given up on this area – and many others like it in South Central. The relative poverty of population and infrastructure means that the large chains don't regard much of South Central as profitable enough for them invest their dollars in. As the supermarkets packed up and left, they left a gap for the start-up entrepreneurs to open the smaller version – the Liquor Mart.

The profligacy of liquor stores in South Central can seem like the cause of its ills, rather than a symptom. There are 17 liquor stores per square mile here, rather than 1.6 per mile in the rest of LA County.

As I pull the car back out on to Western, Tibu says, 'Damn. My mom is coming. She's got, like, a '98 Chrysler.' This is the sort of neighbourhood where I'm grateful to be driving a beaten-up old Rabbit.

He opens the packet of blackcurrant pastilles, hands one pastille to Sir T and then sets about sucking one himself.

In the spring of 1991 a 15-year-old girl called Latasha Harlins walked into the Empire Liquor Market, just south-east of here on the 9100 block of South Figueroa Avenue. In the two years the store had been open it had been shoplifted and robbed frequently, so the Korean Du family who owned it began to keep a .38 calibre pistol under the counter.

It was hot, and Latasha was thirsty, so she went in to buy some orange juice. She picked up a bottle and put it straight in her backpack. She didn't make any attempt to hide the bottle: the top half was clearly visible, poking out of the top of the bag

Latasha was approaching the counter to pay for the juice, money in hand, when 51-year-old Soon Ya Du – a woman family member who worked only at weekends – grabbed the girl by her sweater, obviously assuming that she had intended to shoplift the bottle. Latasha fought back, punching Soon Ya several times in the face. Soon Ya retaliated by picking up a stool and throwing it at the teenager.

Soon Ya's husband, Heung Ki Du, was asleep in his delivery van outside the shop when he heard the gunshot. He ran into the shop to discover his wife, passed out behind the counter, and the body of Latasha Harlins lying dead on the floor, a single bullet hole in the back of her head.

Later Soon Ya told her family that the girl – who she thought was about 25 – had attempted to take cash from the till. Unfortunately, the security video didn't corroborate her story. It clearly showed that after Soon Ya threw the stool at her, Latasha appeared to have decided that a $1.79 bottle of juice wasn't worth the struggle. She placed the bottle back on the counter and turned to leave the shop, at which point Soon Ya grabbed the .38 and fired it at her.

In the aftermath, the LAPD rushed to say that there were no racial overtones to this incident – it was, they said, 'simply a business dispute' – but this declaration didn't cut any ice with many in the local African-American community. Latasha Harlins's death touched a nerve.

The ethnic composition of South Central has been changing rapidly over the past 30 years. Many African-Americans have left the poorer areas on the east side, moving westwards towards Inglewood and Hawthorne, or south-east towards Downey and

Long Beach, just as Tibu's family had moved to Bellflower. Across South Central as a whole, the African-American population was declining rapidly – it fell by 6.5 per cent in the years between 1980 and 1990. The older heavy industries were closing down throughout South Central, laying off their workforce.

During the same period the Asian population of LA County more than doubled. Some were businesspeople, others refugees: many moved into South Central, though often not as residents but as entrepreneurs. Koreans and some Filipinos invested in convenience stores all over the area. The shop owners who set up in South Central were in many cases poor families themselves, trying desperately to find a foothold in the world of American business. The older Jewish store owners had employed local labour. The Koreans, by contrast, relied on family labour: generally they couldn't afford to employ local labour, even if they had wanted to. This caused the slogan 'Don't buy where you can't work', which recalled an earlier rights struggle, to be resurrected. Not only did the Korean store owners not employ locals, but as soon as they had built up enough capital they would sell up and move to a more profitable neighbourhood. Their capital didn't stay in South Central.

What probably didn't help much, either, was that some of the incomers who bought leases on the cheap stores in South Central were unused to American ways. Coming from a straight-laced Asian background, many were shocked by the apparently lax mores of African-Americans. Given their lack of knowledge of the society they were moving into, it was inevitable that some would take the myths that still permeate American society at face value. In short, some arrived believing the old racial stereotypes, that blacks were lazy, dishonest and sexually profligate. Added to that, communication between black and Korean Americans was hampered by the fact that two-thirds of the new immigrants couldn't speak English properly or at all.

Some African-Americans began to see Koreans as merely predatory – sucking money out of the community. To them, it looked like incomers were thriving at the expense of their own dwindling population.

The slaying of Latasha Harlins sparked an ugly wave of anti-Korean protests. Some African-American community leaders organized a boycott of Korean shops, and many stores were attacked. In June 1991, an African-American called Lee Arthur Mitchell was shot dead by another store owner during a befuddled, stupid robbery attempt. Mitchell had tried to swap a piece of jewellery for a bottle of wine. Furious African-Americans picketed the store at Western and 79th, carrying signs that read: 'GET OUT OF OUR COMMUNITY.' Later a protester lobbed a Molotov cocktail on to the roof of the shop. In August of that year, in a dry run for the following spring's riots, three Korean stores were fire-bombed.

A few months after the killing of Latasha Harlins, Ice Cube released the album *Death CertifiKKKate*, which included a track called 'Black Korea'. In the rap, Cube walks into a Korean-owned grocery store in South Central to buy a 40-ounce bottle of beer. He's followed by the store owners, who clearly suspect him of being a shoplifter, and he bristles under their racist assumptions until he fumes:

Don't follow me up and down your crazy little market
Or your chop suey ass will be the target
Of a nationwide boycott.

Towards the end, the lyrics became even more aggressive:

Pay respect to the black fist
Or we'll burn your store right down to a crisp
And then we'll see ya
Because you can't turn the ghetto into Black Korea . . .

Ice Cube was playing outrageously to the crowd, treading all over one of the most sensitive racial disputes in South Central. He was reducing the problem to straight territoriality, that familiar battle-cry of South Central.

The Koreans, a tiny minority within a minority, dug in. Their own mood darkened in October 1991 when a nine-year-old Korean girl was shot during a robbery of a gas station at Century and Broadway.

The situation degenerated even further when Soon Ya Du received a light sentence for killing Latasha Harlins: five years' probation for involuntary manslaughter. As far as the African-American community was concerned, the underlying message was clear. Los Angeles regarded it as reasonable to take lethal action when facing a confrontation with a black person: blacks were a toxic quantity, to be dealt with brutally. It was a message that would be amplified the following year when Rodney King stepped out of his white Hyundai on Foothill Boulevard.

In the early nineties, murder rates in South Central were rising at an alarming speed. Racial friction was at a new high. Everyone there seemed to know that something was about to explode.

The fires that burned so wildly around this area are often portrayed as a blind act of rage, or as a spontaneous anti-white uprising inspired by the King verdict. In fact, in some ways the rioting was remarkably focused. Seventy-five per cent of the liquor stores that were burned down were Korean-owned.

At the time of writing, in 1998, it is seven years since the Harlins killing, six since the uprising. I remember, back in March this year, Hal Fishman saying reassuringly on KTLA how 80 per cent of the buildings damaged had been repaired. In fact, little has really changed here, despite all the warm words. Stores are still built like little fortresses. The owners still have guns tucked beneath the counters, behind the security glass, the grilles and the surveillance cameras. The sense of shock had been the same after Watts burned, and there had been the same earnest promises to change the way things were heading.

The Christopher Commission recommended sweeping reforms of the LAPD in the aftermath of the King beating, but by the mid-nineties Los Angeles was already back in boom time. Crime fell again. The LAPD now happily take the credit for adopting a more community-orientated approach to crime, though it is doubtful whether anything substantial has changed. The appetite for reform has vanished as the economy has prospered. The Commission created the position of Inspector General, to be filled by a civilian appointed to oversee allegations of police misconduct. The post was effectively neutralized when the pro-LAPD LA Police Commission decided that the Inspector General, Katherine Madar, should make her reports in private to them alone.

When it came to revitalizing the riot-ripped area, a private corporation called Rebuild LA (RLA) was established, amid a fanfare of publicity, to draw funds into South Central, so that the healing could begin. In the ideological climate of the times, it was believed that the task of rebuilding the area should be led by private investment. In the early days, when the media spotlight was still on South Central, large companies lined up to announce that they were pledging to invest fantastic sums of money into the ruined neighbourhoods. The supermarket chain Vons led the pack, claiming that they planned to pour in $100 million into a dozen new supermarkets. A tiny handful of medium-sized companies, like Smart & Final, Taco Bell and Chief Auto Parts, did move into the newly vacant lots, but anyone who imagined that, once the PR dust had settled, worthy entrepreneurs would be queuing up to invest in a sprawling inner-city neighbourhood with a severe image problem, was crazy. As time went on, they did their sums, figured out the poor returns they might receive on their investments and quietly scaled down their noble ambitions. Vons built only a quarter of the number of the supermarkets it originally promised, and those were in the neighbourhoods that were already more financially secure. 'It would not serve us or the community to build stores where it doesn't make economic sense,' a spokesperson announced later. Smaller investors were also understandably reluctant to bring their capital into an area where hundreds had already had their livelihoods torn apart.

The regeneration followed already too familiar patterns. North of the 10 or Santa Monica freeway, the recovery had proceeded well. Poorer areas, like the blitzed lots on Vermont, south of Pico-Union, remained neglected.

When RLA was wound up after five years, it estimated corporate investments totalled only $389 million, a tiny fraction of the $6 billion it had estimated was needed to put the city's deprived areas back on their feet. Despite their boasts, corporate investors had contributed less than half the figure raised by government agencies, and even this figure of $389 million is questionable. All inward investment was counted into the equation, and it's impossible to determine how much of this investment would have occurred in the normal course of events. Given the city's history, it would, perhaps, have been uncharacteristic of LA to have thrown itself wholeheartedly into such a grand public scheme.

From the outside, the big hall at Florence and Western, next to Valeries Hair Connection ('Wraps Curls Drys') looks as dead as ever. One room has been designated a dressing room; Sir T and Tibu are told to wait in there until it's their turn to perform. Rowe is fussing around the building: he sticks his head round the door every now and then and peers at the artists. He is wearing a clean white shirt and tie. His lackey, Leonard, is today dressed in a black shirt and an old pair of nylon black and white patterned trousers that have gone bobbly and baggy at the knees.

The room is unfurnished save for an old tape recorder, a dingy brown sofa, a fan and a dartboard with three darts buried in it. The thin office carpet is rumpled, worn to nothing in places.

An r'n'b trio who call themselves MSO have taken the sofa: two good-looking women in their early twenties and a boy who looks like their baby brother and must be only about ten years old. The women are dressed in black formal clothes, like they're going to church. A male singer who calls himself Kenny Byrd – he looks about 18 and is dressed in a fancy embroidered brown and beige shirt and shiny patent-leather shoes – stands nervously next to them. 'I got to do my breathing exercises,' he announces. He closes his eyes and fills his chest.

Rappers and r'n'b singers eye each other like they're different species. The two subcultures that always share the stages at these talent shows are so entirely different: the churchy soul singers and the gangsterish rappers.

Tibu is hyped up. In a voice loud enough for them to hear, he says, 'Look at them fools, all dressed up. I just got out of bed and threw this T-shirt on.' He's wearing an XXL Helly Hansen shirt.

Pretending not to notice, the girls watch him with a mixture of nerviness and contempt out of the corner of their eyes. One of them tries quietly to loosen up her voice.

'Shit,' says Tibu, more quietly to me. 'If Patrice was here she'd beat her.' He still hopes that Patrice stands a good chance of getting a deal of some sort from Todd's demo. He wants to manage her, although Patrice doesn't seem to be sure about what is in it for her. 'She still wants to fuck me, though,' he boasts. 'She could really go somewhere.'

'She just have to wear a bag on her head, that's all,' adds Sir T.

Tibu laughs. 'She got a good body, but she's got a kind of goofy face. She fucks, though. How many people in the click she fucked?'

'Shit,' says Sir T. 'You and me. I don't know.' Tibu giggles.

Sir T pulls the darts out of the dartboard and starts hurling them into it. He has an aggressive throw, stabbing them at the board so their points sink right in. When he's bored of trying the conventional method, he tries underarm, stabbing the darts into the wall.

Then he turns his back and starts throwing them over his shoulder, blind.

Sir T is relaxed, not taking the whole thing seriously, but Tibu is full of nervous energy. He is cocky and domineering, talking in a loud voice. A young guy comes in, in jeans and suede shoes. Tibu looks him up and down. 'Wassup, homie? You rap?'

The boy is 16. 'Yeah,' he says defiantly.

'You got a click?' Tibu asks.

'Yeah.'

'What they called?'

'JB and Triple C.'

Tibu shoots a glance at Sir T, as if to say, 'Wack.' He doesn't regard him as competition.

Then in walks another boy. He's 19, but looks younger. He has a soft, dark-skinned, round face. His hair is tied into tight bunches, one on either side of his head, and he's wearing a blue number-12 basketball shirt.

Tibu sizes him up. 'What's your name, homie?' The newcomer is short: next to Tibu's bulk, he looks tiny.

'Blue Diamond,' says the boy in a quiet voice. Blue clothes, a bunched gangsta hairstyle and a blue shirt; he's even wearing what looks much like the favoured Crip footwear of the moment, blue suede Hush Puppies. Despite all the rules about no sneakers and no caps, and nothing that might show any gang affiliation, the Crip signals Blue Diamond is giving out couldn't be less subtle.

Instantly there is a competitive spark between Tibu and Blue Diamond. Each is sizing the other up, looking the other over, trying to figure out if he represents some real competition. 'They got some good sounds out there?' Blue Diamond asks Tibu. 'Last show I did, it was wack. It was like that,' he points to the small, cheesy tape recorder plugged into the wall. Tibu and Blue Diamond are more or less the same age, both trying to prove that they're the best.

Rowe appears with a young guy in a suit in tow. 'OK, everyone, can I have your attention. I'd like to introduce our Master of Ceremonies for tonight,' Mr Rowe says proudly.

A young man who looks younger than his 18 years stands next to Rowe, who seems to tower over him. He's an actor who used to have a small part in the black Warners sitcom *Hangin' With Mr Cooper*. The show has recently been cancelled by Warners, but having a bona fide TV star, albeit a very minor one, in the house is something of a coup for Rowe.

'Shit,' says Tibu. 'I thought I recognized him.'

Blue Diamond is still surveying the room. He feels he should announce his presence in some way, that he should assert himself. Once Rowe and the actor have gone, Blue Diamond looks Tibu in the eye and says: 'You battle?'

'Hell yeah,' says Tibu.

'You got a beat?' asks Blue Diamond. The familiar gladiatorial contest of two boys doing battle with rhyme starts. Tibu puts a tape in the machine and starts pacing the room. He freestyles, staring Blue Diamond out:

I'm comin' at you with a cleaver – you best be a believer
And your Tek 9 better spit more rounds than mine when I come down . . .

It's the usual hyper-aggressive wordplay, Tibu killing off his opponent with couplets. In Tibu's rhymes, Blue Diamond is slaughtered a hundred times. Blue Diamond steadily returns Tibu's gaze.

After two minutes of extemporization, Tibu draws breath and says triumphantly, 'It's on you, homie. Shock the hell out of me.'

Blue Diamond bursts into life. Though he's short, and his features are almost babyish, he's so overwound by pre-show tension that his words spill out so fast I can't make them out. There is something desperate about his performance; it's so intense it verges on the psychotic. He leans forward, pushing each word into Tibu's face. Sir T and Tibu make a display of listening intently, making out they're unfazed by the aggressiveness of Blue Diamond's tone. The gospel-singing girls are watching too, but with distant, vaguely contemptuous expressions on their faces, as if to say, 'Yeah, right. Boys.'

When he's finished, Blue Diamond seems to visibly deflate, as if someone has exorcized his demons. 'I don't freestyle,' he says, as if apologizing for his performance: they were rhymes he'd already prepared, unlike Tibu's improvised tirade. 'I'm just trying to get ready for the night.'

'I hear you,' replies Sir T. The tension between Tibu and Blue Diamond has gone. By going through this display, and hearing each other out, they have shown a sort of mutual respect.

'You got a click?' Tibu asks Blue Diamond.

'No. You?'

'Oh yeah,' says Tibu proudly. 'Vietnom. Victory Is Everything To Niggas On My side.'

Rowe pops his head round the door again. He looks at Blue Diamond. 'Where's your tape, homie?'

He's using a Tupac track for his backing music. 'I got to wait for my homeboy to bring it.'

'He's not here yet?' Rowe looks at his watch. The show is about to start.

'I'll go see.' And Blue Diamond leaves the room in search of his homeboy. After he has gone, Sir T turns to Tibu and says, 'Ciscoed up.'

'Hell yeah,' says Tibu. 'I smelled that cisco on his breath the moment he came in.'

'Cisco' is slang for any drink that has 'sherm' added to it: 'sherm' is the popular name for embalming fluid – formaldehyde. The drugs people inject, inhale and ingest say so much about the times they consume them in. Speed – even the name was perfect for the urgency of the punk era. The grim symbolism of heroin, say, with its elaborately ugly paraphernalia and the antisocial psychotropic cocoon it created, was perfect too for the doomed, dead-end aesthetic of white suburbia in the early nineties. More recently the white-boy drug of choice has been Ketamine: an animal tranquillizer. But rarely has a drug had as impressive a symbolism as sherm: what an appropriate drug it has been for these ghettos through their most murderous years. Not only a symbolic substance, but a plentiful one too.

Sherm has become a popular reference point in West Coast rhymes. The most famous anthem to the drug is Jayo Felony's hit 'Sherm Stick':

> *We gon' smoke a dip, all of it, not a little bit*
> *We gon' smoke a dip – sherm stick . . .*
> *I took four hard hits then passed it to the next man*
> *Now it seems like I got powers like the X-Man*
> *Sittin' on the kerb for fuckin' hours . . .*

As Jayo's rhyme goes on to say, part of growin' up is throwin' up. The legendary potency of the drug has become a familiar metaphor. One of Sir T's stock lines runs:

> *My raps will get you high like sherm, they always laced . . .*

The fad for using formaldehyde as a drug began in the seventies. Authorities were first alerted to its use when funeral homes in New Jersey, California and Maryland started noticing that their cavity-embalming fluid was no longer working. Ghoulishly, corpses continued to decay. On closer inspection they discovered that their bottles of the fluid had been watered down or their contents entirely replaced with water.

Drug users have always been remarkably resourceful in seeking out even the most obscure new high, and then fetishizing it, creating a unique vocabulary for it. Sherm connoisseurs prefer cavity-embalming fluid to the arterial fluid pumped into the blood vessels – it contains more formaldehyde. Originally dope dealers used the fluid to disguise the poor quality of their weed, but quickly discovered that some consumers found that they preferred it to marijuana. It probably acquired the name sherm when users started dipping Sherman cigarettes in the fluid, choosing the brand because its cigarettes are more robustly constructed than most, and don't fall apart when steeped in fluid. (To keep things confusing, 'sherm sticks' also became slang for cigarettes dipped in PCP (phencyclidine), or 'angel dust'.) Meanwhile some users preferred to cut out the cigarette and simply started adding the mortician's fluid to Cisco – a cheap but potent brand of wine – and soon 'cisco' became the standard name for any alcoholic drink laced with the stuff. Ultimately, and probably appropriately for a drug born in the mortuaries, sherm is a lethal habit. Formaldehyde is a very effective carcinogen.

I notice that Sir T is making eyes at the older of the black-dressed soul singers. His eyes are fixed directly on her large breasts. 'I want to squeeze those things,' he whispers.

Before he can make a move on her, Rowe bursts into the room. Blue Diamond is back with him. He has found his backing track. 'OK?' he says. 'Everybody ready?'

'Yes. We're ready.'

'Now,' Rowe addresses the whole room. 'I've kept my part of the promise. There are A&R guys from all the record companies out there, just like I told you there were going to be. Now it's up to you. I want you to keep your side of the promise.' He holds out his hands and says, 'Form a circle.'

The performers link hands and Rowe intones: 'Dear God. We thank you for bringing us here tonight.'

The r'n'b singer Kenny Byrd nods devoutly. Rowe continues: 'We thank you for giving us the talent that we have, and for letting us share it tonight, for letting is have the opportunity to show it tonight.' Everyone has their eyes shut, apart from Sir T, who is still greedily eyeing the soul singer's bosom. 'We pray that we can all give you the best performance we can possibly give.'

'Amen,' everyone says loudly.

On the way out of the room, Tibu gives Blue Diamond some avuncular advice: 'Remember – don't curse.'

'Yeah,' says the singer from the r'n'b group MSO that Sir T has been gawping at. 'Don't curse, 'cause my momma is out there.'

'Oh, I won't curse,' says Sir T. 'I love your momma.'

Tibu asks her, 'How old are you?'

'I'm 23,' she says, as if to say she's way out of his class.

'Ooooh,' mocks Tibu. 'Twenty-*three*! I thought you were 40.'

The girl looks at Tibu sourly as he leaves the dressing room and prepares to take his turn on stage.

There are only about 70 or 80 people in the hall. Rowe has stocked his large bar but hardly anyone drinks. No one smokes. A few buy fried chicken from the kitchens. People have paid their $10 to come here to support their friends, their sons, daughters and brothers. No one looks particularly interested in paying out any more than that. Rowe is never going to become a millionaire doing this.

The judges are lined up at a desk at the front of the stage. The audience, gathered around the candle-lit tables on the concrete floor, are the friends and relatives of each performer. Cavi and a few others of the Belltown click, to whom Tibu has sold tickets, huddle at the rear.

Tibu is on. He takes the mike. 'Check it out,' he booms. 'This is my man, Sir T, representing Bellflower, California.'

He waits for the playback to start. Instead a horrible noise grinds out of the PA system, then silence.

A few seconds pass. Tibu grins nervously. 'They don't gonna get this tune up.'

The backing tape still doesn't start.

'Come on,' says Tibu gamely. 'All the ladies in the house say, "Oh-oh."'

Several women answer, 'Oh-oh.'

'Oh-oh,' says Tibu, trying to keep a spark of interest alive.

'Oh-oh,' repeats the smattering of voices.

Fortunately for Tibu, the music suddenly kicks in now and he starts to rhyme, stomping around the stage:

We're going for the ghetto medal
Walkin' over these broads even if they delicate like rose petals . . .

It's a lousy performance. For all his pre-show bravado, the delivery is ragged, and he looks like he doesn't really know what to do apart from march up and down. Sir T tries to act the part of hypeman, but because they've never actually rehearsed, he looks unsure of when Tibu is going to leave him space for his turn. By the second chorus of Tibu chanting, 'Hustle, hustle', they've lost the crowd and people are talking over the music.

Tibu and Sir T walk off the stage to lukewarm applause. Big Al is in the crowd, dressed as always in white denim. He's clapping politely. In the past year's he's performed at James Rowe's talent shows too: he's performed at just about every talent show there is. Tonight he has just come along to lend his support. By the time he and Tibu shake hands, Tibu has already started to blame the quality of the PA system for his faulty delivery.

'I liked it,' Al insists magnanimously. 'That was phat.' Tibu nods. Al always has a civil word for everyone, even though he never seems to get the prize he feels he deserves himself.

It's the thin r'n'b singer Kenny Byrd who wins the crowd over. He's chosen 'My Heart Will Go On', Celine Dion's overblown show-stopper from the movie *Titanic*. He gives it his all. Behind the stage, Rowe and Leonard have arranged a semicircle of white Christmas lights, a low-tech attempt to add some glamour to the proceedings. The left half blinks on and off. The right half doesn't seem to work properly.

As the tune rises to the final chorus key change, Kenny Byrd closes his eyes, rapt, hands out before him.

'Look at that pansy,' sniggers Tibu.

This is only Blue Diamond's second performance. The week before he appeared at a talent show at the Vision Theater in Leimert Park. He had seen a poster in a church advertising the talent show, and had decided that he was good enough to compete. It cost him $25 just to appear at the audition for the show, but they promised that there was a $500 prize for the winner.

When he got to the theatre, the show was a shambles. There was no PA system, just a tape machine on the stage, and the prize money had shrunk to $100. Blue Diamond didn't get anywhere near winning. It wouldn't have mattered if he had. When he left, disgusted, the organizers were asking the winner if he'd take a cheque, because they didn't have the cash on them.

Waiting to go on stage tonight, Blue Diamond notes cynically that all those stars who Rowe promised would be here tonight don't seem to have materialized. 'He was talking about how Ice Cube was going to be here,' he remembers wryly. After the Leimert Park fiasco, he's learned not to expect very much from these talent shows.

But when it's his turn, Blue Diamond bursts on to the stage. Where Tibu seemed to shrink up there, the small Compton rapper fills the auditorium. All eyes are on him.

His delivery is furious: his fast rhymes are full of the usual bravado about his rhyming skills, but they're also full of pent-up fury:

Through the hood I float, blowin' the smoke
God please ease my pain, I'm really missin' my locs . . .

He's rhyming about lost friends, some killed in shooting incidents, others killed in the stupid car accidents which young people get killed in. It's not a particularly polished performance; it is the obvious bitterness of his delivery that makes it so electrifying.

Afterwards Rowe grabs the mike and beckons all the competitors on to the stage, where he arranges them in a semicircle behind him.

'Hopefully we impressed you,' he says, looking down toward the judges. The panel of well-connected major-label A&R representatives that he promised on his flyers has not materialized. Most of the judges are from small South Central labels with names like Hightime or Ambassador. 'I appreciate you guys coming here tonight.'

The audience claps them. 'We put a lot of money up to get the building. It's not completed, but God is great . . .' Another smattering of clapping. 'And He knows how hard we've all been working to get this building ready. What this evening means,' Rowe pontificates, 'is that there are no longer any excuses for our young boys and men. They can no longer say they don't have the opportunity. If they decide to go astray, they no longer have an excuse to say, "It was the government's fault . . . it was this guy's fault or that guy's fault." '

The audience haven't come here for sermonizing: they've come along to see if their son, or daughter, or friend has won a prize. Nobody is really paying any attention to Rowe's self-aggrandizing speech. 'Hey,' he protests. 'Come on. We got more to say.'

Leonard gets up from his seat in the audience, raises his arms and tries to shush the crowd.

'Listen,' orders Rowe loudly. 'We have no more excuses! It's all bullcrap. "Oh, my dad gave up on me." "My mom gave up on me." It's all bullcrap. This is the beginning of the end of that. You got to figure out what you goin' to do. It's all bullcrap now.'

James Rowe, impresario, has somehow become the Reverend James Rowe, flinging the rhetoric of a church preacher at his audience, elevating his role as small-time music business entrepreneur to that of saviour of the ghetto.

'It's no good saying we are getting left out. You can blame the Korean and the Hispanic, coming in here. I say, come on in, buy our property if you want to. If they want to take it from us, we've got no excuse if we're doing nothing to keep it.'

It is an achievement to have organized this small show in this run-down part of the city, where there is so little else to go out to see, but it's hard to see how he has reversed the decline of African-American South Central. The uninterested hum of the small crowd starts to drown him out.

'Please,' he pleads. 'Quiet please.'

Leonard stands again and tries to hush the crowd.

'Now we know that the devil's in here,' Rowe admonishes the audience preachily. But he has lost them now: they just want to find out whether the people they paid to come to see have won or not.

Rowe tries to reassert control by beckoning the actor from *Hangin' With Mr Cooper* back on stage. 'Look at this man,' he demands. 'He is a role model.'

There is applause for the TV star. 'What's a 15-year-old gang-banger not got that he had? Nothing at all. We should be proud of young men who are not afraid of making something of what they have.'

Blue Diamond, dressed all in Crip blue, listens to all this

cynically. He's heard all these pious words from his elders many times before. He's tired of grown-ups like Rowe looking down on young people like him. They don't look for the good in you, only the bad. They don't really understand what it means, being young, growing up here now.

Thankfully, Rowe grinds to a halt. 'OK, now for what you all have been waiting for. Can we have the trophies up here?' The trophies are huge. Rowe has done them proud. Three tiers of gilded plastic. On the top sits a large musical note.

Rowe takes the results from the judges and reads: 'In third place, my man, Blue Diamond.'

Blue Diamond is disappointed when he hears his name. He feels he should have won second place at least. But it's only his second show, and the first prize he's won for music. Tibu is more depressed, though. The moment he hears Blue Diamond's name, he guesses that there isn't going to be a prize for him. Tibu thought it was going to be easy, that his talent would be obvious to everyone here. The boy from *Hangin' With Mr Cooper* hands over the trophy and asks, 'You want to say anything, Blue?'

Blue Diamond, who had been so articulate a few minutes before on stage, takes the mike, pauses and then says briefly, 'Thanks.'

MSO get the second place, and Kenny Byrd's eye-watering version of the theme from *Titanic* takes first price.

People start shifting their chairs to go home. No one wants to hang out around here any longer than they have to. 'Congratulations to the winners,' the guy from *Hangin' With Mr Cooper* is gushing, 'And believe me, just because you didn't win a trophy, doesn't mean you didn't win. We're all winners in here tonight.'

It's not all bad for Tibu. He has done his first live show. He has learned that it is not as easy as he imagined.

His mother, who kicked him out of the house because she was tired of his go-nowhere delinquent behaviour and his layabout friends, came to see him perform. 'You were good,' she tells him encouragingly. She's a small, neat, well-dressed woman, young-looking and fresh-faced. Tibu dwarfs her.

Tibu tells me proudly: 'All this time, she didn't know what I was doing. She probably thought I was just wasting my time.' Tibu is pleased she came.

It's past ten when we leave. The Sunday night congregations are spilling out of the storefront churches on to the dark streets. Rowe isn't the only one to have taken advantage of the empty properties to preach his gospel of hope and regeneration. The small churches on Western all have such grand names: the Christ Apostolic Church of America, the Calvary Life Assembly International and the Celestial Church in Christ are all within a few hundred yards of the HQ of the Unlimited Break Talent Show.

Small, ramshackle storefront churches constantly sprout and die here, as if this part of the city is struggling to remember the way things were in the Southern Bible Belt before the big migrations of the forties and fifties.

Here the pastors preach of damnation and hellfire to prostitutes and crack addicts. Many of the preachers at these small churches are those who've been themselves saved from a life of sin, like Michael 'Ice Mike' Rowles, once the murderous leader of the Main Street Mafia Crips, now a Minister at Holy Temple Four Square Com-munity Church on Crenshaw. Or Robert E. Manuel, once a pimp and dealer, now Bishop of the Emmanuel Church of Christ Apostolic Faith's headquarters on South Central Avenue. Faith and sin exist here in such close proximity.

Just across the street neatly dressed Seventh Day Adventists emerge from the building on the corner opposite, on which is painted the words 'Ephesus Church'.

A young woman in a neat blouse and cardigan, clutching her handbag, calls out, 'What's going on over there?'

'A talent show,' answers Tibu. 'You been going to church?'

'That's right,' says the woman.

'Can I come to your church?' asks Tibu.

'Of course you can,' the woman answers generously.

'Well then, why don't you give me your telephone number, so I can go to church with you?'

The woman scuttles hastily off down the sidewalk.

'The man's a fool,' giggles Sir T happily. But a fool after his own heart.

By the time we hit the 710 freeway, Tibu has rationalized the evening. Maybe Sir T wasn't hype enough, wasn't lively enough to give him support, but aside from that, his performance was great – they just couldn't see it, that's all. If the real A&R men from the Hollywood labels had turned up, they would have recognized his talent.

The performance itself was a washout for Sir T, but he's done rather better tonight when it comes to hitting on girls. 'I picked up three phone numbers,' he says proudly, holding up a scrap of paper with some numbers written on it. 'Did you see that girl in the bodysuit? She was fucking coming on.'

PART FOUR

'He was a detective-lieutenant attached to the 77th Street Division and we talked in a bare room with two small desks against opposite walls, and room to move between them . . .

He lit half of a cigar and threw the match on the floor where a lot of company was waiting for it. His voice said bitterly:

"Shines. Another shine killing. That's what I rate after eighteen years in this man's police department. No pix, no space, not even four lines in the want ad department."'

Raymond Chandler,
Farewell, My Lovely, 1940

20

C Walk

BABYBOY

The summer boils. Up in the Hollywood Hills it's at least ten degrees cooler than down here on the flat plain of South Central, where the temperature is rising towards 100.

For Sunday breakfast, Babyboy takes me to Jack's Family Diner on Leighton and Western. It's as if we've stepped into the South of 50 years ago. Old men in trilbies and stout women sweating in their church best, ranged around the counter that rings the small kitchen, look up from their chicken, eggs, steaming collard greens, pale, soupy grits and bright-yellow cornbread.

In the city, the African-American culture has had many changes forced upon it, but the cookery has remained resiliently consistent: a fixed point by which people can anchor themselves, whether it's at Stevie's On The Strip on Crenshaw, Roscoe's Chicken And Waffles on Pico, or Bertha's Soul Food on Western. Restaurant food in South Central can be exceptional. Everywhere you go, there are thousands of tiny BBQ joints, with dubious-looking frontages which belie the excellence of the cooking, like Woody's on Crenshaw, or Big Joe's at the junction with Slauson, whose excellent motto is: 'YOU DON'T NEED TEETH TO EAT MY BEEF.' Compared to the chi-chi restaurants up in Sunset Plaza, these offer feasts, yet very few people ever venture down from the hillside to try them.

South Central has few places where people can sit down together and socialize, and this fact is one of the eternal complaints of those who want to eradicate gang-banging. Jack's Family Diner is a local treasure, cherished by people from all over the locality. It's open every day from six in the morning until two in the afternoon on weekdays, three on Sundays. For a while it was in danger of closing when Jack became hooked on crack a few years back, but the local 'big-ass ballers' from the community banded around to help him kick it. They didn't want to lose their diner. This is a place where the Rollin' 30s Crips can sit down next to the Rollin' 40s Crips from south of King without there being a beef.

It's too full to find a seat, so we order our food to go: immense steaming paper bags full of food wrapped in napkins for warmth. We drive the two blocks back to Babyboy and Marlene's house. Marlene's parents have just pulled up outside, supermarket bags full of shopping.

'Let me get them,' says Babyboy, taking the bags from Marlene's mother and hauling them into the little house.

Marlene stands there with Chanel on her hip. Babyboy takes the baby proudly and holds her up in the air. Marlene looks on anxiously. 'Come on,' she says. 'She don't like that.'

Babyboy just stands there, holding the baby in the air.

'Give her to me, Kimeyo. She don't like that.'

At first the baby likes it. She smiles as Babyboy holds her defiantly up in the air.

'Please.'

The baby is starting to whine now, wanting to be put down.

BLUE DIAMOND

It's late afternoon when I pull in to the kerb at the address Blue Diamond gave me: strictly speaking, Bullis Road is in Lynwood, just outside the City of Compton, though its young residents count it as Compton too. I am curious about Blue Diamond. When he was up on stage, performing to win that huge, gaudy third-place trophy, it looked like it was the most important thing he'd ever done in his life. I asked him for his number after the show, and told him I wanted to talk to him. He told me to come and visit him here, at home.

I arrive later than I had intended. I have had a long day, and I'm tired. The first thing I notice as I pull up is that the wall on the offside of the car is covered in gang graffiti. These days I automatically try to read the spidery writing on walls, to see what it tells me about the locality. The spots where gang graffiti accrue are palimpsests, the letters overwritten, resprayed, crossed through and angrily painted out. It's an obscure language, not intended for me.

So I'm trying in vain to decipher them even as I'm reversing my car. 'WHHS Pirus': Something Holly Hood Something Pirus? The Pirus are a subset of the Bloods who thrive here in Lynwood. It suddenly dawns on me that here I am, visiting a Crip and, from the writing outside his house, this appears to be a Blood neighbourhood. I'm trying to figure this out, and also what 'WHHS' could stand for, when my notebooks fly off the dashboard.

'Fuck.' I have reversed into another car that must have parked right behind me after I last checked the mirror.

I jump out of my car and, in that paranoid moment, I imagine I've hit the car of some young Blood, who will not want to back down from a confrontation. But it's a van, driven by an elderly black man in a brown T-shirt. 'Sorry,' I say. I lean down to check his fender. There's a dent in it, though no dent in my car. I'm not sure whether I caused the mark or not. But the old man just looks at me warily, resentfully, and scurries away, avoiding any confrontation.

I hazard a guess that is a bad neighbourhood. Looking around, I see all the houses have bars on the windows and doors. Blue Diamond's single-storey house is painted dark green and stands on the corner. Old trees overhang it.

Blue Diamond's grandmother opens the door and beckons me inside. 'Michael is just having a shower,' she says, and after offering me a drink, returns with a glass of Pepsi and a coaster. I sit on the sofa and wait, looking at the neat living room, the house plants and the photographs on the walls, the ceramic dolphin that sits on the middle of the dining table.

Blue Diamond finally appears, towelled dry and dressed, approaches and shakes my hand shyly. In the security of his own home he is far calmer than he was the other night at the talent show. He tells me we should talk in the bedroom he shares with his younger brother; he spends a lot of time in there.

Blue Diamond tells me that his first name is Michael. When he sleeps in this bedroom, Mike often dreams that he is a star. The other night he dreamed he was having sex with Brandy, the beautiful r'n'b star. The first thing he'd do if he made some money would be to get some clothes, buy a car and get right out of here.

There is a chest of drawers, and a set of shelves with no books on – just a stereo, a TV and a Sega Megadrive. There are two beds, one for him and another for his brother. The walls are covered in posters and pictures torn out of magazines. Many are of Tupac Shakur. There's a black and white photo of Suge Knight there too.

Mike is a fan of Tupac: he feels a communion with him. 'I like him because he talks about real stuff: stuff that was happening to him, around him. He wasn't just makin' up stuff just cause it rhymed.' He smiles his small, reticent smile and explains further: 'My life is so similar to his. His mother was on drugs. Mine is. He didn't have a father. My father has been in jail, like . . . half my life.'

Stuck to a Formica shelf, just above a mass of old blunt butts, are two pictures of Michael when he about six years old. The colour has faded into oranges and browns. Blue Diamond sits on his father's knee. His father, smiling proudly at the camera, is wearing an extravagantly lapelled shirt.

Mike was born at the start of the eighties: his father was a big man in the Crips. 'An O.G.,' he says. Mike's father grew up poor. He was dark-skinned too, like Blue Diamond. It's fashionable to be dark-skinned now, but back in those days people looked down on you if your skin was so dark.

Blue Diamond isn't just a rap name Mike has dreamed up himself. He was christened Blue Diamond. 'See, the Crip rags are blue. Way back in the day, though, the original rags had diamonds on, so that's where I got my name. My whole name is Michael Blue Diamond Lil' Magic Jesus Mairoba Lil' Cuzz Bracks.'

He used to be embarrassed about the extravagant name his father gave him, full of his daddy's pet names for his son, and reminders of his daddy's loyalties to his Crip set. Now, when Michael recites it, he sounds proud of it.

'From the time I was born,' Michael says, 'he was in jail for, like, drugs. Then when I was, like, 11 years old, he got 15 years for murder.'

I ask: 'How did you feel that he had murdered someone? And that he was going to prison?'

'Thch.' Mike sucks his teeth. He looks up and says, 'I wasn't surprised.' Then: 'I was hurt.'Cause I thought I wasn't ever going to see him. I was a little kid. I cried. But it really didn't surprise me that he had killed somebody.'

There was a gang battle of some sort going on, and, whatever the reason, Mike's uncle was shot and killed. Mike's father retaliated, in the way of gang wars. They kill one of yours; you kill one of theirs. Mike's father murdered the man who had killed his brother. 'It was for self-defence,' insists Mike. 'The man who killed my uncle was going to kill my daddy that night. You'd do the same if I was going to kill you,' he adds. 'That's what it was like.'

'I don't know,' I say. I've been hearing stories like his for a year now, yet when he says that I'd do the same, it exposes the gulf between my life and his. I don't know if I would do the same, but I would like to believe I would not. I have never encountered any situations in my life that would let me know how I would react, how I would feel in those circumstances, yet I am tired, and the fatalism in what he says irritates me. 'I'm from London,' I say exasperatedly. 'It's like a different planet.'

'I know,' the 19-year-old says. 'You can't understand it unless you're here. It ain't 'cause you're white,' he adds generously. 'Some white people live out here. They're messed up the same way too.'

Mike's father completed his sentence in January of this year and was released. Almost immediately afterwards, he was arrested for a parole violation, and now he's back inside. He is due to be released in 1999.

Mike started rapping when he was about 17, which is late. Most boys I have been meeting started much earlier, but Mike had always assumed he was going to be a professional football player. Though he's small, he was always a talented sportsman. He was never much of an academic, but then he never really had much of a chance to be one. At his high school they had to share books, one to every four or five students on occasion. Sometimes there weren't enough chairs and students had to sit on the floor.

He missed a lot of school, anyway. Getting there was difficult. 'You don't just go to school,' he says. 'You got to *get* to school.' He remembers the passengers in the car who flicked the 'B' hand sign at him on 104th, thumb curled round to meet the forefinger, before swinging into a U-turn and driving back at him, with guns firing. Or the time he was jumped by three guys and eight girls with sticks and canes. Born into a known Crip family, he was a target, both at school and on the way there.

His home life was chaotic too. With their mother taking drugs and their father in prison, Mike and his brother became used to poverty. They ate irregular meals and slept on the floor. They were lucky if they received presents on their birthdays or at Christmas.

So Mike focused on that more traditional fast track out of the ghetto: sport. He believes he stood a chance, too. For a while the

Los Angeles Unified Schools district tried bussing him out to schools in the Valley. There, Mike played in football teams with white kids, and made friends with some, but he still can't get over the shock of how stupid they seemed to him at times. Well-meaningly, they would call him names: 'Hey, Michael Jordan', as if everyone who was black was Michael Jordan. One time, he heard a team-mate talking about him and a girlfriend of his: 'Hey, Mike got into it with Sherylnn.'

'Which Sherylnn? Sherylnn who?' another football player asked.

'You know, Sherylnn the nigger,' said his team-mate. Mike went up to him and hit him in the mouth. Ignorant stuff like that, he recalls.

His great ambition to become a professional American-football player fell apart about four years ago, when his drug-addicted mother could no longer care for him properly. With his father in prison, he had no choice but to live with his grandmother in this house on Bullis Road. She's been looking after him ever since, and receives a small income from the state that contributes to his upkeep.

The problem is that Bullis Road is a major Blood area. 'All around here is Bloods,' says Mike, with a tiny wave of the hand. Not just any Bloods either: these streets are Piru territory. 'So I don't go outside,' he says simply. Raised a Crip, Mike is now living in the heart of enemy territory.

That put paid to his ambitions to be a sportsman. Sometimes Mike goes back to the old Crip neighbourhoods he grew up in, north-west of here, but in Lynwood he can't show his face. 'This is really a bad neighbourhood. Really,' he laughs quietly.

The streets in Mike's neighbourhood are run by the Leuders Park Pirus, one of the Compton Blood sets who take their name from the small recreation ground a few blocks further south on Bullis Road. He spends pretty much his whole life in his bedroom. It's hard to pursue a career in sport when you don't go outside much.

'Does it bother you,' I ask, 'being cooped up in here?'

'It don't bother me,' says Mike, "cause I'm used to it."

'Three years not going out?'

'You get used to it. I can go outside. I can go out and chill in the front yard for a minute, but I don't walk anywhere.'

An old colour line dividing black and white somehow became a new one dividing red and blue. Not that it's as simple any more as just Bloods versus Crips: the territoriality of local gangs is far more complex.

Compton has long been an epicentre of gang conflict. There are now Crip and Blood gangs all over America, and in fact gangs have sprung up all over the Third World, styling themselves after the Los Angeles gangs. But some of the original battles that drew up the bloody lines between those in red and those in blue were fought on the streets around here.

The phenomenon of black gangs can seem like a monster that crept out of nowhere, but it has been a long time in the making. The first era of black gangs may have been easier to understand as a simple response to the welcome they had received from white Angelenos in the first half of this century, when African-Americans had had to fight for territory and each street was precious. In the sixties, though, black gang activity began to decline rapidly, and towards the end of the decade it had almost entirely disappeared. Quite why is a mystery, but the growth of the civil-rights movement may have had much to do with it.

In the sixties, a generation became radicalized. They sensed the possibility of change; they were impatient for it, even. The gradualist policies of Martin Luther King were no longer enough. When the civil-rights leader came to speak at the Westminster Neighborhood Center auditorium in the aftermath of the Watts uprising, he was booed off the stage.

One reason for the low gang activity could be that several radical political groupings emerged in their place. In Los Angeles, a former member of the Slausons gang, Bunchy Carter, set up the city's first Black Panthers chapter. Maybe the Panthers were a sort of gang themselves – they certainly weren't above using strong-arm tactics – but their polemic and political aspirations were real enough, and anyone who's hung around contemporary gang-bangers, whose political ambitions stop at the next street corner, would know that the Panthers represented something radically different. Meanwhile a black nationalist called Manuela Ron Karenga also emerged in Los Angeles, creating the Afrocentrist political grouping he named US. Karenga's most lasting achievement may turn out to be the invention of a brand-new tradition, Kwanzaa – a black Christmas-time holiday – which he created so that African-Americans would have their own reason to celebrate. Today, shops all over America are filled with Kwanzaa cards every year.

The decline of LA gangs coincides with the rise of these organizations. Maybe more significantly, the sudden and brutal resurgence of gang warfare at the end of the sixties also coincides with the crushing of radical black ambitions.

Los Angeles police set up the Criminal Conspiracy Squad to target the Panthers. Nationally, J. Edgar Hoover declared that the Black Panthers were 'the greatest threat to internal security in the country'. The activities of the FBI Counter Intelligence Program, COINTELPRO – which targeted black political groupings and leaders, including Martin Luther King, over this period – are now well documented. By the last year of the decade, 27 Panthers had been killed by the police and 749 had been jailed or arrested.

As part of COINTELPRO, the FBI deliberately fostered enmity between black radicals, infiltrating the groups, employing *agents provocateurs* and forging letters that heightened tensions between the leaderships. It was depressingly easy to spark off the bitter feud that followed. The militant, political Panthers quickly clashed with Karenga's cultural, Afrocentrist US. Panther leader Bunchy Carter was shot and killed at the University of Southern California in the ensuing internecine battle. A generation of political leaders had been quickly eliminated. In their place, a new set of leaders began to emerge, the O.G.s.

One of the first groupings to emerge were the Piru Street gang, who originated in the Compton area and were a clearly identifiable entity by 1969, well before separate Blood and Crip gangs appeared.

The Crips were almost certainly the creation of a Fremont High School student named Raymond Washington, who, ironically, had been impressed with the Panthers' charismatic mixture of revolutionary politics and strong-arm tactics.

Washington was a young tough who walked with an exaggerated swagger, clutching a silver-topped cane and wearing a Panther-style leather jacket. Many have speculated that the gang were called Crips as a short version of the word 'cripples', because the new gang members copied Washington's habit of walking as if he had a limp and carrying a cane.

The Crip Walk, or C Walk, is still in evidence. You can see stars like Snoop Dogg Crips, who still drops the LBC – Long Beach Crip – tag frequently in his songs, doing the exaggerated lope of the Crip Walk in some of his videos. Former Death Row artist Kurupt's track 'C Walk' is an even more direct reference:

Get your walk on – C walkin' homie.

Alejandro Alonso, a young former Blood gang member, is now a postgraduate student at USC. He studies LA gangs. He has his own theory about the origin of the name Crip. Raymond Washington, he believes, must have remembered an old local gang called the Avenues who had once run the area he grew up in, because for a while the original Crips had been known as the Baby Avenues. Some of the members soon gave that a twist, exchanging the word

Baby for Crib, and the gang became known as the Avenue Cribs, or the Cribs.

Somehow, Alonso believes, when local journalists first came across the gang they must have misheard the name as 'Crips'. The word first appeared in print in 1972 in the black newspaper the *Sentinel-Times*. Journalistic recognition was enough for the O.G.s. Soon they started calling themselves Crips too. It says something for the Crips' origins in the post-Panther era that one of the acronyms gang members derived from the letters was 'Continual Revolution In Progress'. They certainly inherited the Panthers' ambition to take power, though this notion of power was devoid of political content.

In the early seventies, Washington's gang rapidly formed alliances with other groups. Those who didn't ally were often brutally crushed: schools were attacked and businesses were held up and robbed. The Crips quickly made a name for themselves as being more violent than their predecessors.

By 1972 the 77th Street Division of the LAPD were tracking the Crip gangs that were spreading with remarkable speed from Inglewood on the west side to Watts and Compton on the east. Already there were 18 black gangs operating in Los Angeles County. That was the year when the first Crip murder was recorded, after a young Crip demanded that someone give up his leather jacket at a concert given by Curtis Mayfield, War and Wilson Pickett. The guy refused and the gang-banger killed him for it.

The Piru Street Gang were one of the gangs who originally allied themselves with the Crips, even down wearing the blue 'rags' that served as a uniform and calling themselves the Compton Piru Crips. But soon the remaining independent gangs rebelled against the growing dominance of the Crips and formed their own alliance. According to some O.G. memories, the first gang that began identifying itself with the red bandanas that defied the Crip blue was the Compton Pirus. The Compton Pirus called a meeting with a gang that was then known as the Leuders Park Hustlers, and the two sets allied to form a new grouping which became known as 'Bloods'.

Unfortunately for him, Blue Diamond lives in the middle of Leuders Park territory, one of the most fought-over turfs in one of the oldest gang rivalries in Los Angeles.

The red and the blue were now firmly pitched against each other – an underclass divided by a fight for control of their own neighbourhoods. The fight over territory has intensified and fragmented. Instead of becoming the unified force that the original Crips appear to have dreamed of, gangs fought over their small local territories. By 1978 there were already around 70 gangs in the Los Angeles area, and the majority were Crips.

The celebrity ex-Crip gang banger 'Monster' Kody Scott, who now calls himself Sanyika Shakur, describes the Crip–Blood confrontation as an unseen war. 'The death toll,' he wrote, 'is in the thousands – wounded, uncountable, missing-in-action, unthinkable. No one is keeping a tally. No one has noticed.'

Kody Scott was initiated into the Eight Tray Crips five years before Blue Diamond was born. He was given a pump-action shotgun and taken on a ride to kill a group of Brim Bloods who were edging into Crip territory. The gun had eight rounds in it; he was told to make sure he came back with it empty. He remembers being dropped off in a Ford Mustang with five other Crips, and blasting away at the group of Bloods. He remembers his seventh shot bringing down a Blood who tried to escape – the first of the many that he would kill. And afterwards he remembered the senior gang member debriefing him and welcoming him into the set: 'Bangin' ain't no part-time thang, it's full time, it's a career. It's bein' down when ain't nobody else down with you. It's gettin' caught and not tellin'. Killin' and not caring, and dyin' without fear. It's love for your set and hate for the enemy. You hear what I'm sayin'?'

Kody was 11 years old when he killed his first Blood. The Crip who inducted him into the gang was 15.

By the time Mike 'Blue Diamond' Bracks was born, the war had already been going on steadily for ten years and the LAPD were estimating that there were already some 15,000 Crips and Bloods in the Los Angeles area.

There are now around 300 gangs in the Los Angeles County area. The figures for gang-related murders in LA County peaked at a staggering 803 deaths in 1992: two-fifths of that year's total number of homicides in the region. After 1995, the figures declined, paralleling the decline in national murder rates. But gang membership continued to grow, and it is now at an all-time high of 150,000. Forty years after the great migrations to escape the constrictions of the old South, the new neighbourhoods were busy re-creating their own new forms of segregation.

Mike used to run with the Crips: after all, it ran in the family. When he gave up his ambition to become a sports star, he decided he would become a rapper instead. The first rhymes he wrote were all about banging with the Crips. 'But I had to get away from that,' he says. 'I wasn't going to be a gang-banger and do nothing. I was going to do it to the fullest. I was going to be a murderer. I was going to sell drugs. And I know too many people who are in jail from doing that type of stuff. So I learned from my daddy,' he says. 'I didn't want to end up like him. I wanted something more out of life.'

Mike says he doesn't bang any more anyway. At 19, he'd already be on the old side. Police in Long Beach estimate that most gang-bangers are aged between nine and 18 years old. As RZA from the Wu-Tang Clan – who grew up in some of the most murderous housing projects in the New York area, on Staten Island – once told me: 'Sixteen, 17, 18 – that's the most violent, uncontrollable age for the black teenager. At 19 you catch on to a few things. Like women.'

It would be hard for Mike to continue banging, in this neigh-

329

bourhood, anyway. And God helped him too, he insists. 'I started going to church. I started praying a lot and the more I prayed, the more I stopped doing the bad things I was doing.'

I say, 'You quit the gangs, but your rap name is still Blue Diamond?'

'My name came to me at birth. I just chose Blue Diamond as a rap name. I was brought into this. It wasn't my choice.'

To me, it's bizarre. Mike still clings to his Crip inheritance, even though it has kept him locked up in this room for most of three years. The other night at the talent show, he still wore his colours. He's been shot at and beaten up for wearing them, but he still 'represents'. The complex web of loyalties and pride seems to hard for me to fathom. But then the secure middle classes of the world don't need to pledge such loyalties to know who they are.

I ask, 'Do you ever wish you weren't christened Blue Diamond?'

He answers a little more hesitantly this time. 'I don't wish I wasn't.'

The fact that Tupac affiliated himself publicly with the Bloods doesn't stop Mike admiring him. On the wall is the photo of Suge Knight, who wore a gold ring with the letters 'MOB' picked out in diamonds: Mob Piru. At first, that appears shocking, but several other Crips I've met also say they are Tupac fans. The real battleground for the African-American gangs is fought over turf, over geography, not over culture. 'At times, Tupac hated his father for what he'd done to him,' I say. 'Do you sometimes do that too?'

'I wish my parents had been something different. But you can't change things. I feel everything happens for a reason and that happens to make me stronger.'

This part of Lynwood was Suge Knight's turf. Tupac used to come here to hang out with the local Pirus, driving around the neighbourhood with the Leuders Parks Pirus in his open-top Jaguar. Once he'd signed to Death Row, he embraced the whole imagery of the Blood gangs. For anyone as confused as Tupac was about his own manhood, gangs are, peculiarly, a refuge. To be a gang-banger is to deny any weakness, to banish it entirely. Gang-banging is the most desperate assertion of maleness.

Mike remembers Tupac coming by around Christmas 1995. He stopped outside the house to admire the Christmas lights Mike's grandmother had put up. She does it every year. Tupac told her how much he liked the lights. 'I'll come back and see them next year,' he promised.

Mike was right here in this room, when he first heard that Tupac had been shot in Las Vegas. He felt bad about that. After all, most people believed it was a South Side Crip, Orlando Anderson, who had assassinated him.

In the days after Tupac's shooting a war broke out between the Pirus and the South Side Crips. The first attack was on a South Side Crip called Darnell Brim, in a store right next to Underworld Records on Alondra Boulevard. Over the next few days police counted 12 shooting incidents and three fatalities. Local gang-bangers claim that there were more. Rumours flew that Bloods were being offered $10,000 for every South Side Crip killed.

Mike stayed inside. Every time the Pirus who were seeking to revenge Tupac attacked the South Siders, the Crips from south of Lynwood, in Compton, retaliated.

After several days of warfare between the north and south sides of Compton, the police intervened. On 2 October 1996 they launched a massive series of raids on addresses in Compton, Long Beach and Paramount.

Orlando Anderson – the man suspected of killing Tupac – was at his girlfriend's home in Lakewood when they burst in and arrested him. Ironically, in interviews given after the arrest, he claimed he had been listening to Tupac's *All Eyez On Me* at the time. The warrant the police used that night was for another murder – that of Compton resident Edward Webb, who had been attacked and killed at a party by 'several black males' the previous April. But Las Vegas detectives were also there to question Anderson about the killing of Tupac Shakur. In the interview, he insisted doggedly that he had returned to his hotel room, where his girlfriend had nursed the wounds he had received from Tupac and Suge Knight's assault in the lobby of the MGM Grand Hotel. Las Vegas police weren't able to find anything to link him to the killing of Tupac. Compton Police released him: the DA had told them that they didn't have enough evidence to link him to the murder of Edward Webb either.

The tension between north and south Compton remained. Nobody in Mike's neighbourhood ventured out after dark much that autumn. In his room, he heard bursts of gunfire and then waited to see if they were followed by the wail of an ambulance. If he heard the sirens, then he knew that somebody had been hit.

At some point in the darkening evening, Mike tells me that his favourite book is the teenage gothic favourite *Flowers In The Attic*, in which a deranged mother and grandmother keep children locked away in an attic. Do you ever feel like you're locked in the attic here? I ask him.

'Yeah,' says Mike.

The street lights are on by the time I leave. The sky at the horizon is the sort of rich, smog-drenched pink you see only in Los Angeles. A bright, tiny fingernail moon shines above the horizon in the west. Mike and I stand at the door, looking up at it, saying our goodbyes.

He goes back inside the house in which he has spent so much of the past three years, and I drive along 110, relishing the silhouettes of palm trees outlined against a sky which changes from red to maroon to purple. As a newcomer I have found LA a hard city to love. At this time of day, driving headlight to tail-light towards the lit skyscrapers of Downtown, and the black outlines of the Holly-wood Hills, with the sun dying so splendidly over the Pacific, it's also hard to hate. I wonder how often Mike gets out to see sunsets like this.

21

Dance Underwater

TIBU

Tibu has taken to calling me collect. He's discovering that General Relief doesn't stretch as far as he'd hoped. 'I just found out some hurtin' news,' he says. 'You remember that girl who rapped with me? That time we were over at Dave's studio?'

'Ms Chevius? What's happened to her.'

'I just spoke to her. She's gone and hooked up with Short Khop.'

'You're kidding?'

'No. She's going to do a song on his album. She just told me. She's going into the studio this afternoon. She met up with this guy called Kidub at Roscoe's or somewhere and told him she was a rapper. He put her on to Khop and now she says she's going to be on his album.'

'Well, maybe she'll put in a good word for you.'

Tibu sighs. 'Maybe. I told her to give Khop my number and say I got plenty of beats. But I doubt it. Once people get in there, they're just looking out for theyself.' He sounds depressed

When I call up Khop about it some time later, he laughs. 'What?' He says he doesn't know who I'm talking about. 'I get a lot of people who're claiming they know me now,' he giggles. Maybe Kidub was trying to impress the girl, to try and get into her sweatpants. Maybe Ms Chevius was just trying to wind Tibu up. If she was, it worked.

'Where have I got to be? How do *I* get hooked up?' Tibu complained sorrowfully. 'When am I going to meet someone who asks me to be on their album?'

The Vietnam click is drifting apart. Tibu pretty much does everything himself these days. The others just aren't as committed as he is.

Sneak has found work in Las Vegas. The Italian Stallion has been sent out of town by his parents. And Tibu's stuck at his grandmother's in Long Beach.

After the summer Tibu is going back to school. This puts off the day when he has to get a job, and besides, he is realizing that he will need some qualifications if he's going to get on.

'I didn't do too well when I was at high school,' he says.

'Why not?' I ask.

He laughs as he says, '706.'

'What do you mean?'

'I had to show that I was with it, that I wasn't a pushover. I was always thumping people.' He reflects for a second. 'I still am.'

For Tibu, staying with his grandmother in her small apartment makes life hazardous. Long Beach is not his territory.

One July day a short Hispanic guy comes up to him and says, 'Where you from?'

If you're a teenager, those can be the scariest words you ever hear in Los Angeles. If you are affiliated, the question is a challenge to your manhood: are you brave enough to admit your affiliations, even before you've heard what they other guy's are, the guy who's calling you out? Because if you say the wrong thing, you know you are going to fight.

Tibu sees the guy go to raise his shirt, and he wonders for a millisecond whether he's going to pull out his strap and shoot. He wishes he had a gun himself.

But the boy turns out to be just raising his shirt to show off his belly. On it, tattooed in dark letters, are the words 'Westside Longo'. The Longos are one of the biggest Hispanic gangs in the area: the Eastside Longos have been embroiled in a bloody battle for territory for years now with groups like the Samoan gang SOS, Sons of Samoa.

If Tibu said he was a member of, say, the Insane Crips, the Longo would have no option but to fight him. Usually Tibu finds it hard to back down from such a challenge, and if this was Bellflower he would fight. After all, he's spent years just doing that for the 706s. If he took this skinny little guy on, he knows he could beat him up easily. He would love to show this teenager that he's not a pushover. But this is Longo turf, a long way from Bellflower. To challenge the guy on it would be to overstep the mark.

'I ain't from nowhere,' says Tibu. It's the standard way of backing down from such a confrontation: deny any affiliation to anything. It sticks in his throat to make such a conciliatory reply to the challenge, but he feels he has no choice. He adds: 'All I am is someone trying to make some money – that's the only place I'm from.'

The Westside Longo nods. 'I hear you.' Having maintained his dominion over any newcomer to the area, he has done his duty to the gang. He wanders away.

Tibu is left fuming. Somebody called him out and there was nothing at all he could do about it but back down.

The last decade – especially the years since the '92 uprising – has seen a new element dominate LA gang battles. Increasingly the fiercest and most protracted battles are not usually between Bloods and Crips, but between gangs whose animosity is based on ethnic differences. During the eighties, Hispanic and African-American gangs shared turf, fighting among their own kind. But now, as Hispanic influence continues to grow and black families move out, the battle for territory is between working-class black kids and the newly dominant Latino gangs.

The gangsta world depicted in the South Central raps has largely been superseded now. The days of Blood and Crip may be numbered. The whole region is changing. South Central is no longer a ghetto in the traditional meaning of the word any more. A ghetto implies a single ethnicity. That has not been true here for years.

To the west, in Venice, black Oakwood gangs have been engaged for most of the decade in one of the most protracted battles, with Hispanic gangs from Culver City. In Compton, a relatively newly emerged Latino gang is fighting a battle with several of the black gangs. They call themselves the Tortilla Flats. How post-modern can you get? Do they know, I wonder, that their name comes from a Steinbeck novel? The Tortilla Flats are huge: if Latino gangs continue to prosper, they will soon dominate the older Blood and Crip groups that they're warring with.

'Tortilla Flats?' says Tibu. 'Oh, they hate black people. I used to buy drugs from them, back when I was dealin'. They always used to say, "Hey, homie. What set are you with?" "I ain't with that shit," I'd say.'

Though he wished he'd had a gun during that confrontation with the Longo, Tibu has never owned one himself. It's always Sneak who owned the weaponry. He's had about every type of gun you can buy, from a .22, up to a .380 and a sawn-off 12-gauge shotgun. Once a relative of Tibu's offered to sell them an AK, but Sneak said they should leave it alone. 'It's too big to carry around,' he counselled. 'That's a drive-by weapon.' Which would be of no use at all to them, since they didn't have a car.

America is never going to get over its love affair with weapons. Of the 36 richest nations in the world, it is not only the richest, but it is also the one with the highest rate for gun deaths in the world, with 14.24 per 100,000 people, beating Brazil into second place and Mexico into a poor third. America has a gun-kill rate 28 times greater than Japan, accounting for almost half of all gun deaths in the developed world.

Driving along Slauson one day, I ask, 'Tibu, just out of curiosity, how much do guns cost around here?' I've heard that you can buy an Uzi or an AK for as little as $200.

'Depends how big a gun you want.'

'Say, a .38.' A number plucked from thin air. I have no idea what a .38 would look like. All I know is that it seems to be a frequently mentioned calibre around here.

'If it's dirty, about $60. If it's fresh out of the box . . . $150.' Fresh out of the box, like it's a pair of new sneakers.

Tibu keeps having another dream about the music business. This time he is in a recording studio. He has unlimited money to spend. He can record whatever he wants to. Then he wakes up and realizes that he is broke as fuck.

'Damn. Why did I have to dream about that shit?'

He thinks that if only it was true, he could record the tracks that would make people realize his talent. It feels like he's this close to it, but he can't touch it. Sometimes he wants it so much that it hurts. Since losing his job and being thrown off the Cal State campus, it's been hard to keep the music going. Tibu doesn't have enough money to rent a studio any more — not at Todd's rates anyway.

He cadges a ride from his grandmother's one day to see his friend Sick Mick, who has a home studio, to try to wheedle some cheap time out of him. Mick lives with his wife Kim and their two kids in a two-storey block built around a courtyard south of Pacific Coast Highway. Tibu steps into the lift and presses the button. He always hates this lift: the stench of disinfectant is so strong it makes his eyes water.

In the apartment, Mick is at the mixing desk in the small living room. His wife Kim is glued to an interactive role-playing game on the Yahoo internet site. Their four-year-old boy is just back from nursery school, and their baby, dressed in a nappy, is playing quietly in the crib.

Mick sits in a wheelchair. He's a thin, spindly man, with shiny, jheri-curled hair, slicked back in a perm like Eazy-E's used to be. He's only 24 but he looks much older. 'I can't do a session right now,' he tells Tibu. 'If you'd gotten here at one o'clock we could have done something. But I got someone coming at four.'

'Oh,' says Tibu, disappointed. 'OK.'

They have known each other years, since before Tibu's mother moved out of Compton to Bellflower. Mick used to go out with Tibu's sister. 'I must have been around 12 or 13,' he laughs. 'I've known Tibu ever since he was a little boy.'

They shared in the excitement of the days when Eazy-E and NWA and later DJ Quik were first coming up, putting their own City of Compton on the map. NWA filmed the video for the track 'Straight Outta Compton' right outside Mick's house. He still remembers how Eazy-E wore a bulletproof vest that day and how Ice Cube was ribbing him: 'Eazy! Don't nobody want you, man . . . you got no need to be dressed like that . . .'

No new artists have come out of Compton for a while. Though he lives in Long Beach, Mick thinks of himself as still representing Compton. He dreams that one day he'll come out and help Compton regain its true status.

Mick was a gangsta rapper – not one of those who just pretend they were. He figured that things in Compton were so intense that people were going to label you a Blood or a Crip one way or another: 'So you end up joining in whatever happens.'

He became one of the Front Hood Compton Crips. These were the days when MC Eight came out with his group, Compton's Most Wanted, so Mick and his friends formed their own group, LA's Most Wanted. They recorded a little independent album, but

it never did anything. Mick had a gangsta verse on a track called
'Livin' A Ruthless Life':

> *I live a ruthless life every day in the street*
> *You gotta smoke motherfuckers, playin' for keeps . . .*

He'd never write a verse like that today.

He was 18 when he was shot in the spine. Tibu says the shooting
was funny, in a sick way. Apparently Mick was trying to have sex with
this girl in his car in a local park, when some guy came up and tried to
rob them. The robbery ended in a scuffle and a shooting. Mick's
paraplegic now. He carried on performing, but the episode changed
him. Instead of writing gangsta raps, he now writes party music. In his
wheelchair he performs a comedy song called 'All Monkeys Love
Bananas', monkeys being women and bananas being . . . well,
bananas. He's performed it at all sorts of shows. The gimmick is that
when he performs it, he throws bananas at the girls in the crowd.

'And hey,' Mick smiles. 'Eating bananas is good for you too.'

There's a signed photo of the actor Cuba Gooding Jnr on the
wall. The actor once presented Mick with a prize for a talent show
he'd won, up in Hollywood at the Roxbury. But he never
managed to get a real break. He thinks he probably didn't want
it badly enough back then. He wasn't ready. He's ready now,
though. He dreams of selling platinum and being a household
name. 'I want to sell big units. I want to stick out like a sore thumb.'

He has acquired an Ensoniq ASR 10 keyboard, a Bose drum
machine and an eight-track. He charges $10 an hour, and works in
the living room with Kim and the kids all around him. There's a
sign above the keyboard that reads: 'Rules'. One rule is that there is
to be no drinking while recording; another is that all sessions must
be paid for in advance. 'You can't go into a liquor store and say,
"I'll pay you another day," ' says Mick, laughing.

The keyboard is arranged so it's easy for him to get to in his wheelchair. He tries not to think about the shooting much: he doesn't like to dwell on anything that would make him depressed. It was just a case of being in the wrong place at the wrong time. That's all. It was bad for a while after he lost the use of his legs, but he's over it now.

Mick's four o'clock appointment is about to arrive. He prepares the eight-track, checking the connections. Tibu sighs and stands up. 'I'll call you, then,' he says. He leans down and shakes Mick's hand. Kim waves goodbye from the computer screen.

The other day Mick was watching a *Spiderman* cartoon on Fox 11 when the station suddenly pulled the cartoon and started showing live footage of some white man who had gone nuts on the inter-change between the 110 and the 105. The man was standing on a ramp 100 feet in the air. He was making some sort of protest. He parked his Toyota truck, unrolled a banner that said: 'HMOs are in it for the money. Live free, love safe or die.' The man was dying of AIDS, it turned out, protesting about Health Maintenance Organizations – private health plans. Once the man had stood around looking up at the helicopters for a couple of minutes, he climbed back inside his truck, poured petrol everywhere and set light to himself and his dog. The explosion showed up really well on TV, and it killed the dog, but somehow the man walked shakily out of it. So then he stood on the edge of the road, high above the ground. You could almost see it going through his head: Shall I jump? Finally he went back to the truck and grabbed a gun, put it in his mouth and blew his brains out, on live television. Cameras kept on rolling. They interrupted children's programmes just so they could show you it.

Mick took a kind of heart from the performance. Look at that guy, he thought. His predicament is way worse than mine.

Tibu makes his way back to his grandmother's.

Ice Cube has just released a new song called 'Ghetto Vet'. It's on the soundtrack to Master P's new movie, *I Got The Hook Up*. If drugs were the illegal ghetto activity of the eighties and early nineties, things are more sophisticated now. Cloning cellphones makes big money, and P's latest movie is a comedy about a gang of South Central cloners.

Ice Cube's song includes background vocals by Mack 10 and Khop. West Coast rap's forte is ironic narratives of ghetto life, and Ice Cube's grisly, voyeuristic storytelling style makes him one of the masters of the genre. 'Ghetto Vet' is quintessential Cube. He plays a mad gang-banger, convinced that it's never going to be his turn to die:

Fool, I'm a vet,
You can bet
That I can dance underwater and not get wet.

And his new sidekick Khop adds:

It's rainin' bullets and I'm still there . . .

Khop remembers hearing Cube's lyrics for the first time and thinking: Damn – this is some of America's Most Wanted shit. He could hear right away that it was going to be one of Cube's best songs. 'I was so happy to get on that motherfucker.'

In the end, inevitably, the veteran gang-banger's luck fails him. Two rivals roll up and call him out:

Are you from the west side?

Khop's brother Binky was in the studio at the time: they used his voice for that part. The rivals shoot the vet before he has the chance to find his own gun. In hospital he wakes up to find he's been shot in the back:

341

I met Dr Who at King Drew
Medical Center as I enter ICU
He said the bullet hit a nerve that was vital
I said I can't move my legs he said don't try to . . .

The fearless gang-banger is now a paraplegic; incontinent and emasculated:

At night I jerk and jerk but my dick don't work . . .

But he still remains dogged for the gang:

Same corner, same hood, I'm still there,
With bandanas tied to my wheelchair . . .

'That's right,' says Tibu, listening to the track. 'I seen 'em do that. Niggas in wheelchairs and they still tie their gang colours to the chair.'

Tibu loves the song. When it's finished he says, 'I wonder what Sick Mick thinks when he hears that. I bet he thinks: Shit . . .'

22

Like the Ocean

'LANDO

The stretch of land south of Watts was once a sandy, treeless flood plain. On the main rail artery between Los Angeles and the docks at San Pedro, it calls itself, boastfully, 'the Hub City'. Compton was named after a local temperance minister, though temperance is not exactly what the Hub City is known for now.

In the sixties, the City of Compton became the first in California to have an African-American political majority. Any optimism that era might have enjoyed is now long gone: joblessness, drug addiction and gang crime have been endemic for so long here that the whole neighbourhood wears a weary air.

At the centre is a bland mall. Drinking coffee at the IHOP there, I spot an article in the local *Press-Telegram* which dourly notes the results of a recent community-safety survey of residents of the Washington School neighbourhood, on North Wilmington Avenue. A majority said gangs were a serious problem, and that there wasn't enough for teenagers to do. Fifty-three per cent of respondents noted that 'there was nothing they liked about their neighborhood'. The gang territories which spread out in each direction from this mall have been some of the most bitterly fought over in LA's history.

Young people who live here have almost inevitably seen things few of us ever have to witness. The rapper Coolio grew up in South Central, idolizing East Coast rappers like Melle Mel. Before Coolio made it as a rapper, originally as part of WC's Maad Circle, he used to live in Compton.

Artis Ivey, as he was called then, moved here with his mother when he was eight. Unlike most rappers who grew up in the area, he never felt the impulse to claim Compton for his own, to shout out for it continually on his albums as the ground-zero of West Coast gangsta rap. His memories of it aren't the prettiest ones. His father moved out early, there was little money in the house and his mother became fond of the crack pipe. 'I always knew things weren't normal,' he said. 'I had friends who had a mother and father at home. They had a cool-assed life.'

> It's really fucked up when there's dope in the crib
> No food in the kitchen for the motherfuckin' kids,

he rapped on the track 'Can O Corn'.

He once told me how he remembered being at school one day, taking a piss ('sorry, a leak,' he corrected himself) in one of the cubicles, when a gunshot rang out. Artis stuck his head around the door and saw someone lying on the floor dead. When he emerged from the bathroom, everyone was staring at him. 'I didn't do that shit!' he shouted, terrified.

Artis quit that school, but stayed in Compton. For a while he was drawn into gang-banging – until at the age of 16, that is, when he witnessed his second murder. That was the day his homeboys turned on another boy they had a beef with and started to hit him over and over again with a hammer, until he was dead.

He said he still remembered the taste of vomit in his mouth that day. He was horrified at what the boys he had called his friends had done. 'Crazy shit,' he said, 'seeing that.'

After that he moved out of Compton and went to live for a while with his father.

I remember something Marion 'Suge' Knight once said too.

'Compton,' he said, 'is like the ocean. It's real pretty, but anytime, something can happen.' He has always been a man of few but choice words.

To call Compton pretty, one would have to be partisan, which of course he is. It looks such a minor suburb, such an unremarkable place, yet since Eazy-E, the one-time Kelly Park Crip, put it on the map it has become known as the epicentre of gangsta rap. Kelly Park Crips are a subset of the many Compton Crip gangs. This tiny, gang-ridden neighbourhood has produced not one but two of the most influential record labels in hip hop, and a disproportionate share of the West Coast's rappers. Eazy founded Ruthless Records and launched NWA from here. North of the Kelly Park territory, on the border with Lakewood, where Blue Diamond lives, is the turf of Suge Knight's famous set, the Mob Pirus.

I drive around both turfs, Crip and Blood. Only here, driving around them, do I realize how close the two gang territories are to each other. Gang warfare has balkanized this city. Geographically the battle between the Compton Crips and the Mob Pirus has been such a provincial war. Pirus to the north, and Crips to the south of Compton, feuding over a tiny parcel of the great mass of crossed streets around here.

When Eazy ran LA hip hop, the south side of Compton was on top: when Suge Knight muscled Eazy out, the north side ruled. All that's finished now. The Tupac shooting had a devastating side-effect on the Los Angeles rap industry, bringing down Knight and curtailing Death Row's domination of the LA rap scene. Knight had become accustomed to believing that he was legally bullet-proof. But that night in Las Vegas he had overstepped a mark: at the time, he was still on parole for several offences – including the vicious 1992 assault of two young would-be rappers, George and Lynwood Stanley, whom he had caught using a telephone in his studio. He had threatened them with a gun, ordered them to strip and pistol-whipped them.

When Tupac had attacked Orlando Anderson in the hotel lobby, Knight had clearly joined in the fray, stomping on the South Side Crip in full view of the surveillance cameras.

At Knight's subsequent parole hearings, Anderson was ordered to appear as a witness. Las Vegas police say that when they interviewed Anderson after his arrest in Los Angeles he had confirmed that Suge Knight had assaulted him. But on the witness stand, dressed in Crip blue, Anderson reversed his testimony. 'I seen him pulling people off me,' he claimed. Suge was 'the only one I heard saying, "Stop this shit!"'

Los Angeles Superior Court Judge J. Stephen Czuleger noted at Knight's probation hearing that Anderson was clearly lying. Tibu tells me that the rumour that was going around at the time was that Knight paid him off.

Knight was sent to jail. Death Row's time as the dominant label in hip hop was effectively over.

One day I'm sitting with Mike (Blue Diamond) in his bedroom, and I start talking about Orlando Anderson. He says simply, fatalistically: 'Just like something happened to Tupac and something happened to Biggie, Orlando Anderson was doing bad things, and bad things were going to come back to him.'

He talks in an offhand way: as if the whole subject is one that wearies him. 'He was only 23 when he died,' I protest.

'It's not really that big a thing. It's, like, the norm. Out here he's just like anyone else.'

'I know,' I insist. 'There are thousands the same age who die. It may be the norm, but . . .'

'He probably didn't think he was going to live to be 23,' Mike interrupts brusquely. 'I didn't think I was going to live to be 19.

That's just how it is.' I realize I have offended him. Why should I be fascinated by such a loser, such a doom-bound gang-banger? It reflects badly on my interest in him.

'People like us who live out here, we don't even want to hear about it. It's, like, it just keeps going on. We got people we lost. We got to put that stuff in the past, because it's going to happen again, to someone we know.'

Orlando Anderson sticks in my mind, though. Millions of hip-hop fans the world over knew his name after he was publicly identified as 'the man who killed Tupac', yet in all the column inches written about Tupac's death no one has ever explained who Anderson was. He was just a zero, a loser, an embarrassment; at best a minor player in somebody else's grand tragedy.

Driving through Compton, I turn down towards South Burris Road, looking for the house where Orlando grew up. It's a short street that leads down to the row of massive electricity pylons that stretch east–west along Greenleaf Boulevard.

I find it easily: a nice-looking, ordinary suburban house, painted blue. Wind-chimes hang outside the front door. The neighbour-hood around it is not welcoming, though. There are bars on most of windows around here. The concrete fence posts on South Burris are scrawled with 'SS': the territorial markings of the South Side Crips. A 'Stop' sign has been redesigned in blue aerosol paint to read: 'Can't STOP SSC.'

On Alondra, just to the north-west, a white storefront church has a sign outside which says: 'Outreach Ministries. "And all thy children shall be taught by the Lord, and great shall be the peace of thy children. If not, great will be your tears and sorrow and pain." Isaiah 54:13.' Great will be your tears and sorrow and pain. This section of Compton is bleak.

Further east is Colin P. Kelly Elementary School, a neat, blue-painted building designed in the fifties in the optimistic, streamlined style of that era. Behind it lies Kelly Park, where Eazy-E had hung out when he was a Kelly Park Crip. To the right of the huge doorway someone has painted the desperate injunction: 'Reading is the key.'

Next to the school is a small, dusty shopping mall. The most thriving business there seems to be the record store: Underworld Records. This is the record shop where, almost a year ago, Babyboy's group Ya Highness had refused to perform because they were scared that it was such a well-known gang hang-out.

Despite appearances, Underworld is one of the more influential mom and pop stores in South Central. The posters outside announce that the r'n'b singer TQ was here last week, promoting his new single, 'Westside'.

I ask Joe, the round-faced, dreadlocked man behind the counter, if he knew Orlando. He says guardedly, 'Yeah. Orlando used to come in here sometimes. Not too often.'

We chat some more about music. I buy a couple of CDs. Joe loosens up. He gives me the number of the store's co-owner, Greg Cross, and tells me I should speak to him instead. 'He knew him better than me.'

Two young schoolgirls enter, hair in bunches. They've seen me pull up and they're selling candy to raise money for the school next door. Giggling, they offer a form to me to sign. Would I like Snickers, Lifesavers or Hershey bars?

Greg Cross is a large, solid-looking man. He's a well-known figure in the Compton record industry: he was friends with Eazy, and gave an oration at his funeral, and used to manage the seminal G-Funk gangsta rap group Above The Law.

In their apartment on El Segundo, Greg's wife is cooking dinner for the kids. Greg sits in an armchair in his living room and tells me categorically that Orlando Anderson did not murder Tupac.

'Orlando was a very quiet-natured person,' he says, sitting back in his big armchair. 'He was, like, "I don't want to harm anybody. I just want to take care of my children." He always talked about how he was the victim.'

Orlando had four daughters. Greg shows me a photograph of him, sitting with the four of them on the carpet at some family occasion. 'That's the real Orlando,' he says, and tells me to keep the photograph.

Greg explains that the reason he got to know Orlando so well is that Orlando was trying to make it in the music business too, like so many other young boys that I've met. He was another boy with hip-hop dreams. At the time he was fatally shot at Rob's Car Wash on Alondra, Orlando had recently finished building his own home recording studio. He was also in the process of setting up his own record label. Ironically, he was going to call it Success Records. Greg knew all this because Orlando used to come and ask him questions about how to go about setting up a label. 'I was,' says Greg slightly grandly, 'his business adviser.'

I ask him how Orlando could afford to build his own studio.

'It was the money from the law suit,' he says vaguely. When I ask what law suit he means he sighs and says, 'Well, it's no secret. Death Row had made some payments to him. That's the money he was using.'

'Sorry? Death Row had made some payments?' I say, thinking about the rumour that had circulated in South Central a few months earlier – that Suge Knight had paid Orlando not to testify against him at his parole hearing.

'Oh yes,' he says.

Two days later I'm sitting in my hotel room with a Compton rapper – a confident, well-spoken man in his early twenties, who used to be friends with Orlando. He doesn't want to give his name in case any of the bad luck that rubbed off on Orlando comes his way.

He too says that Orlando couldn't have shot Tupac: he was nothing like the gang-banger he was depicted as.

He and Orlando were hip-hop fans together. Back when Eazy-E ruled South Central's music scene, they used to hang out with a man called DJ Train. Train used to DJ for all the local acts like Eazy, JJ Fad, Dr Dre, MC Ren and the DOC. Orlando would watch DJ Train come home from foreign tours, rich and happy. Rap, to use Babyboy's phrase, was the new dope game. DJ Train would tell Orlando and his gang-banging friends: 'All the stuff that you're doin' that's bad? *Rap* about it. Make something positive of it.'

The man who's come to my hotel room became a rapper as DJ Train advised him, but Orlando was less of an extrovert. He dreamed of getting involved in the business side of things. That's why he was setting up his own label.

DJ Train was killed in a house fire in the early nineties. 'Train was the only friend of ours who died due to natural causes – and that wasn't even a natural cause,' the rapper says. 'All our other friends were murdered.'

'How deeply involved in gangs was Orlando?' I ask.

'Not really deeply,' says his friend guardedly. 'It wasn't even *really* gang-bangin',' he says. 'A gang is just a bunch of people who hang out together . . .'

I think to myself: They were both members of the South Side Crips. Perhaps that's no surprise. Having driven around the area, looking at the graffiti, it's obvious that the South Side Crips are as solid a part of the local geography as the lamp posts they tag.

But the rapper looks at me as if I can't possibly understand what he's trying to say. ''Lando was *not* some failing, getting-drunk, gang-bangin'-type person,' he insists. He was a popular boy, but a fairly quiet one. He liked to drink a little, but he never smoked weed. He was not a murderer, his friend also says. Others around here were, but not Orlando. 'I feel that some of us started out good – but those were the days when a lot of us had parents on crack. A lot of us had parents in jail. In the eighties, growing up here, it was like Beirut. You had people dying for no reason. We lost so many friends.'

He says Orlando may have flirted with gangs when he was a teenager, but he got out. He didn't need the gang life. 'We all had problems with our parents. Our mothers were on crack and our dads in the pen, or not even around. Orlando had something I didn't have and that was family. He was still in school. He ate every day. There were really no problems.'

The house on South Burris Road which I drove past belonged to Utah Williams, Orlando's great-grandmother and the family matriarch. She had been born in Texas just before the start of the First World War and moved to Compton in the fifties, when it was still a thriving suburb.

Orlando Tive Anderson was born on 13 August 1974 to Utah's granddaughter, Charlotte Davis. Charlotte and Orlando's father, Harvey Lee Anderson, split, so Orlando was raised at the family home on South Burris. Charlotte worked 12-hour shifts as a bookkeeper to raise her children, but there were always aunts and grandparents around to look after him. It wasn't a case of a broken home. Orlando stayed in touch with his father. Most weekends there was a large family gathering.

At school he was known as a bright boy. Though it's obvious he became caught up in the gang culture when he was a teenager, it's hard to believe from his school record that he remained a hard-core gang-banger. Orlando graduated from Dominguez High School in Compton in 1992, and went on to study at Compton College. Gang-banging is pretty much a full-time occupation: bangers don't have the time to study, or to graduate.

'He wasn't that type of person at *all*,' a girl called Tyise who knew him at Dominguez High told me. 'He was a real friendly person – real cool.'

His class graduation ring remained his favourite piece of jewellery. He wore it all the time. There's a picture of Orlando in the Dominguez High School Yearbook for 1992 taken at that year's 'Too Good to Be True' prom. He's there with his girlfriend, Rashena Smith. That was one of the most murderous years in the history of LA's gangs. How many school yearbooks contain full-page adverts for local mortuaries? Orlando's did.

If Orlando dreamed of getting into the music business, he hadn't made much headway by 1996, the year he first hit the headlines. By now he was living with Rashena, a nurse, in her apartment in Lakewood. They had two daughters, Crystal, then two, and Courtney, aged one. But he was also having an affair with Teice Lanier, who had just given birth to a girl called Ariel. He was 22, had never had a paid job, and now had three children dependent on him. But that summer Orlando's older half-brother, Pooh, returned from college to Compton, and the two finally began to do something they'd talked about for years: set up their own record company.

Success Records still exists. It's a small studio set up in a garage in Compton, premises that Orlando found for them that summer. Pooh still works there, producing tracks. He plans to put out a CD soon, featuring some of the tracks his brother worked on. There are a couple of couches in the studio, a tiny recording booth and a mixing desk. The walls are covered in posters advertising movies like Soul Food, and Janet Jackson's latest album.

Pooh is a light-skinned young man with dreadlocks: he talks fast and intensely. He doesn't fit the stereotype of the brother of a local gang-banger. From Compton, he won a scholarship to a private boarding school in Massachusetts and from there, a place at Berkeley, where he graduated in film. The whole extended family raised money to see him through college.

Pooh loved Orlando. 'The most charismatic person that I ever knew. Ever. Absolutely,' he says. He too doesn't deny that his brother ran with the gangs when he was younger: 'Let me say what he said to me. He said, "When I was a child, I did as a child, but when I became a man, I let go of my childish things." At 12 and 13, that was a common thing to do. But those things were not part of his life, lately. He had children, for God's sakes!'

Pooh believes in his brother's innocence: he would love me to believe in it too. I ask Pooh where the money for the studio came from. He tells me he borrowed it. So I repeat what Greg Cross told me: that it was a 'known fact' the money came from payments to Orlando, made by Death Row.

Pooh blanches. He stares at me for a second. He is shocked, as if he's never heard that rumour before. 'That's so *ridiculous*!' he explodes finally. 'If Suge Knight paid him, where is the money then? I'm sure his kids need it. We were close in age. A year apart. Something like that. There is no doubt in my mind that he would have told me.' Pooh sighs. 'If that's a well-known fact, where's the *money*?'

Angry at Greg Cross for putting flesh on the rumour, he insists that the money for the studio was all his own: Orlando never had much money, and any he got he had to spend on his kids. (Orlando's attorney, Renée Campbell, also insisted to me that the rumours about Suge Knight paying him off are ridiculous. He changed his testimony, she says, because he was terrified of testifying against Knight. 'He lived a life of complete fear,' she says.)

The police never discovered the truth about what happened that night in Las Vegas; I'm not exactly in a position to do better. But what I am beginning to understand is that South Central can be a maze: rumours take on lives of their own. In this divided place whispering and innuendo turn half-truths into hard fact.

The day before Tupac died, Compton Police filed a report from one of their informers, known as 'CRI#3', the acronym standing for 'Confidential Reliable Informant'. The informant appeared to have good information about what local Bloods were saying about Tupac's murder. The informant claimed to have overheard Travon 'Tray' Lane – the same Blood who had pointed Orlando Anderson out to Tupac in the lobby of the MGM Grand Hotel – talking in Suge Knight's 662 club after Tupac was shot. According to CRI#3, Tray identified the man who shot Tupac as the same man they had assaulted in the hotel lobby: he was, according to Tray, 'Keefee D's nephew'. Keefee D is Orlando's uncle, Keith Davis, a man identified by Compton Police as a member of the South Side Crips.

Over the following days Compton police say they received several other reports by people who claimed to know that Orlando Anderson was the killer. All these were included in the 'probable cause' affidavit that was compiled in order to obtain a warrant for Orlando's arrest.

The reports were circumstantial. Ultimately they were not enough for local police to use against Orlando. Whether what was contained in the reports was ultimately true or not, the evidence was based basically on what local Bloods were saying about a person from enemy Crip territory: hardly the most reliable foundation on which to build a case. Yet the details contained in the affidavit were leaked to the press on the night Orlando was arrested, and were widely reprinted. They are the reason why Orlando Anderson became the man most people believe to have killed Tupac.

According to his friends, life changed radically for Orlando after the press identified him as the main suspect in the case. When he went out he realized that people were looking at him. They know who I am, he would think.

One day he told Renée Campbell: 'You know? I don't think I'm going to have a long life.'

To be known as the man who shot Tupac lent a surreal edge to his life. Greg Cross showed me a photo of Orlando in his store,

Underworld Records. Montel Jordan had come by to do an in-store signing session. Orlando is standing between Montel and the LA rapper Kokane. There's a story that goes with the photograph. While Montel was busy signing albums, a young girl was looking at a book the store was selling called *The Killing of Tupac Shakur*. The back cover blared: 'WHO did it and WHY?'

The girl looked at it contemptuously and mouthed off: 'Tupac's not dead. He's alive and living in Cuba.'

Then she turned two pages back and found the photograph of Orlando, captioned: 'Orlando Anderson is later identified as the beating victim.' Suddenly she looked up at the real Orlando standing there in the tiny store with her. 'Damn,' she said. 'That's the guy that killed Tupac.'

For a glorious second, everyone laughed: 'Didn't you just say Tupac was still alive?' The girl watched Orlando, scared.

'People reacted to him like that because they thought he really was a killer,' says one friend.

But by 1998 Orlando's reputation still hadn't killed him. Things seemed to be looking up. He would wake early and exercise his two pit bulls, Blue and Na-Na, riding a bike along the sidewalks. He and Rashena had a third daughter, Cierra. 'God is with me,' he would say. 'I'm not going to spend the rest of my life worrying about Tupac.'

Success Records was finally starting to take shape. He recorded some friends of his from Compton, who called themselves the Young Gunz. One day early that summer he came across a teenage rapper named Na-Ijah at The Spot record store in Del Amo Mall. She had a ferocious, gravelly voice that belied her years. Excited, Orlando took her right away back to the tiny recording booth in the garage and laid down a track called 'Ride 2 This'.

On 29 May 1997, Utah Williams, the 85-year-old heart of the family at South Burris Road, died in the hospital where she'd been taken after a fall a few weeks earlier.

'Oh Lord,' said one of her granddaughters. 'Momma has started something now, 'cause we always go in threes.'

Pooh and Orlando's mother, Charlotte, had been at the hospital all morning, so no one had made lunch. Orlando, who had been waiting at the family home, decided to go out and get a burger with his friend Michael Reed Dorrough. They had known each other all their lives: Michael was one of Orlando's closest friends.

A little after three in the afternoon, Orlando pulled into the parking lot of Cigs Records. This is a Corner Pocket Crip hood, though Latino gangs have made serious inroads into their territory recently. He was driving a black Chevrolet Blazer. One of the rumours that circulated was that the Blazer was a gift from Suge Knight – part of a bribe to keep his mouth shut. In fact the car belonged to girlfriend number two – Teice Lanier. It was the same car he'd driven to Las Vegas in on the day Tupac was shot.

According to the police, Orlando saws Michael Stone, a Corner Pocket Crip, at a car wash across the intersection and confronted him about some money that Orlando believed Michael Stone owed him. What happened next has been hotly argued over. All that's clear is that furious shooting broke out between the two men in the Blazer and two Corner Pocket Crips who were at the car wash, Michael Stone and his nephew, Jerry Stone. Within a few minutes, all four were injured, three of them fatally.

Orlando, with Dorrough in the passenger seat, tried to drive to safety. He only made it a couple of blocks, to the corner of Willowbrook and Cocoa, on the far side of Compton High School, before the truck ground to a halt.

Michael Dorrough held his friend as he slipped into unconsciousness. Orlando's last words to him were: 'I love you.'

Anderson and Jerry Stone were both pronounced dead at King-Drew Medical Center, the hospital locals call 'Killer King', because so many of the young men who go there, often with gunshot wounds, are dead by the time they leave. Michael Stone died there the following day.

Around 4 p.m. that day, the pagers began to go off. The story of Orlando's shooting spread fast. A rapper friend rushed to the scene. He noted that the police hadn't even taped off the shot-up Blazer. To him it was as if they didn't even think Orlando was worth it.

'What happened?' he asked a cop.

'Well, the guys from the south side and the Corner Pockets got into it. Jerry Stone and Orlando Anderson are dead.' Then he said something like, 'They took a job of work off our hands.'

Orlando's friend looked at the cop and thought: That's fucked up. Then he walked over and looked at the bullet holes in the Blazer and imagined where the bullets had hit and ricocheted.

Pooh hadn't even made it to his audition when his pager flashed up 911. He phoned his sister Uganda, who told him the news, but by the time he made it to King-Drew, Orlando was dead. Pooh reeled from the shock of having lost two of the people he loved the most – Utah and Orlando – in the same day. It didn't seem real. He kept thinking he was in some Sidney Sheldon story. He says things have never seemed quite the same since. 'I still feel like I'm living in a fictional world,' he says.

I drive over to Rob's Car Wash to try to imagine the furious fire-fight that took place here in May. The car wash is busy, vehicles lined up outside, for a special hand wash and valeting service by the men in overalls outside.

At the back of the service bay I find the boss, a large, deep-voiced man. Rob, I presume. He greets me cordially, wiping his hand on a cloth to shake with me, but his smile drops when I tell him I'm interested in what went on here the day Orlando died.

He shakes his head and says flatly, 'I don't even want to get involved.'

Orlando's friends insist that he was unarmed: that the gun was Dorrough's. They claim that Jerry Stone probably fired the first shot and that Dorrough retaliated. Greg Cross thinks that it was Orlando's reputation as the man who killed Tupac which led to the fire-fight. Greg used to gang-bang himself, when he was a kid. He says he knew all of the four people who were involved in the shooting. He reckons that when Jerry Stone saw Anderson arguing with his uncle, Jerry pulled his gun, thinking: Man. This is the guy that killed Tupac. I got to be quick with the draw.

But at Dorrough's murder trial in July 1999, the prosecution presented forensic evidence that they claim showed powder burns on Orlando. They claimed that it was Orlando who fired first. After he was wounded, Dorrough picked up the gun and continued to fire at the Stones.

When I hear of the prosecution case I call up Pooh and tell him. This is the first he had heard of it. His voice goes quiet. 'That's impossible,' he says, clearly shocked. His voice is choked. It sounds like he's crying. This is the third time his brother has been accused of shooting someone: first Edward Webb, then Tupac Shakur and now the Stones. Whatever the police evidence says, Pooh still believes his brother to be innocent.

In the meantime Dorrough's defence attorney has moved for a retrial. She too believes the prosecution evidence was unreliable, but retrials are rare. Dorrough is currently serving a sentence for murder.

The Testimonial Church of God in Christ was so packed for the joint funerals of Orlando and his great-grandmother, that there wasn't space to accommodate everyone. Orlando's family circle was large, but others turned up too, to stand outside the church as if to show emotional support for the man from Compton's south side.

Michael Dorrough, who at that point was still awaiting trial in the smart new Lynwood Detention Center, just by the courthouse, wrote a eulogy that was printed on the obituary that was handed out that day: 'Man, I love you so much . . . Lando, your last words while I held you will always remain the most special words I've ever heard.' It ends, full of that bravado of comradeship: 'S.S. Like always, I got your back in the end.' S.S. – South Side.

Orlando's reputation remains that of Tupac's killer. In Las Vegas Sergeant Kevin Manning admits, 'We don't have any suspects in the Tupac case. There were certain occurrences, being the altercation at the MGM, which obviously made Anderson of interest to us, but, um, there was not enough that would actually point to him as a suspect.'

'Have you ruled him out as a suspect?' I ask.

'No.'

'You don't consider him a suspect, but you haven't ruled him out?'

'It may be a play on words a little bit,' replies the sergeant, 'but that's just the way we do business around here.'

The Compton police department has backed away from linking Orlando to either Tupac's murder or the murders that happened in the area in the following days. 'We were not able to make that connection,' says Lieutenant Danny Sneed. The Compton police insisted, however, that they were still in the process of forming a case against Anderson for the murder of Edward Webb. 'Our impression was that he was involved in a homicide.'

Pooh shakes his head furiously. He thinks it's about race and politics. He thinks each one of the police cases against his brother was false. If they had evidence against him for killing Edward Webb or Tupac Shakur in 1996, he'd have been locked up long ago. 'Orlando Anderson is an African-American,' he says. 'Do you think that if there was one shred of evidence against an African-American male of his age, that he would not have been behind bars?'

Now he's dead, thinks Pooh, they say they have conclusive evidence against him. He doesn't believe it.

Myself, I don't know whether Orlando was a killer or not. I know, at least, that people found it a little too easy to fit Orlando into their picture of a killer from a failing inner city. He was a grainy face on a security video from a nothing neighbourhood, a place outsiders expect to be full of murderers. They know. After all, they've heard all the records.

On the south side there is still bitterness about the whole affair. Orlando was blamed for Tupac's death, but the people I spoke to see it the other way round, almost as if it was Tupac that killed Orlando. Suge Knight pumped up the Blood neighbourhoods to the north. Tupac stoked the gang animosities. Tensions rose everywhere.

In a way, that's the trouble. Real life and art became confused. 'Tupac started everything,' is the way a one-time Crip tells me. 'You hate him for what he started.'

Tupac wasn't from Compton: he was from the East. Yet when he came to LA, he took on all Suge Knight's local animosities as if they were his own and magnified them with the loud voice of a hip-hop star:

Fuck the rap game nigga
This is M.O.B.
So believe me
We enemies,

he says on his track 'Against All Odds', putting it down for one of the most notorious Blood gangs in Los Angeles, dressing up for photograph sessions in red bandannas and giving 'B' hand signs.

Greg Cross shakes his head sorrowfully. 'It's not to take anything away from anybody, but the thing is, God bless his soul, Tupac was *not* a gang-banger.' Greg, tut-tutting in his role as the older, wiser man, insists that Tupac didn't understand the way things were around here. He didn't understand the territorial niceties that go with gang loyalties in LA. He came in, beating his breast, and the rest of the world lapped it up, platinum-style. 'It's a big difference,' says Greg, 'growing up in gang activity, as opposed to being a artist who is now being with gang members.'

'And you think,' I say, 'he played the role wrong because he didn't understand the territory well enough?'

'Exactly,' agrees Greg.

'Before Suge,' says Orlando's rapper friend, 'it wasn't out and out warfare. Tupac started everything. You got to hate him for what he started. For Orlando to be a fan of someone, and to never know him, and then for Tupac to come up to Orlando with some gang stuff . . . To me that's the root of it all. He was trying to live out his lyrics too much. Tupac crossed the line by coming up and saying, "Where you from?"'

Where are you from? Such an innocent question with so much fear and history lying behind it.

23

This Weird Dream

CAMP ZERO

The Jackson Limousines HQ is in Inglewood, just south of Slauson, a small, neat office, with a line of shiny black cars parked outside. 'I started two years ago with two cars,' the middle-aged proprietor, Elsworth 'EJ' Jackson, says proudly. 'Now it's a multimillion-dollar business.'

It's a neat office, upholstered in thick cream carpet, with black smoked–glass cocktail cabinets, and coffee tables. A four-foot TV screen fills the conference room.

Before he founded the company, EJ used to be in the music business, managing the singer Vesta Williams, who had a hit with 'Once Bitten Twice Shy'. The limo company has been good to him. It kept him close to the entertainment business he loved, but he found himself hankering to return to a more direct involvement in it. Then he came across T–Bob, the energetic centre of the Camp Zero click, and heard some of the tracks he produced. He liked the whole 'Camp' concept. It was different from gangsta rap's clicks and posses.

Now the limousine office is the HQ of Scooter Records too. 'That was my name when I was a little boy,' EJ laughs. 'Scooter. I used to scoot around the floor, buck naked.'

Camp Zero have arrived for one of their rare group meetings. In a 4WD parked outside, Kimmie G is playing the rest of the Camp the recording she's just made at the Edge with Babyboy, cranked up to full volume. 'That's bumpin',' says T-Bob proudly.

The Camp agree. Kimmie's response to Babyboy's lecherous verses has done them proud.

The news for Camp Zero is good. EJ is hoping to be able to put out an album by the end of 1998. He says he's talking to the BMG label about a distribution deal. Nothing is signed yet, but he's optimistic.

After the meeting, T-Bob takes me out back. 'Come and look at this,' he says. There, in the yard, off West Boulevard, is where Jackson keeps his celebrity limousines. Two are two rented permanently to the massively successful r'n'b group Boyz II Men; a third is used exclusively by Shaquille O'Neal, the LA Lakers' basketball hero and one of the most famous sportsmen in America. The two Boyz II Men limos have the group's logo painted just above the petrol caps, and their number-plates read 'CRYSTAL', which, along with Dom P and Moët, is the favourite bubbly of the moment. Shaq's vehicle is being cleaned. His shirt number is painted in the Lakers' yellow and purple, no more than two inches high, on the rear-offside wing.

T-Bob asks if he can look inside, behind the smoked glass. Stretch limousines are curiously cramped inside, but they are the chariots of the famous, of the successful. To have your own stretch limo is a sign of greatness. We peer at the black upholstery, sniffing at the sweet smell of soft leather.

T-Bob stares at it for a while. I stare too. I feel we're like children, peering in at a church door.

C-DOUBLE-E

Herman sits on the wall of the parking lot of the Liquor Bank, a store on Crenshaw and Stocker.

Another of the Crenshaw Hustlers, Philly, is five yards further down Stocker selling phone-extension cords, children's giant balloons and T-shirts with the slogan 'God Feels So Good' on them; the two 'o's of 'Good' have been turned into eyes that give the shirts a rather spooky quality.

Philly says, 'I just come here when I'm not working. I'm an actor, really.' Which is the sort of line you expect to hear from every valet-parking man in Hollywood – so why can't a Crenshaw Hustler use it too? 'I was in *Boogie Nights*,' Philly says. 'You see that?'

A nearby lamppost is plastered with faded stickers for the Liks, the shortened, less-offensive name the marketing people persuaded the LA group the Alkaholiks to use. They were almost certainly put there by Transit Crew last summer.

On the corner a member of the Nation of Islam is selling copies of its newspaper *The Final Call*. The headline reads 'Cocaine Import Agency': it's a story repeating the allegation that during the Iran-Contra scandal, the CIA flooded the inner cities with cocaine, raising money for arms and simultaneously keeping the black population from lifting themselves above the poverty level. The newspaper vendor is talking to a man who is dressed in a T-shirt printed with another acronym: 'Return Exact Same Props Equality Community Truthful.'

Herman has ditched his girlfriend Shanté. She was too young for him. Besides, one day she arrived and started to clean up his apartment, which Herman took for a sure sign that she was trying to move in with him. 'I don't have a lot of time to work with girls. I work late.'

A woman in a Buick pulls up at the liquor store car park. 'How much is the incense?'

Herman sells her a bag for a buck.

The day passes. It's hot now in the afternoons, standing here. Around four Herman wanders over to a burger stand and buys a quarter-pounder and fries. It's much more relaxed than selling umbrellas in the rain, but it's not so lucrative. There's more to see, though, on Crenshaw and Stocker.

A policeman on a motorbike stops a woman who's jaywalking across Stocker and starts to write out a ticket.

Herman laughs. Crime is down. 'Trouble is,' he says, 'there's so little going on the cops have got to find something else to do.'

RAH

Rah still hangs out on Melrose. There he meets two of his friends, Anka and Rif Raf, in the Starbucks, just down from Fairfax High, where he went to school. Rah ostentatiously orders a Strawberry Frappuccino. 'Try it,' he tells the other two. 'It's nice.'

All three are would-be rappers. All three used to be street robbers; they're always talking about the old days, about thieving from Tower Records, and about being caught and sent to prison. Rif Raf used to be a Crip. He met Rah in jail, where they were both serving time for robbery. They've stayed friends ever since. Both worked for Cash and Minus at Lockdown, and Rif Raf still does, though he's making his name as a rapper. Anka acts as his hypeman. They recently performed a showcase at Underworld Records in Compton. 'We blew it up,' Rif Raf boasts.

He wears camouflage gear, head to toe, with a camouflage cap perched sideways on his head, and he has the names of two friends, Basic and Spur, tattooed on his arms. They died within a few weeks of each other. Basic was shot in the head on the corner of 39th and Western by gang-bangers who were retaliating for another murder. Spur just loved playing with guns too much: he aimed a handgun at his head one day and pulled the trigger, forgetting there was a round in it.

The deaths tipped Rif Raf over the edge for a while. That year, sherm was back in fashion. Jayo's single 'Sherm Stick' was being played everywhere. Rif Raf started smoking sherm in a big way:

Basic had introduced him to the drug before he died. Rif Raf wouldn't even dress, he'd just lie in bed all day, smoking 'lovelies' with the Puerto Rican girl he was going out with back then. A 'lovely' is sherm and weed mixed together, so called because it makes you feel lovely. But sherm sent him crazy. In the evening he would go out to nightclubs all shermed up, feeling murderous, and get into fights and crawl back home, his body smashed and beaten from where somebody had laid into him with a baseball bat.

Nowadays, he can't even listen to Jayo's last album without feeling drawn back to those days. It was a dark part of his life.

The three finish their coffees and wander down Melrose. They scope the street and nudge each other whenever they see a good-looking girl. They shout, 'Hey!' if they see one, to see if the girls will look back at them.

'She's hot.'

'That janky-ass bitch?' 'Janky' is Rah's favourite word these days. Anything below par is janky.

Elaborately Rah bends to tie his shoelaces to wait for one white girl to catch up. 'You have the time?' he asks.

He stops by a Jaguar and pretends to put a dime into the parking meter, as if he's just got out, waiting for two pretty Latinas to approach. 'How are you doin'?' The ruse doesn't seem to impress them, though.

Rah is happy. Business is good. His self-confidence seems to be greater each time I meet him. Street promotion is finally paying off. At the local Radio Shack on Fairfax he ostentatiously buys a new Sony cellphone for $240, with a $99 monthly rental charge.

Hollywood being Hollywood, Russell Simmons from Def Jam rolls past in his car; and when they drop into the local shoe store, T-Boz, the girl singer from the multi-platinum r'n'b group TLC, is browsing the racks. The three boys act cool. They are used to the surreal way fame butts up against the mundane in this neighbourhood. Still on a spree, Rah picks up a $90 pair of Reebok Iversons.

Coincidentally, it's a brand which has been marketed heavily through street promotion here.

Just outside the shoe store, a rangy Latino in a reversed baseball cap is sitting in a doorway.

'Hey,' he calls out to the three boys.

'Marlon, how's it going?'

Marlon went to Fairfax High School at the same time as Rah. Graffiti is his thing. His tag is Rate. Sometimes he signs it 'R8'. Marlon's grandmother brought his family here from Guatemala. Uprooted, the children changed to fit in with this new world. Marlon's brothers and sisters all became involved in the 18th Street Gang. Marlon dabbled with gang life, but it was graffiti that saved him from it. He became a convert one day while ditching school, when he caught sight of a beautiful 'burner' down on the drab concrete walls that now form the LA river basin. A 'burner' is the taggers' name for one of those big, 15-foot-long works of art.

Gang graffiti and tagger graffiti are different. Unlike tagging, both the message and the style of gang graffiti is simple: block letters that say, This place is mine, you are my enemy. Taggers can paint anywhere; gangs stick to their own territory. Taggers love to paint trains or buses; that way they can create a sort of mobile art exhibition, something that would be pointless to a gang-banger. So it can be hazardous, tagging in gang territory where a gang may regard all walls as its own.

One of Marlon's teachers was Skate One, one of the best-known LA graffiti bandits of his day. Skate One was a hero to him. He taught Marlon how to create burners – showing him how to collect nozzles from domestic spray cans and how to angle the can to achieve various effects. Marlon remembers how back in '93 the phone began ringing at around four in the morning. Skate One had been spraying a wagon in the Woodman Yard up in the Valley, when the train hit him: he had his headphones on and never heard it coming. They gave Skate One a huge funeral. Marlon crosses himself whenever he talks about his dead friend.

It didn't stop Marlon doing wagons. There is something special about the trains that run up from the harbour. It's not like the New York subway trains that never leave the state: here, your artwork travels everywhere. He's had graffiti writers as far away as New Mexico and Florida tell him they've seen trains with 'R8' on them.

They chat for a little while. Rah fingers his new phone. Afterwards the three boys shake hands with Marlon and wander back to Fairfax High, to sit on some concrete steps and watch the joggers who trundle slowly around the running track. As the evening draws on, the three start to freestyle.

Rah's improvisations are brutal, breast–beating affairs:

> *How the fuck you think you going to fuck with us*
> *These rough and tough, scandalous*
> *Villains?*
> *We lay your ass on your back*
> *And lay that nine-inch dick up in your shit . . .*

He has come so far, and yet his rhymes always betray this dark violence; even after all he's been through, this need to prove himself tougher than the rest.

Rif Raf is generous with his praise. 'Whooo!' he shouts. But in contrast his rhymes, about his men friends all sticking together, about loyalty and aggression, sound effortless:

> *Actually, I represent the Lockdown faculty*
> *Give me signals, I have fifty niggas on back o' me*
> *You take Cash and Minus*
> *Two of Los Angeles' finest*
> *Anka and Cron Don hold it down for the alliance*
> *Stickering poles and holding mikes till they turn cold . . .*

Gradually the joggers and basketball players have left. It's completely dark now. For an hour, the three have been trading rhymes under the darkening sky. The stars have slowly come out. Three friends trading rhymes on this delicious, warm California evening.

As a police helicopter moves overhead, Rif Raf rises to a triumphant climax:

A nigga like me don't give a fuck about nuttin' but my click.
You da toilet. I'm da shit!

Laughter echoes off the concrete walls.

BABYBOY

Babyboy pulls a chair outside and sits by the front door. A single cast-iron column holds up the corner of the small white house, leaving a patio just big enough to put two chairs on.

'I get this weird dream,' says Babyboy, 'where I am somewhere and a snake jumps to bite me, and just about where the teeth are about to penetrate the skin, I wake up.'

The grass in the small yard is lush. Cacti and other succulents grow along the side of the house. Above us, the tops of regal palms are still in the windless morning. 'Or it's like I'm getting shot up, and right before I feel the gunfire, and right when I know there is no way I can get away from it, I wake up.'

Babyboy scratches his bare chest. 'And there's another dream too. I'm at this big-ass house, in front of the gate, waiting to go in. But there's always something fucked up about the house. I know it's there, but I can't see it. I know I'm getting closer, but I can't get a clear picture of what it's like.'

High above us, a jet is leaving trails in the blue sky. 'Or, like, there's another dream which is the same: I see myself rollin' in a

Benz and I can see the wood grain on the fascia, and the steering wheel, but I'm driving it and I realize that it don't have no brakes. Or it might be missing the passenger door. It's weird.'

'That's your life, isn't it?' I say.

'Yes,' says Babyboy.

24

The Last Days

I'm back in LA for just a couple of weeks: I have been away a few months. It felt good to get away, but now I find it feels good to come back, too.

I am more familiar with the place now. I remember how the first times I went to South Central I was uneasy. I had no idea of where I was not supposed to go. The flatness and the endlessness made it hard for me to like it. All I really knew about it then was pretty much what Ice Cube had said: 'It ain't the most terrible place to live in the world, but it's just so unpredictable.' Like most newcomers, that upredictability put me on edge. Now, driving around with my radio playing loudly, this familiarity has made me fonder of it, too.

Car radio in Los Angeles is different from anywhere else. Expatriates and New Yorkers I know all swear to this. Songs that sound terrible in London or Boston can somehow sound fabulous on LA streets. I drive down Central Avenue listening to TQ's 'Westside'. It is the tail end of 1998: Los Angeles has taken the song to its heart and 92.3 The Beat is playing it on heavy rotation:

> I was just a young boy livin' in the Hub City
> (Eastside Compton, G)
> Back in the days when Ice Cube and Eazy
> Had every nigga talkin' 'bout, 'Boy, you can't fuck with me'

Remember Ice-T had the power (Ooh, wee)
Hearin' gunshot lickin' by the hour . . .

Out here, the record's heavy-handed romance, its dewy-eyed
vision of LA hip hop's golden years, draws me in. If I am cynical
about why white boys like me like hip hop, I remain fascinated and
seduced by the way it summons such a powerful image of these
streets, whether a real one or a romantic one:

It would seem that long ago
We were stealin' forties out the liquor store
Mama started trippin', so it's time to go
Mob to the park with the loc'sters
Everybody broke smokin' roaches
DJ Quik was the shit,
Had every nigga claimin' he was from the CPT . . .

It feels right to be driving through Compton as the song plays,
through the CPT – the letters designate a Compton number in the
LA phone directory. The turbulent days of the late eighties and
early nineties here are already the subject of rap mythology.
Nostalgia builds, already.

It's not like these aren't still murderous streets – if you're in the
wrong place. I picked up a copy of the *Press-Telegram* this morning.
The night before last there were five murders within an hour of
each other in the Southland; three hours later a 15-year-old was
murdered in a drive-by in Lynwood, not far from where Blue
Diamond lives. Police were treating them all, for the moment at
least, as gang-related murders. Local people are anxious. They
know that little has been achieved here in the past ten years, and
there is a dread that soon the violence may start escalating again,
back towards the murder rates of 1992. Lieutenant Drake Robles is
quoted as saying it's too early to tell whether the recent batch of

shootings over the past few weeks means there has been an increase in gang crimes.

TQ sings:

From Crenshaw to Foothill Boulevard
All I see is lolos in mob cars, Daytons and Five Stars
All the true niggas is hittin' switches with all the finest riches . . .

It's a slickly produced r'n'b tribute to those hip-hoppers from Eazy-E onwards who glorified this drab geography and wrested something from it.

Not everyone sees it this way. The irascible LA journalist Earl Ofari Hutchinson once wrote that he had lived in South Central for 30 years and yet he didn't recognize the territory depicted in John Singleton's movie *Boyz In Tha Hood*. He deplored the negative vision of black men that the film connected to his own geography, and railed against his black friends who praised the film for depicting a realer vision of themselves than any white Hollywood movie. If some people felt it told their stories, it certainly wasn't his story. But his is a lonely voice. It's the story much of America, black and white, wants to hear, though: a culture that recognizes itself only through tales of an underclass:

Don't get it twisted, Ask me what's a real G.
Show me a nigga scrappin' back against the wall until his knuckles bleed
Screamin' 'Death to all our enemies and those who don't believe'
West Coast livin' be the shit to me . . .

On my radio, driving down Alameda, the lush, pugilistic passion of the pop music sounds eerily perfect. The DJ says he has a surprise guest coming up in a minute.

The afternoon has turned into evening. I turn on to Alondra, where trucks labelled 'Maersk', 'Hanjin' and 'Seaco' laboriously rumble past northwards. When the last one has passed, I see a man on a horse, who had been riding behind it.

I slow my car down and stare. A massive Latino, of John Wayne proportions, dressed in a white straw hat with magnificent leather chaps and an elaborate Western saddle, is riding slowly up towards the north. Gradually more horsemen appear, following behind, some with ropes tied up to their saddles, some wearing bright bandannas. Dressed to the nines, these Latino cowboys, I guess, are returning from some parade. They look so alien here, at first, in this landscape. Riding past Mexicali Tires and the other auto-repair shops, up towards Elm Street, they look like ghosts from before the city covered this sandy desert scrub. If I squint, I can see the distant mountains in the north-west, turning purple in the last light.

Cowboys are the stuff of folklore. I wonder idly whether the children of the future will talk about the exploits of Tupac, the gangstas like Monster Kody Scott and the Bloods and Crips in the same way as they talk of Jesse James and the Hole in the Wall Gang, and whether those rap songs that depict life here so luridly have served the same function as the gaudy nineteenth-century pulp fiction that created the cowboy myth, a vision so powerful, so brutally romantic, that for many Americans it drowns out other histories.

Some time after I've watched them pass – I'm not sure how long – the DJ on 92.3 The Beat says, 'I got Mr Short Khop on the line right now.'

'Wassup?' Khop's voice comes on.

'Khop, we got this tape right now that we got through the underground. I got to thank Kidub for bringing it to me. It's kind of, seeped up here . . .'

'Right.' I expect him to say, 'Yee-ah' at any moment, but he doesn't.

'Bring it on, bro.'

'OK. OK,' Khop says, with the casual flair of someone who has

been doing this for a hundred years. 'This is Mr Sho' Khop. I'm stayin'
with Ice Cube. This is the "All My Love" remix, never before heard,
right here on 92.3 The Beat. It's goin' down, y'understand me?'

And the track – originally from *The Players Club* soundtrack –
starts up.

TIBU

I find Tibu living on campus at Cal State, with Keyna again; the
exclusion order has expired now and he's allowed back. It makes life
easier for him. But beyond that, nothing in his life seems to have
moved forward. He is no closer to winning the attention of any A&R
men. He never managed to produce enough tracks that he was
confident enough of to put out on the tape that he always said he was
going to make. The Vietnam click is pretty much defunct now, too.

Keyna and he are arguing all the time. Blu-tacked to the fridge is
a circle of card with the three names of the apartment's tenants on
it, and a list of duties. Each week the disc is rotated so the names
point to different duties. Today it says, 'Keyna: Kitchen, Trash.'

I ask, 'What duties do you do, then, Tibu?'

'I don't do shit,' he says. Then: 'I do the dishes sometimes.'

He's been back to Todd's studios, though. Blue Diamond came
into some money and asked him to produce three tracks for him.
'Guess what?' he says. 'Big Al's going to be on MTV.'

BIG AL

I call Al and we meet over a Chinese meal. It's true. Six months
after he went to the MTV audition for the nationwide r'n'b and
hip-hop talent show *The Cut*, Al had the call-back. They wanted
him to come and perform 'Freez Up'.

The series' executive producer, Kathy Cotter, liked what she saw
of the audition: 'Al has this big presence. He gets out there and

makes the audience work for him. He doesn't hold anything back. His presentation is so positive. Smart guy. Smart track.'

The rapper Xzibit was the judge on the first show. Al and Xzibit know each other from way back; but both had to pretend they didn't, for the sake of propriety.

On that first recording, up at Empire Studios in Burbank, Al took a look at the routines the other performers had and knew that he should win it easily, which he did. He proudly called up all his friends and relations and told them the broadcast date of the show.

When it came to it, MTV were unhappy with the format they'd recorded the first episodes on and cancelled them. Al sat there in front of the television, waiting for the show that never came on. He felt crushed. He couldn't believe it. Maybe this was going to be as much of a let-down as all the other shows.

But it was just those episodes they had cancelled, not the whole series. When they went to shoot the next program, he was listed as a semi-finalist. So he returned to Empire Studios and performed 'Freez Up' once again. The judges were Treach from Naughty By Nature and Compton's own DJ Quik, who was back on the scene with a new album. This time around, Al was more nervous about his prospects, because all the other competitors were singers and he was the only rapper. But again he won.

Afterwards, in a simulated display of spontaneity, the director wanted him to run to embrace the supporters who had come to see him perform. Only Al, who has never had a click or a crew, had come with just his girlfriend, Latonja. A reluctant Latonja, reticent at the best of times, had to ham it up for the cameras as best she could, throwing her arms around the big man on campus.

On the Thursday night the show was finally broadcast, and Al saw it at the family house in Inglewood, by the 105 freeway. This time he hadn't called everybody up. On the program, *The Cut* billed Al as coming from Cleveland. It's where his family is from originally. As the show was being filmed in LA, there were too many local contestants, so it looked better that way: 'Big Al, from Cleveland, Ohio.' Al doesn't need to represent the Westside or the Eastside. Representing Ohio is OK by him if it gets him where he deserves to be after all these years.

Already Al had beaten off around 150 other competitors and was one of the ten finalists. The winner's prize was to have a video filmed for his or her song, for broadcast on MTV.

Never in the 11 years since Al had appeared on *The Gong Show* had he reached this peak. At work all that week he found it impossible to concentrate.

In the end, though, he didn't win the final: KRS-One and the other judges gave the prize to a girl rapper called Silk E, whose style was similar to that of the chart-topper Lauryn Hill. But that didn't bother Al. Getting through to the last session was enough for him. For two weeks in December, the two shows are played, on Thursdays and Saturdays. Signed acts would kill for that exposure.

Finally Al is in a position where he has the profile he needs to win another record deal.

He is excited now. He feels that after 11 years things are about to happen for him. Even if they don't, he feels vindicated. He and Latonja have been discussing what he should call his first album, if he does cut a deal. He's thinking about *It's About Time*, or perhaps *Finally . . .*

Peter Cohen from Sony 550 watches *The Cut*'s episodes. He is impressed: it's an exciting performance. The Monday after the first showing of the final he calls Al, as he promised he would. He tells him he's come a long way since he first saw him, back at the *Rap Sheet*'s Unified Hip Hop IV convention, 14 months earlier. But he doesn't have a deal to offer yet.

A&R men like Cohen want to see that an artist has a following. On the South Central showcase circuit, where the audience is mostly fellow performers and their mothers, this is hard. And despite his extroversion on stage, Al is a quiet soul. He isn't the sort of boy to hang out with a click who can be mobilized to turn up, night after night, to all his shows. Whatever his achievements, he has still not managed to build a fan base.

Cohen urges him to keep in touch, though.

BABYBOY

Babyboy is harder to track down. His phone and his pager have been disconnected. This is a bad sign. Normally it's just his pager that is disconnected when Babyboy is broke. I can't get an answer from the house on Wilton: there seems to be nobody in. I go up to the dub and ask around. 'You know where I can get in touch with Kimeyo?'

'I don't know who you're talking about,' a tall man with his hair in gangsta bunches blanks me and then strides away purposefully.

'He lives around here,' I say.

'Don't know who you're talking about,' he says, quickening his pace, eyes on the sidewalk.

An older man looks out of the screen door, close to where I first met Babyboy a year and more ago. 'You know Kimeyo?' I ask him.

The old man shrugs. 'He doesn't live around here.'

No one around here likes a white guy asking around for a drug dealer. The old makes to close the screen door again. 'Wait,' I say. I write my phone number on a piece of paper and ask him to give it to Kimeyo when he sees him.

The man shrugs again and pockets the paper.

RAH

Gradually I catch up with the news. Stranded's album disappeared without trace. Rodney King's record company has been a failure. Camp Zero and Kimmie G have signed to Scooter Records, and have been promised major-label distribution. They've been waiting months now for the deal to be finalized.

One day Orlando Anderson's brother drops by my hotel and gives me a CD. Almost exactly a year since his brother was killed, Pooh has completed the first Success Records compilation. Some of the tracks his brother recorded with the Young Gunz and Na-Ijah are on it. Inside there's a photograph of Orlando, smiling broadly, captioned: 'Never another like you.'

I visit Blue Diamond too. He's still sitting there in his bedroom. He and Tibu hooked up for a while. Once they travelled over to Todd's studio, and Tibu produced a couple of tracks for Mike. Another night they went down to Inglewood, where Lonzo Williams has opened a new club called The Current Affair. They performed an open-mike spot together. But since then they've not been in touch. They're both so proud of what they do, so sure of their own talent, I guess it's hard for them to work together.

Driving down Crenshaw, I notice that the snipers have invented a new lick while I have been away: they're sticking posters on to large pieces of card and then stapling two cards together around a lamp post. They push the card up the post and start again, until there are eight or nine cards, the highest 20 feet off the ground.

Big Wes from Priority says Rah is one of the most conscientious workers out there. Sometimes Rah still dreams of being a rapper: R. Shottie of the Top Notch click. He thinks that if he becomes a rapper he will still do all his own street promotion. 'My plan,' he tells me, 'is I want to be the first rapper to promote his own album. I want to do all my own retail, to pass out all my tapes. I want to do it all myself.' Other times he dreams of making it big in promotion. He wants to promote everything: Lexuses, Timberland clothes. 'You know what I'm sayin'? Pepsi. Everything. I think I got a lot of character. I'm a go-getter, you know what I'm sayin'? I don't waste time.'

When I ask Rah what made him this sort of person, he answers straight away: 'What made me that is when I met Josiah. When I met Josiah and his brother.'

TIBU

Tibu's trying to earn some money himself now. He is looking for a proper job. He's looking for something that will earn him some money without taking all his time, so he can still do music. But he's tired of being broke: and he can't just rely on hustling weed any more. We drive to the Del Amo shopping mall, where he buys a cheap white shirt and a tie. He spends 40 minutes choosing them, holding the shirt and the tie up in front of his huge belly. The next day I drive him over to Long Beach. He has an interview as a security guard. There is a written examination, a comprehension test, and . . .

'I have to take a drug test,' Tibu grins. 'My friend's given me some jellies – some tablets – that means that nothing shows up in your piss.'

'Good luck,' I tell him, when I drop him off in front of the two-storey office building.

He sighs and gets out of the car, then leans back in again to say goodbye. It'll be the last time I see him before I go back home. We shake hands, stiltedly.

C-DOUBLE-E

Herman, C–Double-E, has 1000 CDs of 'Nine Times Outta Ten' in a box in his small room in the Jungle.

The last time I saw him was at a studio where he and the rest of the group had paid hard-earned money to record the song yet again. The recording session had been a disaster. It was Herman's first time in the studio and he had spent two expensive hours trying to get his MPC 2000 to download the sound before he finally made the machine work. Even Dennis, the genial DJ RBG, had paced up and down shouting, 'Man, man, man, man, man . . . I'm going to roast him later. I'm really going to roast him.'

But they went back to Island Trax a few weeks later and Herman got it right. I have lost count of how many versions of 'Nine Times Outta Ten' I've heard.

But this time they were satisfied with it. They've pressed the CDs up at a total cost of $820. I buy one for $5. They've sold only a handful. Other than selling them on the street, they haven't yet worked out how they're going to distribute them.

Herman plays a copy on his CD player. His rhyme about life here, as a street vendor on Crenshaw and Stocker, sounds good, but on its own that is never enough.

Last week DX had a job as security at a youth club called the Sodapop Crew, at the Living Room on 4th and West 54th. DJ Scratch, a minor turntable celebrity locally, was playing that night. DX said, 'Hey, I got a new group. We got a new CD. You think you could play it?'

Scratch said he'd put it on, but he never did. His attitude angered DX. But then at around half past ten, another DJ took over to give Scratch a break, and DX gave him the CD.

Around 11 p.m. the room was filled with A Nu Creation's first single. When DX tells me about this, sitting on Herman's chair, he's smiling proudly, as if this is one of the best things that ever happened to him. 'Everyone was dancing. Like two, three hundred people. And they danced all the way through. All the way through . . .'

Herman tinkers with the pads on his beloved MPC 2000. 'I know that we're going somewhere now,' he says, ever optimistic. Herman is always happy. I have never seen anything really get him down. 'I feel as if I'm in the last days of me struggling.'

KHOP

I call up Khop and leave a message on his pager, which plays me a snatch of music before it beeps. It's one of the more scatological snatches from 'If I Was Fuckin' You', the first song he recorded for Cube's *War & Peace* album:

If I was fuckin' you I'd let the homie fuck too . . .
Right up in the guts, bustin' nuts . . .

His voice comes out at me. I wonder what his parents make of this, when they call him:

 . . . Cooch screamin'
Meat cleanin'
Creamin'
Tag teamin'
Suckin' semen . . . BEEP.

'That's for all the females that's paging me,' he jokes when he calls me back.

Ice Cube's single 'Pushin' Weight', which features Khop, has been number one in the *Billboard* r'n'b charts for, Khop says, 'I don't know how long'. He says he's finally working on the solo album now: he's going to call it *The Khop Shop*. He's going out on his first tour, not just as part of Cube's band, but under his own name, along with Mack 10 and Bizzy Bone from Bone Thugs N' Harmony.

Things have changed for his managers Charlie B and Casual T, too. They've moved out of their tiny two room office and are converting a much plusher office space several blocks away into a state-of-the-art recording studio. As for Khop – of all the boys I've met over the last year and more, he is the only one who has earned any money from hip hop. The rest are no better off than when they started. Khop, on the other hand, has become rich. He's famous now, too. It has all worked out well. He gets stopped wherever he goes in LA. He says, 'I ain't mad at that. I stop. I talk. But sometimes I think, Damn!'

This is the sweetest time of all, before fame becomes a routine, before the start of the struggle to maintain status, to pay the bills and tax demands and keep the ball rolling.

Khop tells me about the fan mail he is sent. 'It's basically females, man. Send a picture. "Can I call you?" You know how they do it. They're crazy, man.' He laughs. 'I write back and tell them I'm married.'

BABYBOY

I find Kimmie G's number and ask her if she knows where Babyboy is. She hasn't spoken to him for weeks, she says. Camp Zero are still recording their album for Scooter Records, but EJ still hasn't managed to find a distribution deal for the label. It's turned out to be harder than he thought it would be. 'If you track down Babyboy, tell him to give me a call,' she says.

Now I have only a couple of days left, and I still haven't found him. I call up a couple of mutual friends, but they haven't heard from him in weeks either. I start to worry. Has he been caught by the police on one of his deals?

Of all the people I followed, I became closest to Babyboy. For all his paranoia, his moodiness and his mad schemes, he was the one who was most open, who wore his ambition so obviously. He was the one with the biggest dreams, who was always able to pick himself up and throw himself into the next ludicrous idea. In London he would have probably ended up working in advertising in Soho, or on a magazine.

He was the one who seemed to need to succeed more desperately than the others. Nearly everyone who dreams of being rich and famous by becoming a music star will have their ambitions frustrated. But that's never put anyone off. Babyboy could never do the sort of day job Big Al does, inputting endless reams of data into government computers.

When Babyboy phones up and leaves a message for me on my hotel voicemail, I am relieved.

'Somebody passed me a note with your number. My beeper is back on. Call me on that, 'cause you know I ain't got no peazy?'

'No *peazy*?' I say, when I call him back.

'No peazy. No phone.' It has been cut off because he can't afford to pay it. He's flat broke.

He says he's under surveillance. 'Someone dropped a dime on me,' he says.

'Dropped a dime?' I say. I may feel more at home here in South Central than I did a year ago, but I am still always reminded that I am a foreigner, constantly bemused at how different this world is.

'Informed on me,' explains Babyboy. He says that someone on Wilton that the police were about to arrest snitched on him, so he's keeping a low profile for a few weeks. This time it sounds less like paranoia than it has done previously.

I visit him on Wilton. Everything has ground to a halt. For all his big stories of deals, Babyboy survives selling a little weed here, a little there. Having spent time inside, he doesn't want to go back there, so he has been forced to cease work, worried that the police are out to get him. I have often seen Babyboy broke, but never so broke that he couldn't find the cash for his own weed dealers. Now he doesn't even have enough money to pay the guy who's just given him ten bucks' worth of grass, and they're standing on the sidewalk arguing.

'I don't have it.' He's already smoked most of it so he can't give it back now, even if he wanted to.

'That's fucked up. You taken my weed and now you don't have no money to pay me,' the other guy says.

'You shouldn'a given me it then. That's your weakness, not mine,' Babyboy argues testily. Not even having the money to pay for weed is like being caught with your pants down.

Babyboy's album *The Lesson* has ground to a halt, too. He has slid backwards since I saw him last. Even the Iranian producers, Bruce and Benny Ferat, who wanted to work with him have backed out.

Babyboy was working in the studio with them one day when some friends of Badazz's dropped by. Babyboy likes them, but they're a rough bunch. Benny was annoyed when one of them, a guy called Coco Loc, started fiddling with the recording equipment. 'Don't touch that, bitch,' he exploded. Next thing he was laid out, unconscious on the floor from a single punch. Babyboy can't blame Coco Loc for what he did to Benny. You don't call black men bitches. A bitch is prison slang for a gay submissive, or, equally shameful to a macho culture, a gay rape victim.

Bruce and Benny never forgave Babyboy. They have told him not to come around again.

Babyboy still hasn't been paid for the Paul Goldsby movie, either. It seems likely that he never will now. Goldsby has been struggling to find a distributor, but hasn't succeeded yet. Babyboy is still waiting, still focusing on it, because though he has built the dream of himself as a hip-hop entrepreneur, the cheque would be the first legal money he has ever earned from the entertainment industry – if he ever gets it.

Six years he's been doing this, and he's never earned a penny from it. The sad truth is that it's the idea of N Entertainment that has sustained him all this time, not the reality of it. For all the years he has put in, trying to nudge himself close to the epicentre of it all, carrying his neat black briefcase and his business cards, he has nothing to show for it.

We stand on Volume 10's porch on 39th Street. The rapper has just recorded a new record that is doing moderately well: it's his first sniff of a hit since his single 'Pistol Grip Pump' four years ago. Kokane drops by, and greets me like an old friend. He says that things are a little better than last time I saw him at the trailer park. He has a deal on an obscure independent label called Street Institute Records. It's not Lollapalooza yet, but he's still in the game. He and Volume 10 are just about to record with Xzibit.

The morning before I have to fly back home to the UK, I offer to buy Babyboy breakfast at my hotel in Compton. He borrows Marlene's car and meets me there.

He prays, lathers his steak with tomato ketchup and tabasco sauce, and says he has some news. After all these years they've been engaged, he and Marlene have set a date for their wedding, in March 1999.

'Congratulations,' I say. 'How do you feel about that?'

'Good,' he says uncertainly. 'Real good.'

I am not sure how much he means it. Just as it's hard to imagine Babyboy settling down to a steady job, it's hard to imagine him stopping philandering. In my heart I don't really believe the wedding will happen. I doubt he can bear to give up his dreams of making it in the music business.

We gaze out of my hotel room window onto the 91 freeway below us, both staring at the cars speeding eastwards and westwards. The hum of traffic is so even you hardly notice it. A huge concrete sign by the road announces that they are passing through the City of Compton.

'I been in the fast lane,' he says. 'Now, if I want to enjoy life the way it's meant to be enjoyed, I'm gonna have to get off the motherfuckin' freeway. Sell my fast car.'

The fast lane, duckin' in and out of traffic in the fast lane.

That was the last rap he wrote, with the Ferat brothers, before Coco Loc punched out Benny.

'Sell my fast car. I might have to get off that fast lane and start riding a bus. Buy a Hyundai.' He coughs. He looks tired and unravelled. Gradually he's giving up his dream of becoming a hip-hop star. I have no idea what he is going to do next. I don't think he has, either.

'Buy a motherfuckin' Hyundai. But even Hyundai got a little speed to them,' he grins. 'Ask Rodney King.' And suddenly he bursts into a loud, wicked, chest-rattling laugh, while outside the window the cars and trucks rush on past.

ACKNOWLEDGEMENTS

I'm particularly grateful to Alejandro Alonso of USC for generously leading me through his own post-graduate research on the history of LA's gangs. Other valuable sources I leaned on include *American Apartheid* by Douglass S. Massey, (Harvard University Press 1993); *The UNIA and Black Los Angeles* by Emory J. Tolbert, (Centre for Afro-American Studies UCLA 1980); *Ghetto Growing Pains*, Sally Sandoval, MA Thesis (California State University 1974); Ralph Eastman's *Pitchin' Up A Boogie* and Michael B. Bakan's *Way Out West* in *California Soul* ed. Jacqueline Cogdell DjeDje and Eddie S. Medows, University of California Press 1998; *Building Common Ground* by Erich Nakano; *The South Central Los Angeles Eruption* by Armando Navarro; *Jewish and Korean Merchants in African American Neighbourhoods* by Edward T. Chang in *Los Angeles Struggles towards a Multiethnic Community*, ed. Edward T. Chang and Russell C. Leong (University of Washington Press 1993); John F. French; *A City Called Heaven* by Susan Anderson in *The City, Los Angeles and Urban Theory at the End of the Twentieth Century* ed. Allen J. Scott and Edward W. Sosa, (University of California Press 1996); *Monster: The Autobiography of an L.A. Gang Member* by Sanyika Shakur, (Penguin Books 1994); S. H. Fernando Jr's *The New Beats* (Payback Press 1995) and David Toop's *Rap Attack* (Serpent's Tail). I was particularly glad to come across Keith E. Collins' *Black Los Angeles: The Maturing of the Ghetto 1940–50* (Century Twenty-One Publishing 1980) when writing my chapter on the history of South Central. Anyone who had read Mike Davis's *City of Quartz Excavating the Future in Los Angeles* (Verso

1990) will know how much I relied on that book for a broader history of the city.

Thanks, too, to the kind staff at the A.C. Bilbrew Library and the African-American Studies Library at UCLA.

Some of the material in this book has appeared in a different form in *Details* magazine. My editor, Susan Murcko, did much to help shape that material.

Dan Mandel suggested the idea in the first place; Simon Trewin, Geoff Kloeske and Matthew Hamilton always managed to sound enthusiastic about it. Thanks also for support and input to David A. Keeps, Al-Rasheed Dauda, Andrew Harrison, Gavin Edwards and Chris Moore. My colleague Chris Heath held my hand, talked, listened, read, lent me money and bought me drinks throughout the writing. Jane McMorrow, finally, can't be thanked enough.